Introduction 3
Preface 7
On Curating Dialogue Concerts 9

Dialogue Concert #1
Mediality
December 19, 2019
Lecture: Oda Pälmke 21
Discussion 29

Dialogue Concert #2
Interaction
February 6, 2020
Lecture: Christophe Hutin 39
Discussion 51

Intervention 59

Dialogue Concert #3
Transformation
August 14, 2021
Lecture: Daniel Libeskind 67
Discussion 75

Dialogue Concert #4
Structure
September 17, 2020
Lecture: Bernd Kniess 83
Discussion 97

Dialogue Concert #5
Corporality
April 20, 2021
Lecture: Christopher Dell 105
Discussion with Denkstatt sàrl 113

Dialogue Concert #6
Materiality
September 9, 2021
Lecture: Ton Matton 125
Discussion 139

Preliminary Concerts 147

Introduction
Christopher Dell

On the occasion of the 40th anniversary of the Aedes Architecture Forum in 2020, the series *Dialogue Concerts: Conceptual Research on Architecture and Music* presented a groundbreaking pluralistic media format, reenvisioning urban and music research. Within the institutional framework of the world-renowned and now canonic exhibition space for architecture and urban design, architectural practice entered into a dialogue with musical practice. Designed as a montage of lectures, concerts, and discussions, the *Dialogue Concerts* (*DC*) took place as a series of events which examined the interplay of urban space and what the German philosopher Hannah Arendt once termed "acting in concert." Based on this, the aim of the *DC* was to create an experimental platform for exchange on how we live together today as a city and what role architects and musicians may play in this realm. The event series was comprised of six events, which took place between December 2019 and September 2021. Throughout the series, architects and musicians alike were encouraged to address important aspects of procedural strategies across disciplines and to reflect on the issues relevant to the thematic focus of the different events.

In the current state of geopolitical instability, migration, climate change, and housing crisis, professionals in different disciplines are once again questioning the integrity of their field. It is against this background that the *DC* project delineated its pioneering investigation on the disciplines of architecture and music. It showed how architects and musicians alike—as they are confronted with the challenges of a future full of uncertainty—are in the process of shifting the focus of their practice. Two issues take center stage: a realm of research that seeks to shed light on the existing and the quotidian of the city; and a self-reflexive criticism of the procedures put forward by this research. Along these lines, the *DC* sought to demonstrate this, and also how the complex issues of today's urban society demand to be discussed in ways that cross and transcend disciplinary and institutional boundaries.

Curated by the urban design theorist, composer, and vibraphonist Christopher Dell, the *Dialogue Concerts* were realized as an artistic statement and critical *dispositif*. The discussions in the series added to current discourse in society about the future of the city after the spatial turn. By this is meant that the city is defined not as a fixed object, but as a dynamic and collective constellation that is performatively produced. To instigate, frame, and structure its discussions, the *DC* invited, as keynote lecturers, architects who are internationally recognized for their reflective work on the current transformation of architecture and urban design. Representing different discursive backgrounds, their lectures reflected on issues relevant to the specific thematic focus of each event. While featuring emphasized projects, all of the architects' lectures demonstrated the lasting effect that their work has (and has had) on the redefinition of architecture and urban design, as well as reactions and parallels from different perspectives, cultures, and nationalities. Each lecture was followed by a concert. After the concert, a discussion between the presenting architects and performing musicians took place. Both the discussions and the lectures were transcribed and edited for this publication.

Set up as a tentative interdisciplinary format, each event focused on a specific theme. Taking the curated themes—mediality, corporeality, interaction, materiality, structure, and transformation—as points of departure, the *DC* launched a discursive space seeking to illustrate the societal relevance of both disciplines in a new way. It set in motion an intense and often challenging encounter, in regard to both the content and its presentation. The concerts resonated in the atmosphere created by both the architectural lectures and the exhibition settings, which were respectively embedded in the Aedes Architecture Forum. After the musical performance, the architect and musicians would gather for a discursive dialogue, circling around and focusing on the themes sparked by the lectures.

#1 Mediality

The first *DC* examined the theme of "Mediality." Drawing on the observation that the dissemination of images is omnipresent today, *DC #1* raised central questions regarding their mediality. The power of images makes them appear to us as evident and natural. However, as media, they convey a constructed representational-instrumental meaning. Critically reflecting on this meaning and its formation, *DC #1* defined mediality as the inanimate mediation of a medium between imagination and representation or, respectively, between representation and presentation. Within this frame, the images of architecture and music were conceptualized as containing a special, operational mediality: rather than representing what is, they indicate what is to be done, what is to be built, and what is to be played. They ask: How do these operative and strategic "images of doing" work? What do they show? How do they show it? How are they produced? How do they circulate? How do they navigate the categorical interval between image and language, between form, function, and structure? Furthermore, these images do not only appear as relata of our actions. One might claim that human practice is principally mediatic, that is, mediated by representation.

But how does this mediatedness allow us to see and do? What knowledge does it contain? What contexts does it generate? And by which image policies does it create and determine places of the common?

It is through this bundle of evocative questions that *DC #1* addressed aspects of mediality. Starting off the program with a remarkable lecture, the German architect Oda Pälmke highlighted her new book series *Repertoire*. A central aim of Pälmke's book series is to establish architectural research that interprets existing spatial situations as if they were designs. Pälmke's motto is coined by her imperative "to love what one draws." The incisive lecture was followed by a chamber concert. The German viola player Karen Lorenz, the Danish bass player and composer Jonas Westergaard, and Christopher Dell on vibraphone played new compositional material by the latter. The subsequent conversation—to which the Aedes founder Kristin Feireiss also contributed—centered around representation and the study of mediality, investigating the architectural drawing, photography, and musical notation. During the insightful conversation, the artists not only explored their respective work but also discussed the work process behind it. The event took place as an intervention in the Aedes Architecture Forum exhibition *Holzbaugeschichten – weberbrunner architekten zürich & berlin*.

#2 Interaction

Realized as an intervention in the exhibition *Our Urban Living Room: Cobe, Copenhagen* and *Architecture for Pigs: Barn.Slaughterhouse.Shop*, the theme of the second *Dialogue Concerts* edition was "Interaction" including its implications for and conceptualizations within the fields of architecture and music. As the basis for its investigation, *DC #2* defined interaction as a situation in which two or more humans or objects act in relation to each other. Alluding to the thesis of the American architecture historian Lewis Mumford that "each habitat creates new patterns of individuality … by their interaction in the close medium of the city," *DC #2* asked: How can one read such an interaction of humans and objects in a planning context? What knowledge does the process of city as interaction contain, and how can it be said and shown? Can its implicitness be tracked? Can we deal with its indeterminacy constructively? Furthermore, how can we understand the fact that the agency of an interaction also frames, structures, or localizes humans and objects?

French architect Christophe Hutin held a highly original lecture, giving insights into the history of his own working practice and into the curation of the French Pavilion at the Venice Biennale of Architecture 2021 (which, at the time, was in the process of preparation). The lecture raised important ethical questions regarding the notions of building and research practices on site and the improvisation of space. The concert highlighted new compositions by Christopher Dell, performed by himself, the German harpist Kathrin Pechlof, and the German percussionist and composer Christian Lillinger. The ensuing discussion critically reflected on aspects of composition and improvisation in architecture.

#3 Transformation

As both initium and culmination of the series, *DC #3* was framed by the theme "Transformation." A form may be a sensual shape, a *morphé*. But it may also be an idea or eidos, understood today as mental content. To change a form is what is coined as transformation: a transformational process moves across two forms in space and time, from the existing to the yet-to-be. This act of passage implies engaging in two activities at the same time: taking form and giving form. What makes architecture and music so fascinating in this context is that they not only move across forms, but are also capable of letting transformation take place across categories. Both a geometric formula transformed into the material state of an architectural drawing or model and a musical concept transformed into the performance by players let mental content become a tangible/experiential shape. The dualism of form versus matter, of *morphé* versus hyle, collapses here. Matter gains agency in the interplay of transformational procedures. In this perspective, architecture and music become reading machines of immanence in the truest sense: an architectural drawing is blind but makes one see; a musical notation is deaf but makes one hear. Consequently, drawing the city, performing a musical piece, suggests being immersed in an open process of change. The one who aims at being confronted with concrete situations and the transformational possibility of yet another recursive take has to go out to intervene in them and represent them.

Just as music can be related to science in the form of visualization, it can also be related to architecture. Not only do music and architectural notation—through variation, modulation, and invention—elegantly move across forms; they also have the capacity to let transformation take place across categories. For instance, both the translation of a geometric formula into the material state of an architectural drawing or model and the making over of a musical concept into the performance by players allow inner ideas become tangible form. This does not mean that the origin of the shape is the idea. On the contrary, the geometrical and the musical concept are both grounded in praxis (practice). They must—and have historically had to be—activated in order to take place. In a strange way, both the geometrical and the musical concepts are ideal entities that are both historical. While containing an ideal core, they accrete sedimentations in their transmission, their delivery to the present and future, thus transforming their shape.

But how does this concept of transformation allow for a reading and showing of today's urban life? How can an ethic be achieved which allows the urban inhabitants to transform themselves and thereby the collective composition of the city? And how does this change the understanding of urban politics?

In his exclusive and mind-opening keynote lecture at *DC #3*, Daniel Libeskind reflected on the notion of transformation as a method in his spatial and architectural design approach, unfolding these aspects of paramount concern to him: the transformation of society through architecture, by focusing on representation and the transformation of ideas in the translation of drawing to building. At the core of his reflections was the canonical work *Chamberworks*. A set of twenty-eight drawings, *Chamberworks* was created by Libeskind during the years in which he served as the head of the Architecture Department at Cranbrook Academy of Art in Bloomfield Hills, Michigan, in the early 1980s. The drawings explore the relationship between music and architecture, both architecturally and graphically.

Also centered around *Chamberworks* and juxtaposed with Dell's concept of *Formblocks*, the music for *DC #3* was performed by the German cellist Elisabeth Coudoux, the German trumpeter and composer Pascal Klewer, the German composer and percussionist Christian Lillinger, and Christopher Dell. The latter conceives his *Formblocks* as a strategic performative approach to work with indeterminacy. In this sense, *Formblocks* served as a lens through which Libeskind's *Chamberworks* were musically read as scores.

#4 Structure

Intervening in the exhibition *Omer Arbel: Architektonische Experimente in Material und Form*, the focus of DC #4 was on the theme "Structure." Etymologically, the term structure goes back to the Latin *structura*, which describes nothing less than the "orderly assembling of walls" in masonry. In contrast, the modern term structure pertains to a specific quantity—namely, a set of relations linking the elements of an organizational field. By this is meant that a structural relation between different elements is determined in such a way that a change in one element results in a corresponding change in the other element.

In music, for example, a motif can be considered a structural element in relation to the form of the work. In architecture one might think of a building-street situation in relation to the district, or an action in relation to the actor constellation of a building-street situation. One may also speak here of elements being structurally "wired" or "coming into functioning" together. But how can such a wiredness be defined in more detail? How can it be represented? And what relevance does it have in understanding, reading, and producing urban space?

Taking structure as its guiding motif, the forward-looking lecture of *DC #4* held by the German architect and urban designer Bernd Kniess discussed the question of reading the contemporary city against the background of climate change and pandemics by looking at different cases, statistics, concepts, and practices. In regard to this, Kniess argued that it is necessary to develop modes of reading the city which decompose its wiring—making them in turn more visible in retrospect—in order to deduce their structure. *DC #4* included a thriving concert by Christopher Dell, Christian Lillinger, and Jonas Westergaard, presenting their latest super-form work. The discussion following the performance circled around questions of positioning toward structure, the representation of structure, and the structural coproduction of open works.

#5 Corporeality

The fifth theme of the *Dialogue Concerts*, "Corporeality," engaged in the concept of the body in society and its significance for architecture and music. Realized as a stream, *DC #5* was part of the exhibition *HUMAN SCALE REMEASURED*, curated by ANCB The Aedes Metropolitan Laboratory and held at the Aedes Architecture Forum. It can be said that hardly any other topic is currently as popular as that of the body. Every day we are concerned with presenting, equipping, and dressing bodies—our own and those of others. Bodies are the central media interfaces at which social practices become visible and tangible—along with the normativity embedded in them. In particular, the sensuality of the body is at stake: corporeality. But what is to be understood by corporeality today? And how would the city be rethought if corporeality were not representative? Wouldn't the diversity and heterogeneity of corporeality then come into view in a new way?

In light of these questions, the investigative lecture by Christopher Dell, with its transhistorical perspective, examined the influence which concepts of the human body have had on architecture. Due to its streamed format, the fifth *Dialogue Concert* was not held in the exhibition space but at the Emil Berliner Studios. Filmed by Moritz Dirks and Otto Stockmeier of reframe, Berlin, and recorded by the sound engineer Lukas Kowalski, the concert was performed by the German contemporary music ensemble Mosaik. Chatschatur Kanajan and Sarah Saviet on violin, Karen Lorenz on viola, and Mathis Mayr on violoncello performed world premieres of *Streichquartett No. 2* and *Formblock 32* by Christopher Dell. In resonance with and reaction to the concert and the lecture, the Zoom discussion was held with Tabea Michaelis and Ben Pohl of the Swiss architecture office Denkstatt (Basel), joined by the musicians Sarah Saviet and Mathis Mayr. Moderated by Christopher Dell, the debate investigated the theme of corporeality in music and architecture, highlighting concepts such as performativity, embodiment, measure, grid, use, representation, notation, and intervention.

#6 Materiality

DC #6 examined the theme "Materiality" as understood both in a metaphorical and in a literal sense. Realized as an intervention in the two Aedes exhibition spaces—Kéré Architects' *Arbre à Palabres* and Ursula Schulz-Dornburg's *Vanished Landscapes*—*DC #6* took its point of departure from the question "What matters?" Posed ever so often, this seemingly universal question touched on several realms: the ethical, political, and epistemological or the ontological. In all of these realms, the question of what matters relates to inquiries on the material constitution of living beings and things, and on the way they exist as bodily and sensually perceivable phenomena. Along these lines, in both music and architecture, materials and their properties are always subject to social construction, while materiality can be coined as the relationship between a phenomenon and human practice. How do these relationships determine the way we live together as a city? And what are the ways to work with them constructively?

The lecture within *DC #6*'s framework was held by the Dutch architect Ton Matton. Transposing artistic strategies to urban planning and highlighting their role as sources of inspiration, Matton's cutting-edge input embraced contemporary themes such as migration, globalization, and postcolonial thinking. The Danish saxophonist Lotte Anker, the Greek bass player Sofia Eftychidou, and Christopher Dell performed the delicate chamber concert amid the meticulously assembled canopé installation of the Burkina Faso architect and Pritzker Architecture Prize recipient Francis Kéré. Since Kéré had conceived this installation as a community-creating structure, the discussion also took place here. It illuminated characteristics of materiality as performative and sociocultural issues, highlighting facets which make this topic particularly relevant in architecture and music. To date, the performative and sociocultural aspects of materiality have been largely ignored, especially by architects, architectural historians, and theorists. Seen in the light of recent transformations of architectural practices and participation, the discussion debated how new representations, practices, and concepts of materiality may rewrite the discourse of architecture and urban design in society. Referring to her differentiation between structure and texture, Lotte Anker offered astonishing understandings of the question of materiality in musical performance and composition. Francis Kéré, who was present at the event, contributed valuable insights into how he had constructed the installation/exhibition and into the highly conceptual and political background of his specific use of materiality.

Conclusion

As different as they may seem, in summary one may say that the disciplines of architecture and music connect through one main theme: action in concert. By raising fundamental questions about the collectivity of action and its representation, both architecture and music query society as it is and ask how it could be. Presenting different reflections on the agency of architecture and music, the documentation of the *Dialogue Concerts* in this book consequently revolves around the subject of procedure. It is exactly at this point where both disciplines converge: How do practitioners think in action, how do they make practice discursive, and in what way is their work normatively and critically directed toward constructive work with the indeterminacy of the present and the future?

Along these lines, this publication aims to contribute to discussions about how cross-readings of the disciplines of architecture and music might inspire and add to the current debates on political, cultural, social, economic, and jurisdictional conditions within society. It is my hope that the book will provide new insights into and understandings of disciplinary practice and research, and also stimulate further debate on these matters.

Preface

Kristin Feireiss and Hans-Jürgen Commerell
Directors, Aedes Architecture Forum, Berlin

The relationship between music and architecture has a long tradition in European cultural history. It ranges from antiquity through the Middle Ages and the Renaissance to the twentieth and twenty-first centuries. It was always about music as a design basis for architecture.

It was through our friend, the architecture and urban planning theorist, philosopher, and gifted and internationally renowned vibraphonist Christopher Dell, that we first became aware that architecture can also be the design basis for music in its conceptual and emotional dimensions.

In 2012, he had the spontaneous idea of interpreting some of our Aedes exhibitions on site with his vibraphone, like the shows by Coop Himmelblau, UN Studio, or Daniel Libeskind, which had particularly inspired creative implementation in space. Each time, these Preliminary Concerts were a profound space-sound experience. In 2020, for the 40th anniversary of the Aedes Architecture Forum, Dell took up his idea again, now expanding it into an interdisciplinary research project on the mutual influence of music and architecture. The dialogue between architecture and music was thematized and interpreted by Christopher Dell in a performative way, both musically and philosophically. These *Dialogue Concerts*, which took place over a period of two years, were located again in the Aedes exhibitions, accompanied by lectures on architecture and music theory in order to combine both disciplines in an innovative manner. An exciting experience that none of us will forget.

We are pleased that the essence of this unique endeavor is now being made accessible to a wider audience through this book, which is special in its interweaving of mediality and content. Christopher, we thank you for that.

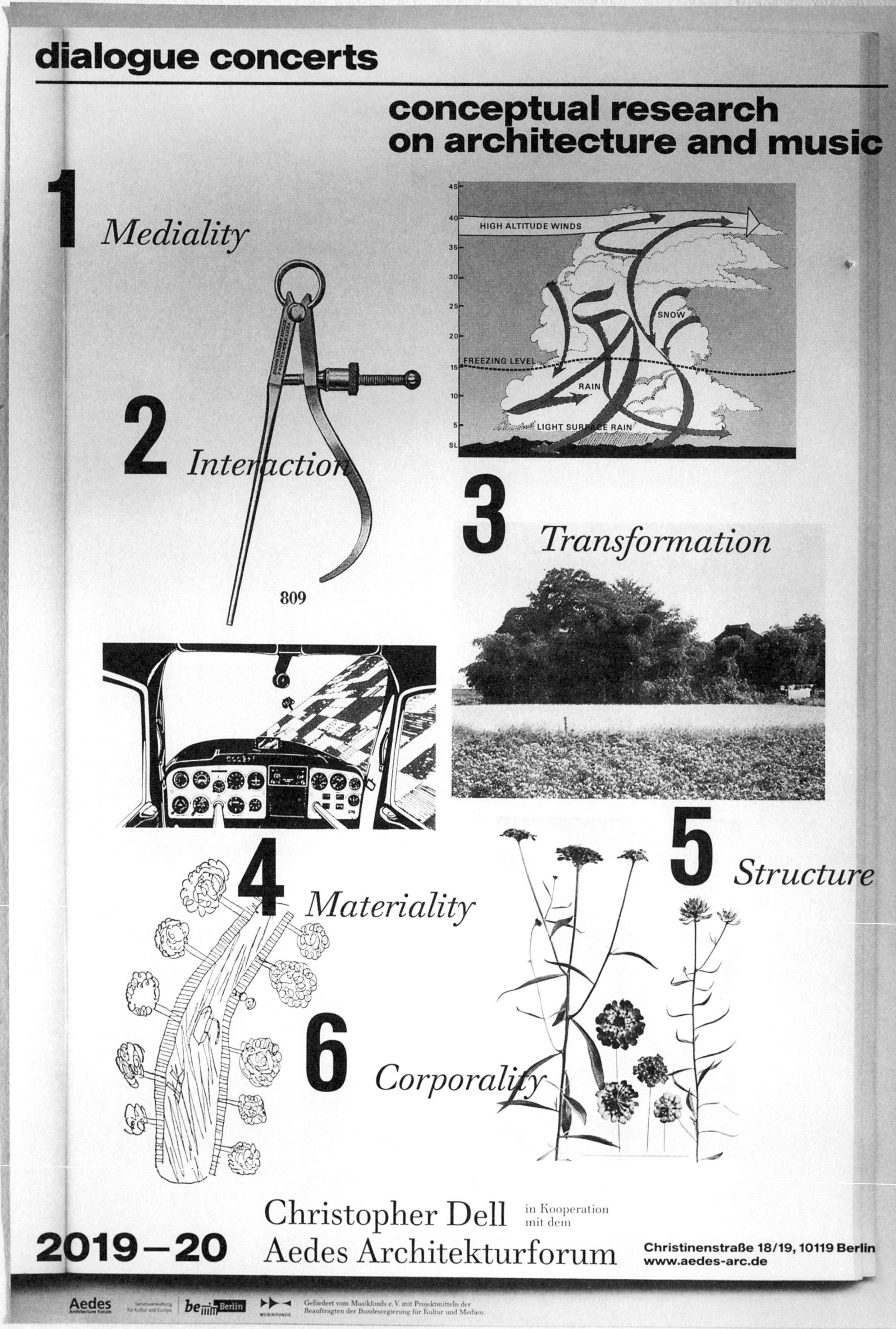
dialogue concerts
conceptual research
on architecture and music
1 Mediality
2 Interaction
809
45
40
HIGH ALTITUDE WINDS
35
30
25
SNOW
20
FREEZING LEVEL
15
RAIN
10
5
LIGHT SURFACE RAIN
SL
3 Transformation
4 Materiality
5 Structure
6 Corporality
2019–20
Christopher Dell
in Kooperation
mit dem
Aedes Architekturforum
Christinenstraße 18/19, 10119 Berlin
www.aedes-arc.de
Aedes
Architecture Forum
Berlin
MUSIKFONDS
Gefördert vom Musikfonds e. V. mit Projektmitteln der
Beauftragten der Bundesregierung für Kultur und Medien.

On Curating *Dialogue Concerts*
Event, Performative Installation, and Book as Form and Medium

Christopher Dell

On Curating *Dialogue Concerts* Event, Performative Installation, and Book as Form and Medium

Christopher Dell

Loud silence. Chairs are being placed, a projector montaged, music instruments set up, a small sound check, visitors drift around the space among the exhibited objects, voices whisper, a tension arises. In the midst of a material constellation of the most different things—models, drawings, displays, tables, screens, shelfs, books, a drum set, a harp, a bass, a trumpet, a cello, a music stand, a wooden bench, metal chairs, downlights, frames—a subtle movement emerges. Slow, but determined. The atmosphere seems to electrify. Are we waiting for something to happen? Is it happening now? Seemingly out of "nothing," the event starts. But hadn't this peculiar "nothing" been meticulously prepared or structured? Or, put differently, hadn't the event been "on" already?

Deliberately, at its own pace, in one corner of the exhibition space a lecture unfolds, preceded by a short opening speech. After the last word has been spoken here, the last slide shown, the whole flock slowly moves to the next spot, where the concert begins to structure the space with organized sounds. And then, gradually, the sound ebbs away. Again, everybody moves, this time toward the assembly spot. The participants and visitors settle in loosely for the discussion. A hang, a gathering, a happening. Finally, the situation gently dissolves. Redensifies elsewhere. Drinks and pretzels are served outside, dialogues continue in duos, trios, or larger groups, just as the evening rhythm takes its own time. All of a sudden, one realizes that the event has ended, again out of the prepared nothing. Still, since it is a series, I know and feel that the next event is about to arrive in the same yet different way.

While the interventions of the *Dialogue Concerts* (*DC*) shuffled through the exhibition space of the Aedes Architecture Forum, placing the lecture, the concert, and the discussion in different sites, little by little the event series instigated a sociomaterial topology, which set in motion performers and visitors alike. Choreographing spaces to make the participants' actions and the visitors' relation to the participants performative, *DC* encouraged an intuitive bodily perception of movement through open navigation. The visitors could reposition themselves freely in the given arrangement. In regard to its material and programmatic framing, the event was conjured through the performative installation as a compulsory, exposing, and showing diagram. Embodiment and dissimulation of meaning as a form of production were never fully determined. Displays became furniture, forming partitioned areas or communal spaces of gathering in places set aside for the lecture, the concert, and the discussion, or for just hanging out after the event in the courtyard in front of the gallery, where drinks and food were provided by the Aedes Architecture Forum team. While each event was conceived as the expression of a strategy for the collaborative production of meaning and being, throughout its duration the *DC* series remained responsive to each invited performer's particular interests in the cross-disciplinary event. At the core of this process remained the objective to situate exceptional and pioneering practices of architecture and music within a discursive, historical, and cultural context, and to reflect on them critically while also examining the specific modes of production of meaning in relation to their dissemination in and use of different media.

It is against the backdrop described above that this text intends to conceptually frame and perspectivize the *Dialogue Concerts* as form and medium. What I aim at is to explore and lay out the conceptual framework that drove and organized the making of the *DC* as a distinct mode of employing medium and form. With this in mind, I investigate the *DC*'s curatorial framework in terms of interaction and dialogue between disciplines. I do so in recognition that critical artistic or scientific research is always moving beyond the boundaries of its field. The position from which I seek to shed light on the theoretical foundation of the *DC* is delimited by two disciplines: urban design and architectural theory on the one hand, and music on the other. I am active in these two disciplinary fields, and also and especially in such a way that I purposely cultivate cross-disciplinary relationships. Yet, I have noticed an astonishing absence of a general forum on interdisciplinarity that is committed to the best possible reflection. This volume is an attempt to fill this gap. However, it does not claim to present a single scientific-theoretical or practical point of view on interdisciplinarity. Instead, a variety of positions are addressed. Anyone who is concerned with inter- or cross-disciplinarity may find inspiration here.

To overcome isolated actions is indispensable for facing the questions concerning today's urban society. What is at stake here is to find new modes of collectively "acting in concert" in support of multilateralism in order to instill critical optimism and positive dynamics around what makes living on this planet possible.

By conceiving the *Dialogue Concerts* as a dialogical practice, I am relating them to a social definition of "medium"—as both stable and transformative—"in which practices and institutions are seen as agencies of mediation in and of themselves."[1] Regarding the definition of the formal aspect of the *DC* as a medium, I am inspired by the French philosopher Gilles Deleuze, who insisted on the fundamental role that mediators play in any process of making: "Creation's all about mediators. Without them nothing happens. They can be people … but things too, even plants or animals."[2] It should be pointed out that, in this definition, mediators are forms that are structurally produced and constituted as collectives of human and non-human actors. Mediators are forms that are in the making, forms of becoming, or, as Deleuze would say, "formations."[3] Such formation receives its structure by means of series. Deleuze argues, "Whether they're real or imaginary, animate or inanimate, you have to form your mediators. It's a series. If you're not in some series, even a completely imaginary one, you're lost. I need my mediators to express myself, and they'd never express themselves without me: you're always working in a group, even when you seem to be on your own."[4] It is in reference to this definition that the *Dialogue Concerts* can be understood as a medium and form in their own right.

On Curating the *Dialogue Concerts*

Realizing the *DC* as form and medium, so as to investigate the newest practices of and reflections on architecture and music, involved employing different curatorial mechanisms. Specifically, my curatorial practice in attaining the formats of the events series, performative installation, and book entailed the selection, coproduction, display, and/or dissemination of disciplinary practices by conceptually and organizationally framing them. The *Dialogue Concerts* gathered their participants to initiate a dialogical project in which the primary objective was to set a temporal discursive process in motion rather than focusing on the outcome of a fixed object. Along these lines, the *DC* invited practitioners with articulate and pioneering positions in their field to discuss what the conditions and possibilities of cross-disciplinary production (of discourse and practice) on a mediating level are today. Through the public discussions within the *DC* event series and its subsequent publication, the select practitioners conveyed a sense of relationality to situate their position within a broader discourse. To this end, through the appropriation of its dynamic and open character, the event as medium provided a means of analyzing and contesting what constitutes disciplinary production.

In today's world, global capitalism is a benign, accelerated process, which embodies not only a transformation of social relations but also, and especially, their spatial organization. Critically discussing this process, the event series *DC* was conceptualized as an inevitable part of the actual urban condition. Homologous to formulating the contemporary city as an amalgam of diagrams, of multiple times and sites, the event series was conceptualized as a performative medium that wires heterogeneous series of content. However, although the *DC* series can only be diagnosed as an outcome and symptom of its conditions—the globalized world—its hybrid and multilayered open form sought to provide minimal moments of utopia, rethinking, reframing, realignment, resistance, dissensus, antagonism, and counter-spectacle to the grand narratives of progress and the market-driven logics of contemporary capitalism.

A collaborative medium of dialogue involving two different disciplines and multiple practices and positions, the *Dialogue Concerts* strove to expand the understanding of both the practices they put on display and the constellation of performer–curator–audience. What the *DC* offered and proposed was a temporary discursive space for intellectual positions from diverse origins and disciplines. The event functioned as a protected space of refuge—an in-between space of hanging out together, of conviviality, reciprocity, and passage. Within this space of knowledge production, the disruptions, misunderstandings, and irritations that come with the cross-disciplinary exchange were not only retained as a structure but moreover inserted as catalysts for constructive learning and unlearning. Sparked to develop new forms of understanding, this reframing of discrepancies sought to render the confrontation of different methods, modes of thinking, and uses of language fruitful in a fresh and inventive manner.

There is reason to suggest that the proliferation of the *DC* manifested a moment in which curatorship in architecture and music opened up to an expanded field beyond mere object display and material production. Therefore, the DC took into account their own discursive and dissemination modes of exchange, while acting as a vehicle for questioning what is commonly understood and known about the disciplines of architecture and music, and the way in which they become known. By hybridizing the performative and the installative, the act of curating the *DC* conveyed a critical dispositive to both disciplines through the organization, presentation, and discussion of events. In this context, my own hybrid role as theorist–artist–curator loosely defined a practice of employing exhibition design, architectural structures, display arrangements, musical instruments, drawings, and other notational representations and curatorial strategies as a way of creating composite research outcomes. In this sense, my work as curator not only included the display of discourses, concerts, and the spatial intervention in the exhibition design, but also the provision of an overall curatorial structure as part of an expanded artistic and scientific practice. Within this framework, the performative installation as event series made

the *DC* a distinctive model of curating—a communicative medium as well as a mode of artistic and scientific production.

Research

To let the research of the *Dialogue Concerts* branch out from the series of events was part of their methodology. As performative installations, the events not only intervened in the very historical location of the Aedes Architecture Forum, but also exemplified the mechanisms that make spaces of contemporary architecture exhibitions both multiple ruptures and rich research resources. Partly a resource, partly an installative exhibition event, the *DC* were defined both as an expanded research project and as a curatorial practice. This double movement indicates that the methodological means through which the research was maintained is situated directly within the structural formalization of the series: the meticulous montage of gatherings of heterogeneous positions assisted in creating and sustaining the cross-disciplinary debate and exchange and the related discursive outcome.

Spatially and institutionally, it was the exhibition space of the Aedes Architecture Forum that functioned as the main context of, and the primary medium for, the performative realization of the *DC* event series. At the same time, it served as the site in which the research was conducted and transformed. Hence, the expansion in understanding the curatorial aspects put forward by the Aedes Architecture Forum and its satellite Aedes Network Campus allowed the *DC* to switch between different areas of activity. This framing increased the potential for a heteronomy of articulation within the field of exhibition and display, as well as in the disciplinary fields discussed and researched. Vice versa, the *Dialogue Concerts* staged a correlation between the various events within the series, which facilitated discourse on specific disciplinary practices. Recontextualizing the main exhibition at the Aedes Architecture Forum, the *DC*'s discussions were orientated around a contextual public cultural formation. The same holds true for the *DC*'s scene of address. One might claim that what is shown at the Aedes Architecture Forum is—or becomes a part of—the architectural canon. As an established institution, this architecture gallery lent its canonizing power to the self-reflexive interrogation of the *DC* related to the redefinition of research in terms of production and representation of knowledge.

Taking this standpoint, the research undertaken by the *DC* aimed at illustrating that (and how) ideologies about the city are shaping how we think about living together as city, and why it matters for scholars in their respective fields to understand how ideologies are formulated and mobilized. While putting the basic objective to work—cross-investigating how practitioners in two disciplinary fields think, how they compose, and how they conceptualize—the *DC*'s conceptual and institutional framing furthermore made it possible to thematize and critically discuss how to represent, what to show, and which media of showing to use.

Form and Medium: Montage I

As a curated event series, performative installation, and book, the *Dialogue Concerts* have constituted a medium of, firstly, active discursive exchange between disciplines and their audience and, secondly, attunement to how the cross-fertilization of individual positions within disciplinary economies propels the transformation of practice. It is from this angle that I understand the *DC*'s space of dialogue and discourse—be it in performative or written form—as a medium in its own right. To operate in this way means to take into account the medium's multidirectional capacity to organize. The mix of formats—as a performative installation, an event, and a creative, semiautonomous, and specifically authored form of mediation and production—structured the experience of the *DC*'s discourse and the formation thereof. Simultaneously, this specific structuring affected the way in which the *DC* could convey the modes in which architecture and music are made and communicated to an audience.

Introducing event groupings and collaborations, the series recognized the limitations of the single exhibition. In this light, the *Dialogue Concerts* were conceived as an expanded plug-in structure for dialogues that transcend the notion of the exhibition as a finite event within the main exhibitions located at and curated by the Aedes Architecture Forum. It is as a medium that the *DC* promoted the idea of the platform as a contested political agent, through which it becomes possible to enact forms of social and disciplinary critique, global commentary, or even activism.

The making of the *Dialogue Concerts* as a discursive space established both the principal curatorial form and the primary medium through which knowledge production and exchange have been contoured. An expansive and evolving project, the *DC* intertwined the spatial constellation and the program as equally considered planes of entangled coproduction. That for instance the floor plans were presented in the program booklet of each event—indicating the spatial relationality of the event to its exhibition context—is an exemplificatory testimony to the image politics of this curatorial strategy. The *DC* made use of a particular method of organizing, framing, and conceptualizing material practices by juxtaposing and wiring agencies of mediation. The event series brought together practitioners to create a specific environment for knowledge production and its performative display. It is important to emphasize that, within this process, the organizational and conceptual framework, the techniques of mediation, and the event format collapsed into one another. By this is meant that by employing the given exhibition site as its medium, the *DC* produced a performative and spatial setting in their own distinct way, which provided the environmental setting for the staging of discussions, concerts, lectures, and visitor engagement.

Visuality, display, and narrative were central to the *Dialogue Concerts*. The emphasis on the event, the video, and the book—as the media through which the *DC* have communicated—was intended to reinforce the transitory moments of discursive exchange between the disciplines. The event does not happen "in" but rather produces time and space, thus creating coexistence, rhythms, transformation, and reordering. The modes of arrangement, display, and of the videos, streams, programs, and the book at hand, should therefore be identified as manifesting a certain aesthetic and political procedure of processing, while imposing a conceptual framework that is similar to many of my other works—with an emphasis on the framing and mediation of dense structure and open formation.

That the *DC* opted for the possibility of outlining the series of events through a set of specific motifs, rather than periods or artists, created a high degree of structuring for the individual agency involved in the performance of events. One might say that the *DC* evolved as a metaform, a plug-in structure that pays attention to and makes use of the functions and potentials performed by curating, exhibition design, and the spatial arrangement of exhibition forms. One can assert that it is in this sense that the *DC* followed the method of montage. Based on the de- and reassembly of fragments, montage demands a calculated heterogeneity of depiction. In this manner, it allows the form to transform into a rich block of material always to be resorted to and drawn from. As a formal procedure, montage fundamentally inscribes itself in the effect of its narrative. It enables the revealing of new connections of reference regarding respective subject matter. For instance, one can act more freely when making use of iconic, tabular, or indexical qualities of any given material. In the case of the *DC*, in a multirhythmic manner, the method of montage allowed structural conflicts, cracks, and fissures of events to be made visible.

The term "performative installation" binds the eventfulness of performativity into the materiality of an installation. The performative installation is characterized by a sense of a simultaneity of action and experience on which the eventfulness of knowledge production (as a process) has a continuous effect. In this way, the performative installation unites presence and representation, ephemeral and static elements, immateriality and materiality. As an immersive space, it introduces a sensory awareness and embodiment of performers and viewers alike.

As a performative installation, the *Dialogue Concerts* were shown and thematized as a cross-disciplinary assemblage of human and nonhuman actors, actions, discourses, and sites that mediate and produce a complex of meaning effects and affects. Based on the assumption that as material practices they become inseparable from architecture and music as discursive practices, the *DC* put forward the thesis that both disciplinary modes of doing can and should be verbalized, spoken of, drawn, or written about. However, far from taking it as a given, this act of "making practice speak" was itself a central subject of critical debate and research.

Far from producing the event as pure presence, the performative installation is not about the dissolution of the work in the event but about the symbiosis of both the event and the work. Regarding aspects of meaning production, the intention of the *DC*'s particular curatorial procedure was to create an open framework within which a recoding of practice as discourse emerged while being transposed onto diverse invited positions. The event as the principal form and the curatorial framing of a series of heterogeneity provided the lens through which alignments could be seen and made between particular practices and statements. By employing the performative installation format, the *Dialogue Concerts* were able to stage questions on a shared reality by means of constructed situations. Their spatial arrangement was understood not as a neutral container, but as a decisive part of instigating and framing discourse and dialogue. I am thinking of their insistence on the embodiment of discourse, which thrust into question general preassumptions of progress in, and mastery over, the planet we live on.

Discursive Practice, Discursive Space

The *Dialogue Concerts* took into account the historical consequence of recoding practice not only by making it discursive, but also by interpreting practice and discourse as dialogically intertwined. Based on this procedure, the *DC* followed the formal concept of letting the spatial and temporal context of discursive production coincide with and intervene in the context of the architecture exhibition. The interplay of spatial arrangement and discursively charged activities was induced by organizational strategies through which the event/exhibition was given form and was experienced. Combined, these strategies shifted the emphasis away from the possible fetishization of mono-disciplines, toward an interdependent relationship between architecture and music and global political/cultural/economic discourse. Focusing on dialogical and local entanglements in this way, the *Dialogue Concerts* located knowledge production beyond disciplinary boundaries. The *DC* extended the reach of single projects by going beyond the parameters of the disciplines as a single narrative and by mobilizing a field of research inquiry beyond the individual disciplinary position, with added significance given to the discussions, lectures, publication, events, performances, and social media dissemination.

Presenting international participants who are working within the expanded field of their disciplines, the *DC* broadened the parameters of the exhibition space to incorporate more discursive forms. Conversational modes centered on the ambit of both the exhibition and its intervention, as a framing device in which discourse was posited as a possible form of practice, while the disciplinary practices themselves were made discursive. Within this procedure, the *DC* interpreted the individual lectures, the discussions, and the publication as discursive moments of the main event series as well as works in their own right. Their iterations acknowledged the fallibility of the mono-event and exhibition alike, taking into account a more dialogical model of practice. And vice versa, in the light of the *DC*, the practice of doing necessitated a discourse as speaking or writing in order to appear as part of an institutional superstructure and to be accessible as an epistemological structure.

The *Dialogue Concerts* promoted a specific understanding of architecture and music. No longer restricted to a realm that is materialized as the objects of architecture or the artifacts of music respectively, this understanding also encompasses the production of concepts about architecture and music, which in themselves can be constituted as decisive and productive parts of their disciplines. As a result, the *DC* mobilized a shift of emphasis in the criticism of works of architecture and music—away from a primary critique of the building or the musical work as an autonomous object of study, toward a mode of process criticism in which the practices and their concepts, procedures, and framings become a central subject of investigation. During this course, architectural and musical practices transcended their traditional boundaries of implicitness to arrive at an explicit state.

True to genre crossing, the *DC* intended to dislodge the scopic regimes of stereotypical characterizations of "disciplines," of the easy interpretations through which the disciplines are read and of the ways in which the institutional canons produce themselves as bounded entities. The *DC* envisaged creating a wider visibility for both the practitioners and their practices, corroborated by an ongoing circulation of related discourse, which employs frames of reference for those involved in the thematic territory of the respective disciplines. In parallel, the event series manifested a set of mediating factors between the invited participants and the audience, allowing the possibility of viewing the participants' work within the paradoxical situation of contextualizing structures beyond market forces yet in the context of a private gallery.

The Book

Conventionally, alongside the development of a practice specific to curating, one important outcome of an exhibition of any sort is the catalogue. As a documentary tool, it secures the exhibition's afterlife. The document allows the content of the exhibition to continue to exist after the latter took place. In the case of the *Dialogue Concerts*, the catalogue subsists long after the event series, as durational entity, has finished. However, utilized to make extended discursive and visual statements, as a curatorial form in itself, the catalogue may also take on an archaeological dimension within the context of the curatorial project. Such a reworking of mediation in a print format induces reflection on a metalevel, inasmuch as it is employed to mobilize discourse surrounding the events and their exhibition, developed in parallel to the critical discourse around certain forms of practice that were, themselves, being developed in the context of the events. Even more decisively, the catalogue allows one to problematize the question of representation, presentation, and documentation of an event series as forms of works in their own right. Understood in this way, the book at hand establishes an extended field of the spatio-temporal nature of the event format involving discussions, concerts, and lectures over the course of the *Dialogue Concerts*. However, constituting a discursive space in itself, the book moves beyond the conventional parameters of documenting. Discussions on practices can then again become, to a large extent, discussions about the showing of these practices and the media that are responsible for their representation or presentation.

Although the events' discussions and lectures have been subsequently disseminated in the form of published texts *after* the events, the texts' transcriptive nature points to and draws on their life character. Manifesting them in this publication implies that they still carry the feel of "taking place," with the participants being present at a physical and discursive space of coexistence. Also responsible for the capturing of such lifeness in this volume are the photographs it contains, all of which were taken by the artist Ruth Hommelsheim. Creating a continuous rewiring of relationships and meaningful juxtapositions, Hommelsheim's installation views make visible the myriad connections and newly established configurations in which the events were reconfigured throughout their duration.

In summary, this volume focuses on how concepts have been expressed and understood in and by two divergent disciplines in recent history, and in what way this understanding has normatively and transformatively shaped their discourse. It is part of an unraveling of how the highly specialized and organized fields of architecture and music result in the formation of cultures of doing that continue to determine and reinvent themselves.

At the same time, providing a mediatic extension to the event series, this book demarcates a discursive position that clarifies the curatorial endeavor of the *DC* as a whole. Through providing a resource for documenting and interpreting, I argue that this book, in its specific materiality and mediality, also conveys the curatorial thesis of the exhibited events and their relationship with other fields of inquiry. With this book, an attempt is made to demonstrate this, and to reflect on how curatorial practices such as cataloguing, selecting, organizing, arranging, mediating, and communicating intersect with the spaces of display, discourse, event, performative installation, and exhibition. The publication queries the relationship between production, display, and conceptualization within the medium of the book space. Inasmuch as it is utilized to mobilize a discourse surrounding the events and their exhibition developed in parallel to the critical discourse around certain forms of practice that were, themselves, being developed in the context of the events, the publication induces a critical and reflexive reworking of mediation in a print format.

Medium and Form: Montage II

To present the history of the *Dialogue Concerts* as a montage is to demonstrate it as an act of becoming. That is why I decided, together with the designer Helmut Völter, by making this book to let the thematic structures interfere with the spatial organization of the representational space showing them. Such montaging of the exposed elements breaks the boundaries between the particular and the history, between the document and the narrative. Its principle is based on the concept that in the spatial organization of interwoven yet particular and heterogeneous visualizations one could work with surprising leaps, clashes, and transitions. To trace such divergent forms of showing back to a single source is neither possible nor intended. Rather, referring to the event series, the serial composition of the book reminds one more of the taxonomic diagrammatics of an herbarium, an inventory list, a structural archive of the most divergent things. I am thinking of the French philosopher Roland Barthes and his seminal text "The Death of the Author," in which he states: "a text is made of multiple writings, drawn from many cultures and entering into mutual relations of dialogue, ... but there is one place where this multiplicity is focused and that place is the reader, not, as was hitherto said, the author. The reader is the space on which all the quotations that make up a writing are inscribed without any of them being lost; a text's unity lies not in its origin but in its destination."[5] By underscoring its multiplicity of idioms, visual strategies, and references, this book—in line with Barthes—invites the reader to actively co-creatively read, collect, and interpret.

Epistemologically, montage is guided by the insight that one of the conditions enabling its capacity to produce knowledge is to bring fragmentation to recomposition and to make the material one intends to examine readable in a certain structure. Essential to this structure is that montage exhibits its mode of showing itself as a form. In other words: the book invests in the recomposition of material without ceasing the effects of interpretation and heterogeneous temporalities, in order to evoke a thinking in the iridescent rhythm of differences and references. The individual documents reveal historical moments in their own right, but mounted—this is in relation to other documents—they guide extended conceptual thinking about the totality of the assembled material. In discursive terms, then, such a formal approach also reveals the position of the one who is presenting. Here, every double-page spread is both reflection and revision in the literal sense of the word, the act of bringing before the eyes, checking, verifying, and testing. The sequencing of page space is not intended to be closed and authoritative, but a permanent public questioning of what is presented, of one's own research work, of one's own episteme. Where it forms a principally unfinished series, the book sequence receives its finality and inner organization from the temporal capacity of the *DC* as event series.

City

To see the city as produced space provides the *Dialogue Concerts* with their agency to affect the social. This is specifically the case regarding the event and the performative installation as sites of looking, seeing, but also socializing. On different scales, then, the city, the exhibition space, the installative event (as people, buildings, actions, and discourse and as a mobilizing concept), and the book can be understood not only as concrete entities to deconstruct or be pluralized, but also as entities to constitute themselves as a collective, open form.

1 Raymond Williams, *Keywords: A Vocabulary of Culture and Society* (London: Fontana Press, 1983), p. 204.
2 Gilles Deleuze, "Mediators," in *Negotiations, 1972–1990*, trans. Martin Joughin (New York: Columbia University Press, 1990), p. 125.
3 Ibid.
4 Ibid.
5 Roland Barthes, "The Death of the Author," in *Image, Music, Text*, trans. S. Heath (London: Fontana, 1977), pp. 142–48, esp. p. 148.

Dialogue Concert #1
Mediality
December 19, 2019

Lecture: Oda Pälmke

Concert: Christopher Dell (vibraphone), Karen Lorenz (viola), Jonas Westergaard (bass)

Discussion: Christopher Dell, Kristin Feireiss, Karen Lorenz, Bruno Margreth, Oda Pälmke, Jonas Westergaard

Aedes Architecture Forum, Berlin

Christopher and I know each other from a Motörhead concert. This happened rather a long time ago. I am an architect living and working in Berlin. I also work as a professor of architecture (Raumgestalt und Entwerfen) at the Technical University Kaiserslautern. A central part of my research as a professor there is the endeavor to publish book series which reflect and accumulate my specific interests. The volumes deal with themes that have been on my mind for a very long time.

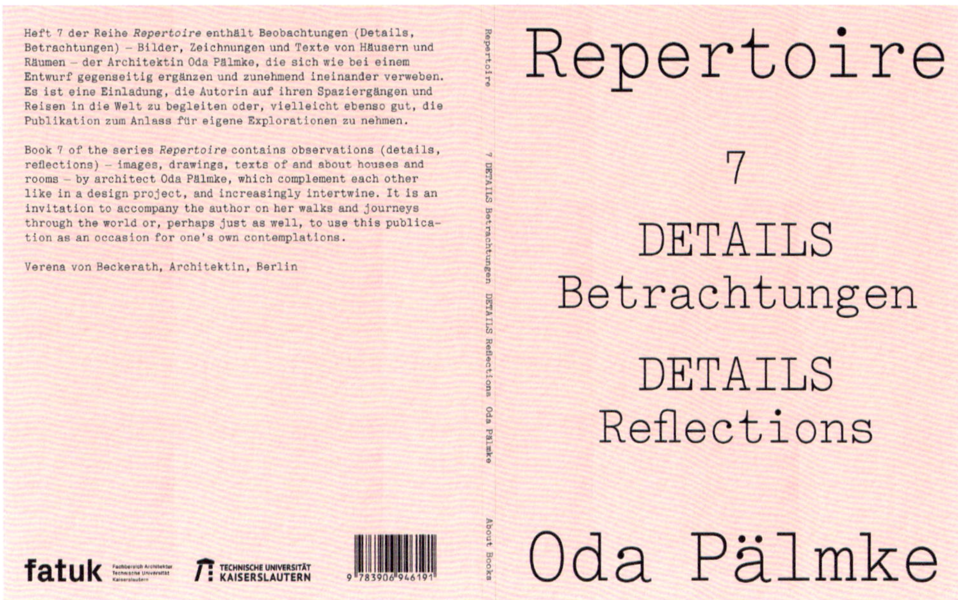

The first book series is called *Repertoire*. It contains collections of drawings and images that I have developed together with the students. One should lay emphasis on the fact that these drawings and images are not submissions or assignments as is traditionally the case in architecture education, but a curated compilation of research. We put together a team and spent three days drawing, cataloguing the drawings, and then writing texts around them. A repertoire is the total number of works an artist or ensemble can perform at any given time. The book series *Repertoire* is about ways of seeing. For example, it explores the fact that the brain learns to look past the distortions in a picture. *Repertoire*. This collection of illustrations and photographs may inspire the expansion of one's own design repertoire. Details photographed on the fly, excerpts or aspects of remarkable works of architecture and art are drawn, and then seen and reflected on as deliberate designs in their own right. Arno Schmidt explains the creation of his prose in *Berechnungen 1* (Calculations 1) as follows: "Recall an arbitrary experience… at first singular, bright impressions ('photos') appear, like a time lapse, around which complementary… 'texts' are placed." Drawing the essential lines—like sketching in front of a building or work of art—is an opportunity to linger, observe, and intensely analyze the decisive aspects of a work, its idea. Complexity *en detail*. When viewed as a whole, the modest elements in the upper living room of the Villa Snellman by Gunnar Asplund form a grand gesture.

The *Repertoire* booklets can be read or worked through in parallel in four ways if you feel like it. There is a text at the beginning, there is a middle section of drawings, there is an appendix at the end, and there is an inserted photobook. We have deliberately chosen the joyfully and at the same time laborious way of showing and reading—the organization of the materials, always flipping back and forth and lingering, sometimes getting it wrong, reading the text for the wrong drawing, seeing that drawing in another set of pictures, looking at a source later on, et cetera.

Dialogue Concerts #1
Mediality
December 19, 2019
Oda Pälmke

15
Kasimir Malewitsch, Schwarzes Quadrat auf weißem Grund, Neue Tretjakow Galerie, Moskau

15
The painting *Black Square* by Kazimir Malevich hangs in the New Tretyakov Gallery in Moscow in a passage connecting two exhibition rooms; it is almost impossible to pause in front of the painting. Surface cracks are clearly visible in the black oil paint.

Florian Illies writes: "For Malevich the square embodies the 'zero state,' the experience of pure abstraction. And the elementary contrast between white and black creates a universal energy for him. It is an end-point for art—and yet, at the same time, the beginning of something completely new."

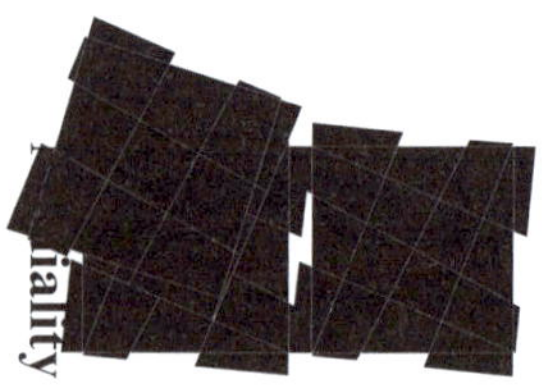

16
The fine lines of the relief *Drei schwarze Elemente mit eingeritztem Liniennetz* (Three Black Elements with an Engraved Network of Lines, 2010) by the artist Karl-Heinz Adler follow geometric rules. The elements in themselves are mirrored twice, yet they cannot be pieced back together. The situation is different in the case of Adler's fine, concrete block walls, which characterize the buildings of the GDR in apparently unending combinations.

"Adler names as two of his four working factors: 1. The secretive, in particular the magical, and 2. The rational-intellectual (the constructive or legitimate)."

17
Johanna Gullichsen, Gaia Rug, Helsinki

16
Karl-Heinz Adler und Friedric
Plastische Formsteinwand, Tierp

17
The pattern of the Gaia Rug by the Finnish designer Johanna Gullichsen, comprised of mirrored, symmetrical, proportionally expanding surfaces, has a spatial effect; the rug makes a wave.

22
Villa Le Lac, designed by Le Corbusier and Pierre Jeanneret for Le Corbusier's parents, is a comfortably furnished machine. At the desk on the linen chest in the guest room, one sits enthroned, back to the wall with a view of Lake Geneva. Le Corbusier writes: "Admittedly, a piece of furniture fastened to the wall appears somewhat immobile and the question may arise—with slight concern—of how one is supposed to live with this situation for years.… Beware of viewing a piece of furniture in isolation.… When it plays the role of an artwork, you can kiss comfort goodbye."

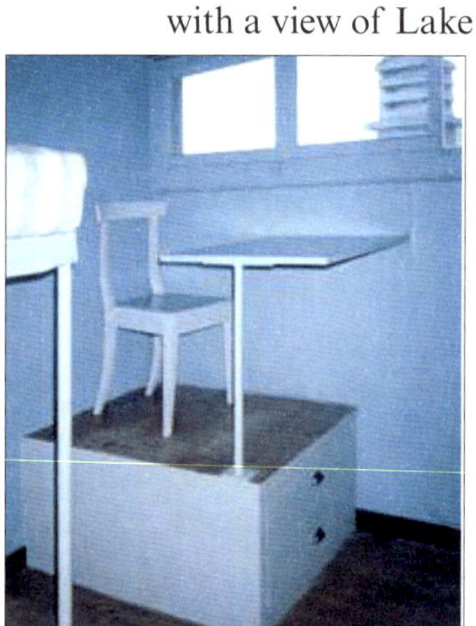

22
Le Corbusier und Pierre Jeanneret, Villa Le Lac, Corseaux

23
The gallery above the living room in Alvar Aalto's own house in Helsinki is reached by a narrow set of stairs. The stairs are above the open fireplace—which serves as a bricked pedestal—and they can also be used as a place to sit near the warm hearth.

"Aalto compared his house … to an old Finnish farmhouse, in which simple materials and simplified, somewhat crude building styles combine to form a harmonious whole."

23
Alvar Aalto, eigenes Wohnhaus, Helsinki

26
Allan Wexler's Vinyl Milford House is a work of art. The diminutive building is too small for all of its functions, which is why the walls absorb the furniture. The empty interior space can be used as needed.

27
Le Cabanon is Le Corbusier's vacation home in Roquebrune, built for his wife. It is a machine for living in the form of a wooden cabin. The tailor-made enclosure with a footprint of 3.66 by 3.66 meters is the result of lifelong research, sufficiently large for an ideal life.

"Through a door, which Le Corbusier had installed in the corridor of the cabin, he had direct access to the restaurant, as well as its food store and refrigerator.... By cleverly outsourcing the more profane every-day tasks, he was able to steer clear of the kitchen activities, thus keeping his Modulor-life pure."

26
d Ellen Wexler, The Vinyl Milford House

Johann Wolfgang von Goethe's Garden House in Weimar (29) is situated at the edge of Ilm Park, and its greenery can climb the trellises on the exterior walls. Individual windows remain closed, and the entrance gate is located directly on the plot's border in order to keep the surrounding landscape out of this garden house tableau.

27
Le Corbusier, Le Cabanon, Roquebrune-Cap-Martin

31
In Haga Park near Stockholm, Gustav III, King of Sweden, commissioned the stage designer Louis Jean Desprez to build a wooden, tent-like building. Its exterior is clad in painted copper sheets. On the interior, the velvety sheen of the sheet metal radiates a sense of summerly cheerfulness.

King Gustav III said about his theater architect Louis-Jean Desprez: "He is the only one besides myself in this country with any imagination."

The residence and studio Hvitträsk in Kirkkonummi, Finland, for the architects Eliel Saarinen, Herman Gesellius, Armas Lindgren, and their wives is a Gesamtkunstwerk or complete work of art (34, 35).

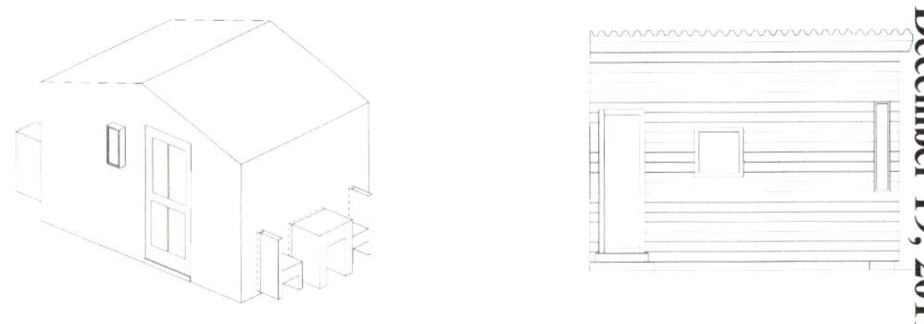

Built-in seating areas are located throughout and in multiple incarnations. Carpets climb the walls, and tapestries are spread out over the floor to form spaces for varying dispositions.

36
Erwin Heerich, Graubner Pavillon, Insel Hombroich

36
The Pavillon 11 (Graubner Pavilion) by Erwin Heerich at Insel Hombroich consists of two intersecting cylinders. The surrounding landscape is captured by the glass cylinder and transported as an image into the space of the completely bricked cylinder. One's memory of this space is like that of a mood.

31
Jean Louis Desprez, Kupferzelt / Koppartälten, Haga Park, Stockholm

41
In a public park across from the main train station in Basel, the artist Erik Steinbrecher erected white picket fences. The dense, existing vegetation is encircled, shielding it from its scheduled removal.

Nature is surrounded. Steinbrecher writes: "As the horizontal slats make clear, the passerby is walking within the fenced off area."

39
For the 2016 Architecture Biennale in Venice, prominent openings in the exterior walls were created according to a concept by the German Museum of Architecture (DAM). They could not be closed, thus turning the German Pavilion into a building for an open society for six months.

"The idea behind the German contribution to the Architecture Biennale was developed during the turbulent weeks and months in the fall of 2015, as thousands of refugees were arriving at train stations on a daily basis. … Six months later, when the biennale ended, the openings were bricked up."

41
Erik Steinbrecher, Landler und Polk
Skulptur, Basel

38 39

39
DAM, Deutscher Pavillon,
5. Architekturbiennale Venedig 2016

38
At the Museum of Modern Art (MMK) in Frankfurt am Main by Hans Hollein, each room is specifically designed, complementing the works of art exhibited to form a holistic situation. The entry to the exhibition spaces at the front of the conical entrance hall has a heightened—thus staged—perspective and makes a spectacular figure.

"Although located aboveground, the Museum of Modern Art in Frankfurt forms a wholly interior space. The museum … resembles a battleship stranded in the city."

44
In the Faaborg Museum by Carl Petersen, the floors of all the rooms are embellished with a specific colorful stoneware pattern. Each hall is an individual, harmonious composition full of character and separated from the surrounding rooms by dark, vaulted, inclined, and curved space-containing walls.

47
The Antonin Hunting Lodge by Karl Friedrich Schinkel possesses a central

38
Hans Hollein, Museum für Moderne Kunst (MMK),
Frankfurt am Main

44
Carl Petersen, Museum Faab

twin fireplace in the form of a free-standing, three-story triumphal column, heroically embellished with trophies—in this case, antlers. As the column can be seen from everywhere in the house, concealing the space behind it, the hunting society is apparently a small and cozy group.

48
Café Bravo by the artist Dan Graham in the courtyard of KW Institute for Contemporary Art in Berlin is a complete building sculpture that doubles its occupants. The illusionary effect of the space, the subsequent preoccupation with one's own mirrored image (Manuel Álvarez Bravo), and the sharp corners of the overlapping, slightly offset cubes are the built manifestations of the idea inherent in this usable sculpture.

47
Karl Friedrich Schinkel, Jagdschloss Antonin, Ostrowo

49
The elongated bar of the residential building on Luisenplatz in Berlin by the architect Hans Kollhoff appears shattered in two by the cubic volume of an existing nineteenth-century *Gründerzeit* building. In fact, two buildings were precisely fit to the sides of this fragment of the historic city footprint. The acute corners—surprising for its use as a residential building—deliberately serve to underscore the vividness of the playful idea.

48
Dan Graham, Café Bravo, Berlin

51
John Hejduk, Wohnbebauung und Atelierturm, Berlin

52
John Hejduk, Wohnbebauung und Atelierturm, Berlin

51, 52
The residential complex with a studio tower by John Hejduk in Berlin forms an emblematic ensemble. The small high-rise building is comprised of five towers; this is impractical for the residential floor plan, but it slims its appearance. The gable ends of the two flanking buildings are unquestionably faces. They have eyes with lashes.

In an interview with Kristin Feireiss, Hejduk says: "I have created a repertoire of objects/subjects that I take with me everywhere, to each place, to cities that I've seen and to cities I've never been."

49
Hans Kollhoff, Wohnbebauung Lu
Berlin

54
The AT&T Building by Philip Johnson and John Burgee in New York is a delicate monument, which thanks to its appearance carries the name "Chippendale." It is a postmodern manifesto in skyscraper form, lent a sense of scale by the buildings in its vicinity.

54
Johnson / Burgee Architects, AT&T Building, New York

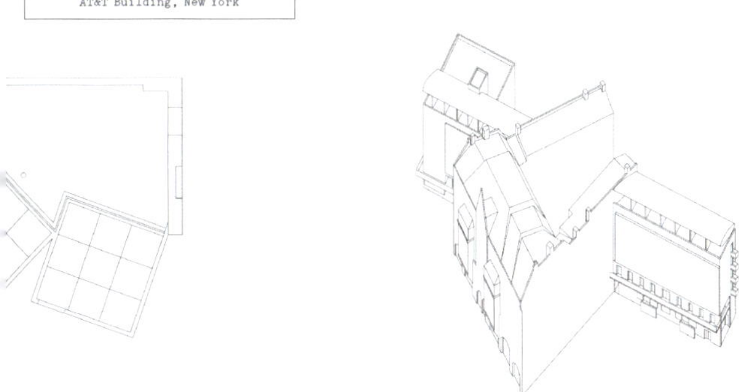

48 49

55
The *Lehrstück IV (Seven Codes)* (1978)—one of the built manifestos by Trix and Robert Haussmann—is a mirrored cabinet draped with a "piece of cloth" made of wood inlay, which dematerializes itself and its surroundings. The Haussmanns insert the scaleless volume like a building into a collage with the New York skyline.

They write: "With the *Lehrstücke* we were completely free to work on our key concerns, with no commission, meaning without having to take any specific purpose or use into consideration. They served as exemplary

55
Trix und Robert Haussmann, Lehrstück IV, Zürich

case studies. And the insights learned from them were then implemented in building projects ...”

60
The pleasure manor Liselund on the Danish island of Møn, with its main building and thematic garden pavilions, is intended to relax body and mind. So that the guests residing in the Norwegian house’s moon room can sleep soundly, the window has wooden shutters with a crescent moon cutout. The morning sun infiltrates the room as moonlight.

In the Liselund visitor’s catalogue, S. I. Andersson and Inge M. Antonsen comment: “The moon, ‘the friend of thoughts,’ was a common figure in the sentimental writings of the time, and it was completely in line with the spirit of the site that artificial moonlight was created for a bedroom in order to evoke this sentiment.”

54 55

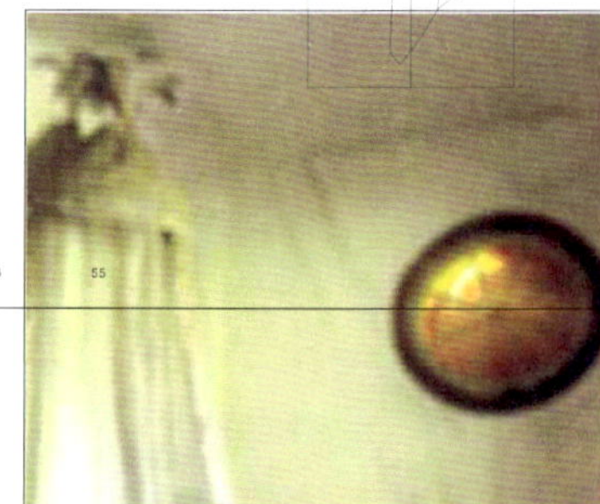

60
Andreas Kirkerup, Norwegerhaus, Liselund, Møn

61
The ceiling of the oval reading room in the Warburg House in Hamburg has a skylight for which Aby Warburg selected the shape of an ellipse with its two geometric foci—thus “the logic” and “the magic” are concurrently present in the room.

“For the great thinkers of the Renaissance ... the elliptical shape of a planet’s orbit was a sign that there was freedom in the cosmos.”

62
Richard Serra, Spot On, Galerie der Gegenwart, Hamburg

62
On the lower level of the squarely proportioned Gallery of Contemporary Art by Oswald Mathias Ungers at the Hamburger Kunsthalle in Hamburg, Richard Serra painted a black circle on the wall. It is not perfectly round and is located in an unexpected position on the wall, neither horizontally nor vertically centered, noticeably perplexing.

61
Gerhard Langmaack, Aby Warburg Hau
Hamburg

62

Dialogue Concerts #1
Mediality
December 19, 2019
Discussion

Christopher Dell
in Conversation with
Oda Pälmke,
Jonas Westergaard,
Karen Lorenz,
Bruno Margreth,
and Kristin Feireiss

Christopher Dell — Oda, when we spoke on the phone to prepare for this event, I asked you to contribute two pictures to the program booklet of this rendition of the *Dialogue Concerts*. You then asked me if I wanted pictures or drawings. Against this background, I am now interested in the difference, that is, in what you understand by picture and what you understand by drawing, and what distinguishes the two from each other.

Oda Pälmke — When you called me, you couldn't have known that at that very moment I was sitting in front of a pile of pictures and a pile of drawings. My counter-question to you was initially aimed at being efficient. In the end, however, I sent all the materials to let you decide for yourself what is a picture and what is a drawing. But if you now put the question to me like this, I must first say that when I speak to my students, I say to them: consider your drawing like a picture. For me, that means first of all: love your drawing. So it's about an intentionality, a position that is articulated through a certain quality of positioning yourself toward something, and that is also expressed in a certain terminology. Specifically: in the case of *Repertoire*, we are not dealing with technical drawings. That is, the representations are not something we make in order to finally transfer them into another reality, namely, a built reality. I say: make the drawing in such a way that you would like to hang it over your bed. But it could also be only a technical question, namely, the drawings in *Repertoire* are black and white, while the original pictures are colored, and I didn't want an illustration of an originally colored picture in a black-and-white booklet.

Christopher Dell — In *Repertoire* you deliberately play with different medialities. On the one hand there are the photographs of specific structural situations, and on the other hand one can find the drawings of the same situations. In *Repertoire 7*, this mode is extended by what one might call phenomenological texts, dense descriptions of the drawn and photographed situations, which in turn operate as their own form of representation. What function do these different medialities have for you?

Oda Pälmke — Drawing is a meditative exercise; it takes time to get involved with something. No matter how—and this also holds true for working with the computer—it takes time until a drawing is perfected, and in our case that means "reduced." For me, drawing means taking away lines. I often think that it is a substitute for what used to be called sketching, which meant looking closely. And that is important to me. I am sometimes asked what students get out of it when they draw in my class. As I just made clear, it doesn't matter. The main thing is to look at a thing or situation intensively and then find your own form for representing it. That is then a drawing, and it is a picture, but it is never the same as the original picture. *(Oda points to the poster of photos enclosed with the booklet.)* The pictures here are snapshots, of really trivial situations and moments taken with some of the worst mobile phone cameras. At the end, all the pictures together, indexically gathered on a poster, make up a picture of their own.

Christopher Dell: In fact, we are not only dealing with different medialities here, but also with specific modes of organization, with different series.

Oda Pälmke: That's why we chose the conservative medium of the book: it can't be extended, it's counted, it has a fixed number of pages—sometimes you're bending over the vibraphone and then you know the piece hasn't been counted to the end, even though I might not have noticed that yet—and so each booklet is finished as it is, as a self-contained form, as are the posters. And then something new has to come again. It's a long way from Instagram.

Christopher Dell: The photographic images are part of an initial situation, an observation, and then the refinement of the observation follows through the drawing. Why was the mediality of the text added in issue 7 of *Repertoire*?

Oda Pälmke: The inspiration actually came from my encounter with Arno Schmidt's work. Schmidt writes texts that are perhaps even difficult to understand. But he explains exactly how his text production works, namely, in such a way that things condense around brief moments. And Schmidt writes in three levels: the story, the fictional story, and the future story in parallel. This process inspired me a lot, and I felt like extending the observation of situations to textual language. In other words, to make texts that go beyond mere explanation in such a way that they limit themselves to the phenomenological method, that is, only describe what is depicted. The selection of what is mentioned in the text is then the decisive thing, and here I select very specifically. It's like studying a source: you pick out moments to add up to a whole. Any claim to explaining something is completely absent here. You could compare the booklet to reading a travel or sticker album: you find something, then you stick it in, and then you have to finish collecting it, but you don't have to have the whole thing—you just need one picture and, starting from there, can dedicate yourself to the whole memory. Experience accumulates like that.

Christopher Dell: What's exciting about *Repertoire* is that on the one hand there is the closed form, as you said: the book is finished and counted. On the other hand, the way it is designed and constructued in a serial fashion, one can browse through the book in manifold ways. Depending on your choice, you can open up the book at any point you like and then wander through it along different paths. Although the book has a closed form, it sparks ever new ways of *dérive*—the modes of reading it never come to a completion. Paradoxically, while fixating the visual singularities such as photographs, drawings, and texts on the pages and in a sequence, they are not "glued" in the epistemological sense. The book offers an organization of visuality that can be activated for the production of meaning in a relational and pluralistic manner.

This leads to the approach of starting from musical nuclei, one could say from material moments. Jonas, we played works from my composition cycle *Formblocks* earlier (see program booklet #1, p. 5). One might claim that these compositions also consist of moments from which movements can emerge. How do you proceed when you see the notation of a *Formblock* as a medium? How do you react to it? How do you work with it?

Jonas Westergaard: I see the material as a structure—for example, the intervals that are there—and translate that to my instrument. I then look for areas on the bass where the structures create different effects, meaning: Where does which interval have special power? Where does it sound soft? I look for favorite interval locations on the instrument in relation to the structure offered on the paper. I look for the favorite harmony, the favorite dissonance. But this is by no means teleological; for example, sometimes surprising consonances occur in the search for dissonance.

Christopher Dell: If I compare your description with Oda's, who says "love your drawing like a picture," here I could say "love the fragment like a composition." One is confronted with compositional input, even if all events in the beginning develop out of points or situations.

Karen, how was the process for you? We played in two different modes. We used one mode, which I call the representational mode, where the whole process is already written down, and then the non-representational mode, where the Formblock dictates the minimal structure of the playing. Which perspective do you have on the differences in approach here?

Karen Lorenz: With the *Formblocks*, I can arrange the sounds and then I wait to see what happens, I react to what you play. For me this is a form of freedom, although it is a very strict construct. In concrete terms: in the first *Formblock* we played, I had two tones at my disposal. That is not much. But in its freedom, it allows much more for me than the completely written piece. In the latter there is a lot going on, but that makes me less free; I can no longer react to a given situation. This results in different sensations when playing.

Christopher Dell: I'll come back to the question of media. In architecture, drawing is clearly positioned as the heart of the work, while in music it is actually more the musical action, the performance, that is at the center. What is your relationship to notation, then?

Jonas Westergaard: I'm not so used to having a lot of sheet music in front of me. The first piece that I played, *Organics*, was a lot more information than I usually get. Sometimes I don't get anything, sometimes a few hints, but mostly I have to compose my own part. That's why with *Organics* I allowed myself to act quite freely, especially in terms of timing, tempo, and rhythm. Some parts I get through faster; others I allow myself to take more slowly. But that was also the premise you gave. And it doesn't run formally from A to Z either. Karen finished faster than I did. And although I still had a good two pages to play, I got to the end. And so the piece was finished there.

Christopher Dell: And Karen, how is it for you? You are used to having a lot of sheet music in front of you.

Karen Lorenz: Yes, when I work with Ensemble Mosaik, my contemporary music ensemble, we improvise very little; mostly everything is totally fixed. In fact, it's much more fixed, because it's more precisely notated, than in the old classical field. What we try to achieve in every new project is to find out what the composer might have had in mind. For instance, some of the compositions we get are technically impossible to realize on the instruments. And our way of dealing with this constructively is to investigate the basic idea that underlies a composition, a written musical text, and then try to make it comprehensible for oneself, to translate it and make it work.

Christopher Dell: When you do that, do you also materially assemble scores yourself, cut them out and put them back together again?

Karen Lorenz: Not really. It's more about my playing position. Of course, you always try to stay as close to the text as possible. So if something is so difficult to play that you would have to practice for three years for a performance, or if it is simply not technically feasible, for example at a crazy tempo, then you try to play it in such a way that the composer doesn't notice. So that it corresponds to what he wanted, even if it is not exactly what he wrote.

Christopher Dell: That brings me to a certain point. What strikes me is that with the three of you there is a central relationship, namely, that between notation and truth. It seems to me that this is about a truth that is linked in a specific way to a proposed reality, a reality to which one is committed. For example, Oda, you start with the *snapshot*, which grows out of a *dérive*. First I let myself go, I detach from any prejudice in order to get *into* situations, then, when in the situation, I shoot the photograph rather spontaneously. But when I have the moment of the situation frozen as a snapshot, then it is important to look closely at this frozen state, to grasp what one might call the essence of the situation, so that, speaking in a phenomenological sense, things come to you, they open up.

On the other hand, it is still relevant for me that you love the process of doing and making as if it were a composition. Or rather: you already read it as a composition. We are then confronted with an attitude toward composition that is aimed at making action coherent. On this topic, I would like to read the following introductory text from *Repertoire 6*: "This collection of drawings and photographs of ordinary situations and elements of the built environment may inspire a natural expansion of the design repertoire. We draw the existing like a design and declare the built to be an architectural work. The method of 'seeing as' sharpens the awareness of the surroundings and enables the appropriation of forms."[1] That is a central point. In my view it is analogous to Jonas's approach. When he says that he plays the *Formblock* by recognizing its structures and transposing them onto his instrument, it means that he can do that because he takes the fragment and the movement that arises from it as seriously as a fixed composition.

And the radical step for architecture that I see in your work, Oda, is that you turn the vector of drawing around. The conventional time vector of architectural design is the one that looks forward, into the future. It obeys the imperative: "This will be built! This is what will be!" And the whole power of architecture has—ever since the Renaissance—historically been established and manifested in this directionality. When you say, "We draw the existing like a design and declare the built to be an architectural work," and you take what is and what was just as seriously as what will be built, no matter how everyday it may be as a spatial situation, and declare it to be a work, then you reverse the vector. Can you explain the genesis of this concept in more detail?

Oda Pälmke I would like to say that the *Repertoire 6* issue is different from what I have shown today. There is a slightly different focus. They are drawings of ordinary situations, and they seem rather reduced, but they are highly accurate, and they have been worked on for a very long time, with several people having been involved. And I find *(Oda picks up the program booklet of Dialogue Concert #1 Mediality and opens it.)* that the drawings look exactly like a *Formblock*. And that's the point. In fact, something has already shifted in my mind now because of this discussion. Earlier I would have skimmed over the musical drawing because it doesn't mean anything concrete to me since I come from architecture. But now I can say that I try to teach my students to show exactly this attitude or ability that Karen and Jonas have, that is, to stay with the *Formblock* for a long time in their own way, in the fabrication of the drawing and the attitude toward the *snapshot*.

Even more radically, I can say: you can design without doing anything. For example, you can design by looking at something. Details are drawn so that they can be built later. But when they are coupled with the word contemplation, details postpone doing. Doing is then not oriented toward doing, but toward concentrating and seeing something as it is—in order to be able to see something in things afterward, and in order to not be able to forget it again.

I don't think musicians can look at a *Formblock* without having to slow down four hours of action, and it's the same with the drawings.

Christopher Dell: Against this background, I would like to talk about the genealogy of *Repertoire*, that is, the series of books and notebooks that you have positioned as the central media of your work since the beginning of your teaching career. It starts out with the exercises at the Bauhaus University Weimar in the late 1990s and continues with the *Salon* booklets of the design seminars at the École Polytechnique Fédérale de Lausanne (EPFL) and later at the University of Fine Arts Hamburg (HFBK). What stands out about the booklets is that they consistently bring together the most heterogeneous materials which were all important for your design seminars and played an essential role. For example, you find floor plans next to photographs and drawings, works of fine art and architectural designs, Rodney Graham's *Millennial Project for an Urban Plaza* from 1986 next to Siah Armajani's *Park Furniture 8* from 1998 in contrast to Nikolay Ladovsky's *Experimental Design for a Communal House* from 1920 or Oswald Mathias Ungers and Stefan Schroth's *Sewage Pumping Station* in Berlin's Tiergarten from 1978, the projects sometimes shown as photographs sometimes as drawings. What interests me is: Why did you choose the medium of the book for this format? What does the book space mean as a form of knowledge?

Oda Pälmke: I would like to pass the question on to Bruno Margreth, the designer of *Repertoire*.

Bruno Margreth: The space of the book provides you with the possibility to tell something. The most heterogeneous materials can be given a narrative in this form. That is important for me. In the case of *Repertoire*, image equals text and you have to get involved with it. For me it is also a format that allows appropriation. Even when I look at a photo and turn it into a drawing, I am appropriating the image. And this process continues in bookmaking: you look at the materials, appropriate them, give them a form, a sequence—and a story emerges. The book provides the space for this story. That's also the case with a poster: the assembly of the whole images makes a picture again. But the individual fragment is also beautiful. Consequently, a space emerges, a walk through architecture, I pass by, the fragments flash, memories come, go. It is perhaps not so much a didactic arrangement, but rather an intuitive one. The book as a medium provides good support for that.

Oda Pälmke: Bruno has dedicated himself to making books, so each series is also a collection. If I may refer to the earlier series, I would say that I always published these small booklets, knowing that they were produced in the copy shop, knowing that they could also be thrown away by the students. With *Repertoire*, I'm taking the next step, and it's already close to the book. Perhaps it is also a sign of a search for continuity. So now my counter-question: How can you stand constantly creating improvised works without someone always being there to record them? Why don't you feel the need to write it down, even in this form? I do it every time.

Christopher Dell: That is a crucial question. The fact that you just mentioned is at times really painful for me as a musician. Everything I do, even the daily practicing at home, is already gone. And, as you know, in teaching architecture it can be the same: you work with the students *on the fly* for a semester, then the semester is over and the work is gone again. In contrast, Oda, you have made teaching a work of art. In this sense, not only the depicted situation, as postulated in *Repertoire*, but also the teaching is elevated to a work of art. I have always been very impressed by the way you have proceeded in this direction.

Oda Pälmke: That has to do with the fact that you don't always get the best result at the end of an effort. Sometimes, however, something like that is much better than the happy ending. Which brings us back to the fact that it's about doing it now and not for something later.

Christopher Dell — I came to interpret this question in such a way that I say: I play for the people who are there. And that is an ethical-political question for me. Those who do not come, who are not present, do not have a part, not even through a CD or video recording. For me, this ethic speaks from the book only in a reversed media constellation. The book arises from being there for a situation, taking it seriously, and, as Bruno says, it also lets you experience the story of being there again, but in a way that you can put together this co-experience yourself, going through it yourself while reading. You are there for the situation that is there and don't make a blueprint for the happy ending. This ties in with Karen's question: I have to assert myself in the face of the score that confronts me, I and my instrument are there, we are there and we are the ones who make the score work. I can't just implement a function.

This leads me to the next question. There are different authors at work in *Repertoire*. Oda, how do you organize this multiple authorship?

Oda Pälmke — Hierarchical. *(Pause)* I curate it. It's like a little machine. It's drawn, brought, put over it, drawn again, drawn again, then it multiplies, and little by little you start to coordinate with each other. And I do that so that in the end everyone can do what they want.

Christopher Dell — In this respect, *Repertoire* and its process of making constitutes, for me, a very good example of the thesis that dealing with the open form is a structural one. One might encounter this quality in music as well, somewhat in dealing with the blocks of form as we have listed them here. Consequently, the talk of the "informal" does not apply here at all. The work with the open form has an extremely formal character; in principle it is formally even stricter than the closed form. I find this also relevant in dealing with mediality: How do you create a medium that has open and closed moments at the same time? What must this medium be able to do? What are its conditions for success? How can it provide both levels in such a way that one can proliferate them with constructive improvisations?

Oda Pälmke — This aspect is directly related to the book *Repertoire*. In order to show the extremely heterogeneous content, we have explicitly chosen a very fixed format. The format is strict so that we can be free—otherwise the open disappears into the arbitrary. Everything is allowed, but not arbitrarily.

Kristin Feireiss — Christopher, you said that you play for those who are there. But I have also experienced it quite differently. At that time, we were showing the exhibition *Urban India*. A video of you playing the vibraphone in the streets of Kolkata was presented there. In the video, you were surrounded by people, but we were not there. We could only watch the video as a proxy.

Christopher Dell — That is a very complex question. To answer it, I would like to refer to the visual arts, just as Oda Pälmke often does to clarify formal themes in architecture. The story goes like this: at that time—in 2007—the Goethe-Institut launched a residency program for musicians for the first time. I was selected to realize a project of my choice in India. Initially, I wanted to make a piece based on the dance performance *Pichet Klunchun and myself* by Jérôme Bel, a piece I had seen at the theater Hebbel am Ufer in Berlin. In this work, the French conceptual artist entered into dialogue with Pichet Klunchun, a classical Khon dancer from Thailand. What was decisive for me was that the two did not dance together but explained to each other what they were doing and why. The result was an open yet transparent and incredibly sensitive dialogue between two artists about choreographic practice and cultural difference—not a blurry fusion project. I wanted to do something similar with a classical Indian musician in musical terms. It never happened. I simply could not get through to the classical musicians in India. In a state of total blockage and despair, I walked the streets of Kolkata and suddenly realized that everything I needed was there. Everything performative happens there. So I let go of my European understanding of a concert. The result was the work *Kolkata Monodosis*. As I performed on the street at points curated together with Patrick Ghose, the city rose to become the orchestra through the performative windows evoked by *Kolkata Monodosis*. At the same time, my practice intersected with the already existing practices of the actors on the sidewalks—the car mechanics, hairdressers, writers, restaurants, in fact everything that takes place in the production of space on Kolkata's streets. The renowned Indian documentary filmmaker Ranu Ghosh was involved as a documenting meta-actor. She and a team of two cameramen recorded the performances at each location and transferred them into a serial film, which was then shown in the exhibition together with the urban research study *Tacit Urbanism* and some original documents. In this respect, the film and the book marked the central inscription of the thematization of mediality in the work *Kolkata Monodosis*.

1 Oda Pälmke, *Repertoire 6, Situation Constellations*, Technical University of Kaiserslautern (Zurich and Berlin: About Books, 2018), p. 1.

Dialogue Concert #2
Interaction
February 6, 2020

Lecture: Christophe Hutin

Concert: Christopher Dell (vibraphone), Christian Lillinger (drums), Kathrin Pechloff (harp)

Discussion: Hans-Jürgen Commerell, Christopher Dell, Christophe Hutin, Christian Lillinger, Kathrin Pechloff, Ulrich Stock

Aedes Architecture Forum, Berlin

Dialogue Concerts #2
Interaction
February 6, 2020
Christophe Hutin

Thank you, Christopher, for inviting me to talk with you tonight. We've known each other for a long time and have discussed the improvisation of architecture. It is not an easy theme to explore because music processes are more efficient and easier to understand than those of architecture. In a lot of ways, my lecture is about improvisation and architecture, and there are many images I want to show. I always

start with this picture from South Africa, because it has become a very important document for me.

When I was eighteen years old, I wanted to be a sailor. But I was not allowed to, because I had failed the entrance exam. So I had to change my mind. This happened in 1994. It was the first election year in South Africa, when later on Mandela was elected. I decided to engage myself in the campaign of the African National Congress (ANC) at that time. And so they hosted me in South Africa and they were asking me to stay in the township. I moved there and lived close to this place, and I took this picture. And this picture became a very important document in my work because my architecture starts from there.

This is what you see when you go to Soweto. In the background you see the Apartheid Museum. And at the back, there is what we call the informal settlement. It is the township of Cape Town. I have worked there for twenty years now. I built a few buildings there.

The story starts with a wedding party. Traditionally, in Soweto, the people do a party for a wedding on a Saturday, and on Sunday they will buy five panels to build a house. That means, after one got married on Saturday, one builds a house to live in on Sunday. Since the wedding guests help out, the building process takes two or three hours. After that one puts the furniture in. For me, this was a really important experience, and I decided that I wanted to work in this field. And for me, it was architecture. So, I came back to France and I said: “Now I know what I want to do.” I want to do architecture. I attended a school of architecture. And I did the academic study, which is very important in life. But the experience in the academic environment was very different from the original experience of architecture that I had had in South Africa. Indeed, the education helps you to make monuments; it teaches you how to draw a perspective. And I was drawing churches and big monuments. But I was very far from the experience in Cape Town.

When you buy your house, the price is very low. And the typology is simple: it’s one room, one room and a half. After you’ve found the space, an empty space, then you build your house, Sunday afternoon. After finishing my studies, I came back to Soweto and did a research program within six months; I was making an inventory of the housing process for (the) people. And I learned a lot from these situations. I learned about the ways in which people, with a very small amount of money, with a lot of freedom and dignity, can build a proper house.

They are very proud. You can see so in this picture. That is very important. It’s not a model; I don’t wish for you to live in this house. But in terms of architecture and thinking architecture, I have learned a lot in this situation.

After that, I worked for a French Jazz musician called Bernard Lubat. He is quite famous in France. He was disturbing me a lot with improvisation. Lubat was very active in Paris, but at a certain moment he decided to move back to the village Uzeste, where he comes from. It is a small village of about four hundred people. And he built a concert hall for three hundred. So, this project could be a success because ten to fifteen people are going to be in the concert. The music is fantastic. And he asked me to transform his building; it was a motel, restaurant, and shop with pigs in the backyard. It was originally his parents’ house. When they died, he transformed it into a concert hall. And we built a space for his jazz production. On the wall he wrote: “don’t come in without desire.” This is the concert hall with a balcony that we did with children of the village.

After that I teamed up with Anne Lacaton, Jean-Philippe Vassal, and Frédéric Druot. We did an urban study in Bordeaux. It was called *50,000 logements*. The goal was to create a strategy for the city to provide a lot of housing. We worked on the study for five years, and our approach was very simple. We started to make a database of what already existed in the city. The network, the pipes, the roads. When you do a project in urban planning and architecture, in fact, you traditionally always start from zero and make a big demonstration of what you are going to do. Instead, our proposal was to look in a new way at what is already existing as a city, in order to find new potential to transform the built structure and increase the city's density and to create more quality. The outcome of the research is a database, which shows and catalogues all the relevant situations in Bordeaux. In this document you can zoom in and see the layout of each apartment in each situation. We studied each case in order to identify the potential and the capacity of each situation to offer new units and new situations for projects.

After that case study we did a project in Bordeaux. It is an eighteenth-century city with a beautiful low-rise panorama. In the background, you see the Grand Parc, a grand housing

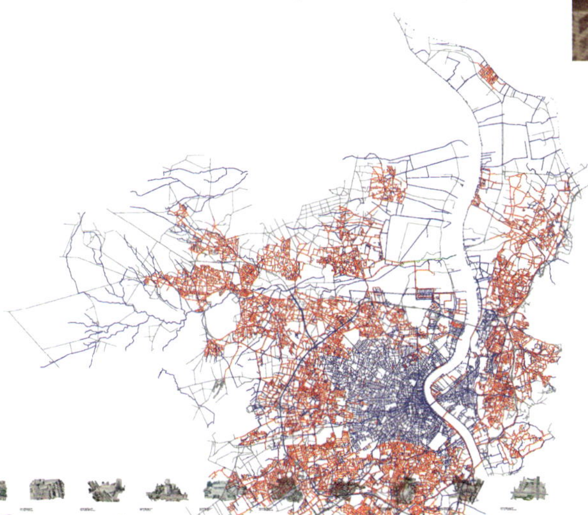

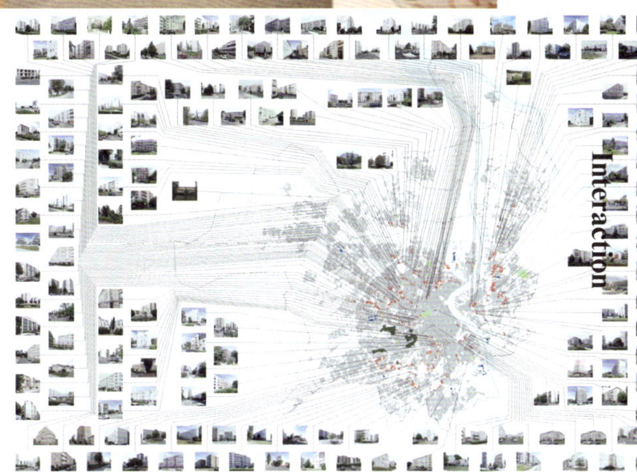

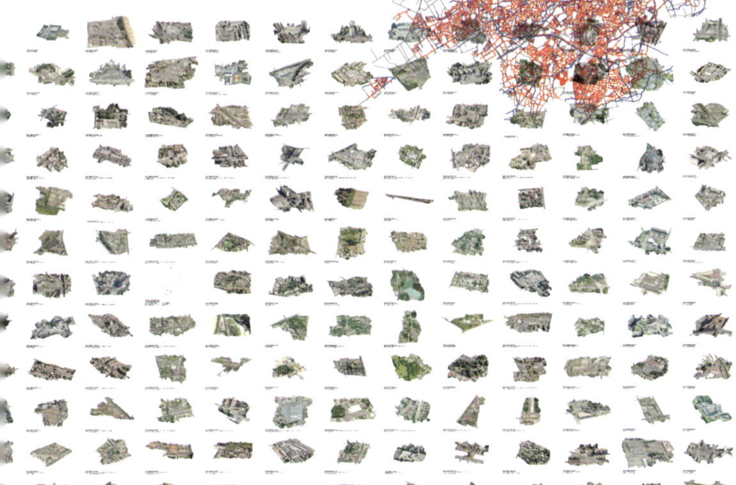

ensemble. The Cité du Grand Parc is a large housing estate north of the Bordeaux city center. It consists of the typical residential bars and towers of the 1960s, with a total of 4,000 residential units.

In France, it's typically the high-rise buildings and grand ensembles that have a bad reputation—for different reasons. The French politicians thought that the social problems are coming from this sort of urban architecture. What they concluded, then, is that the only way one can transform and regenerate the grand ensemble is to demolish it and install a new development instead—usually with less quality. In opposition to this approach, we tried to convince them that the three Grand Parc buildings in Bordeaux don't have to be demolished. You see, it's a typical 1960 ensemble with 530 units. The politicians would say it is a problem. They call it, in a simple way, urban form. Because they need a description of a situation that is coming from the outside. But if you go inside, and that is what we have done—indeed, we created a photographic database of all the apartments with the photographer Philippe Ruault—you find, in fact, 530 different worlds. If you go into the apartment, it is completely different than from outside. In this sense, the project starts with trying to understand daily life and how the people live in this apartment, and to enlarge and to bring new qualities into this building. The next step was to extend the building, the facade, by adding a four-meter-wide concrete floor. We

used the same industrial system as the existing building, and by that you create a structure. After adding the balcony floor, we closed the facade with movable transparent panels and curtains. Let me show you quickly. This is the result. In the existing apartment, we took out the window, the wall, and we inserted a sliding double-glazed window. In consequence, you have winter garden and a one-meter balcony.

Here we see three apartments: one is a two-bedroom, one a three-bedroom, and one a four-bedroom apartment. One can see here that, originally, the building was conceived with a very functional idea of housing in mind. Each space had a different function, and it was very determined in terms of use. Also, the way of moving about in these apartments was very reduced; you only had limited options. So we tried to create—like in a house—another approach to spatial organization, another way to move and live in this apartment and to provide more indeterminate space. The latter aspect is very important because it leads right to the point of the improvisation. This topic is very difficult. For me, one definition of improvisation in this context is the meeting between the skill of the architecture and the performance of the inhabitants.

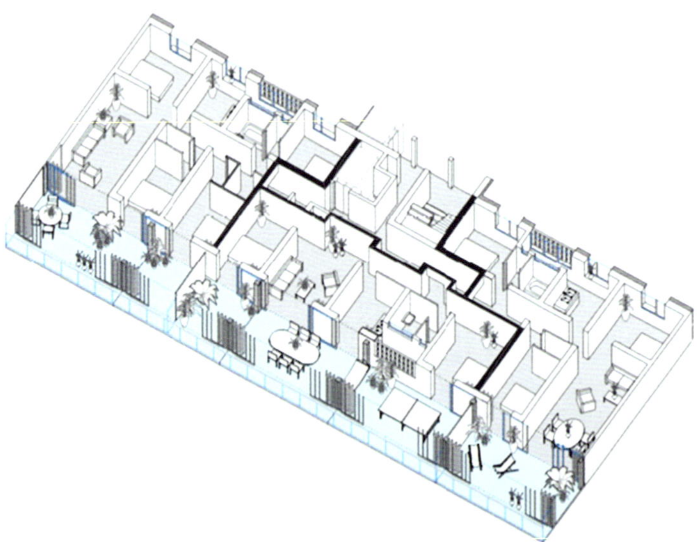

Together with Anne Lacaton, Jean-Philippe Vassal, and Frédéric Druot, we proposed a very simple option. We upgraded the 530 flats with an addition by docking 1,200 prefabricated concrete modules onto the existing built structure. With this extensive measure, we then continued to pursue our strategy of renewing existing buildings by adding additional space. This systematic enlargement of the floor plans is also our response to the urgency of urban redensification.

The added balcony constitutes a new floor. It enlarges the apartment and, beyond that, there's no function, no program. People can invent their life inside this space, and they can live the way they want. This is the process. With a crane we installed the additional floor with a ready-made fence. Immediately, people can even walk there. It's very efficient, and it at the same time works like a scaffold for the construction, but not like a temporary one, for it is long-term scaffolding. That leads to the next important point: people can stay in their apartment during the construction; they don't

have to move out. Actually, there were situations where the inhabitants would watch TV inside while we were building outside. This is very decisive because the project is done for them. We have to keep them in the building during the process and during the construction period. This is because you don't reach the goal of the project if you gentrify the people. And this picture is showing you the new space and the way the people are using their apartments and the way they perform there.

I'm not comfortable with participatory processes because, for me, it's like a paternalistic system lacking democracy. I don't see my role as an architect in determining the way someone has to live in their apartment. Nor do I understand inhabitants wanting to be architects and do the replacement work. I've got my skill, they've got their skills, and it's a deal. I'm sure that at this rendition of the *Dialogue Concerts*, after my performance, we will see your performance. You are playing the vibraphone. It is a skill.

This is a kitchen. So now you can live here. The new openings always allow two possibilities for leaving the space—A + B—which are very important for our lives. And, of course, the balcony is a bioclimatic system where in the winter you can keep the natural isolation, and in the summer you are protected. And we have a curtain and a lot of systems to help people control and deal with the climate. For example, in one apartment, the size of the floor doubled in size; it was enlarged from originally 56 to 110 square meters.

You see, this is the way the people live. Contrary to the general understanding of architecture, this is neither the architects' problem, nor a question of taste. The inhabitants want to live the way they want. In these images, you see the performance of the people; it's very understandable. And each apartment is different. I took

some pictures of the building last week and discovered on the twelfth floor, in one extension, that there is a radio station playing Latino music. It broadcasts to Venezuela and other countries of South America. The employees installed a swimming pool, and they do barbecue inside.

The next slides are from Vietnam. I am showing you this building, which is, in fact, rather the same kind of building as the Grand Parc, and it contains very similar stories. And I realized that we had thought that we as architects had been very clever, that we had had a very new idea. But that is not the truth. In Vietnam, people have been doing this for forty years without asking any architects. Since their apartments are too small for their families, they extend each apartment—yet without talking to the neighbor or an architect. They realize the extension on their own and it's unbelievable. I discovered this phenomenon two years ago, when I had moved to Vietnam in order to make a photographic documentary. The story of the building in this image is amazing because the structure was designed by Kim Lien in Hanoi with a reference to the typology and to the conception of building in East Germany during the 1960s. I want to show you that Vietnamese people initiate a lot of very good building processes, with the aim of making their daily lives better. Do you see the system? It's a culture. All their cities work like that.

Ulrich Stock: But is it safe?

Christophe Hutin: Nobody reported any problems to me. Apparently, it is safe. You see, this one is an extension of extensions. I also like to emphasize the way the people use the public space. During the day, they use the same space in very different ways. You can have scooter parking; you can have a restaurant or a place where you can play in the afternoon. In terms of performance, this is very interesting.

I now return to Bordeaux to show you a project which I am doing at the moment. It's a project in a neighborhood of one-on-one houses. It was built in the 1970s for the people who migrated to France during the decolonization process in the context of Algeria. The people who migrated from Algeria could not apply for a unit in the social housing system, so the government built houses for them. It was conceived as a temporary city, and now the third generation is living there. The settlement is evidence of fifty years of dwelling practice, and now (today) the social housing agency decided to do a renovation. I won the competition to transform this neighborhood. As usual, the project was envisioned as a demolishing of the houses to make a new development. And I started differently: I always work with the people.

I took this picture, and I talked to the project comissioners of the social housing agency. I said: “No, we have to work with the inhabitants to transform this neighborhood. Otherwise the project is not possible.” The inhabitants are the key resource for the project of transforming this neighborhood. Nothing had been happening there for fifty years regarding official building activity. The state had completely forgotten about the place. Against this background, I as an architect claimed that if we wanted to transform and to rehabilitate the houses, now we had to pay attention to the inhabitants and their practices and also to the story and the people.

Kay Geipel — Can you say something about the people who were living there first. Are they still the people from fifty years ago?

Christophe Hutin — Yes.

Kay Geipel — In all the houses?

Christophe Hutin — Yes. Because they were forgotten. They regulated the process of moving in and out by themselves. Someone left a house, and someone else moved in while the social housing company did not take part in the process. This is very interesting. The territory is “under the radar,” so it’s full of freedom and improvisation. I will show you.

Here you can see a picture of the beginning of the settlement. I did the mapping of the family connections in the neighborhood. It’s unbelievable. The lot is very close to the airport, and there is a military base adjunct to it. Here you see an object we installed last week because we are working with artists and preparing a ball for people to dance on Saturday, which is very important. This is the house. On the street front, it’s very regulated, very quiet. At the back, it’s

another story. It’s exactly the same process as I had been documenting in Soweto. One might claim that it is a universal theme: people need more space than their house originally offers and they expand the house. Indicated on the drawing in black is the original structure of the building. Indicated in red are the extensions that people made. It is amazing to see what people can do, how they improvise.

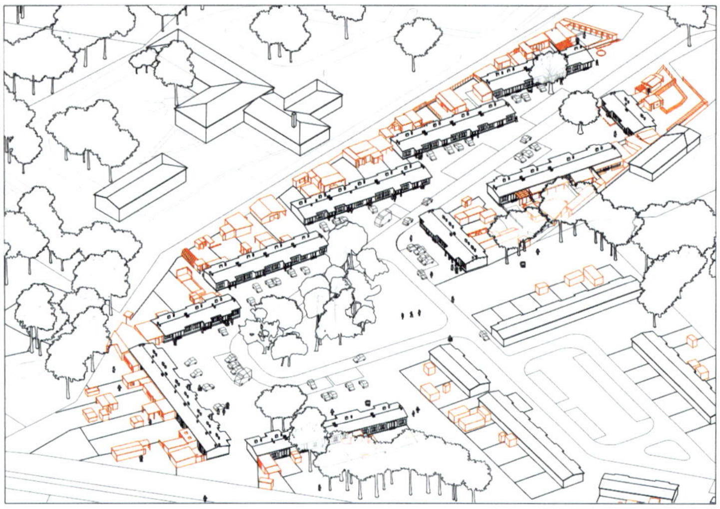

With the extensions, some homes now have 200 square meters. You can't demolish that. I believe that you cannot overwrite this life with any social paternalism, because you cannot delete the personal stories. And it is the goal of our project to recognize and to put value on what people have done for fifty years and to help them to continue this process in a better way. What we add is our skill.

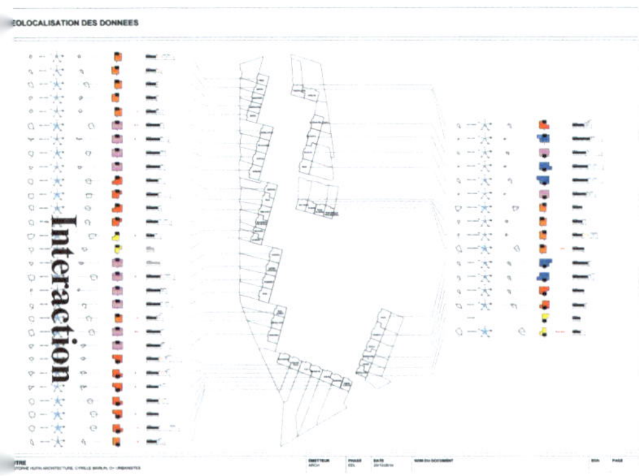

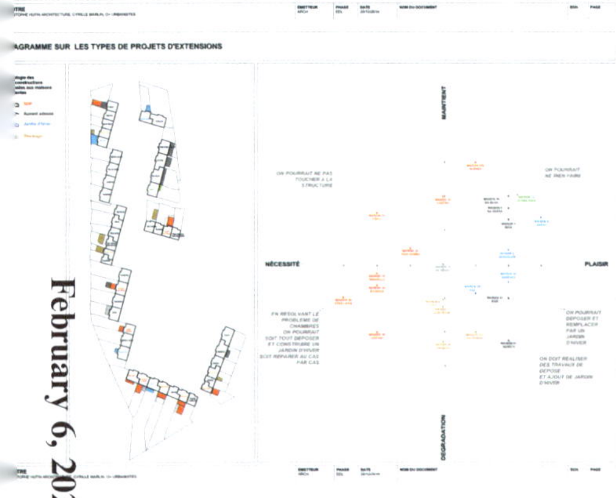

I want to show you some documents. I don't have time to explain, but we work with diagrammatics. We want to work and represent in a different way. Therefore, we invent new tools. The traditional tools of architecture are not able to go through that kind of process and that kind of project. Our diagrammatic work is like diagnostics, but it is technical, numerical, and social. It is mixing the categories. For example, this diagram shows the relationality of needs and pleasure within the built structure and its uses. This picture shows where maintenance happens and which part of the building was not maintained. This mode of drawing is a way to show the processual working of the houses and to know where to intervene and which channel to pick.

However, the problem is the following: in France, our government suddenly said that it is wonderful that the people transform the architecture themselves. In other words, the government doesn't have to contribute money, it's perfect. But no, it's not perfect, because some have the skill and capacity to do it and others don't. The result is an increase in inequality between the inhabitants of the houses. On the contrary, our project is about reducing the inequality between the situations of the families.

This is another drawing we are making. It shows the original house. The people are paying rent for this each month. And they built the second part of the house in the garden. And then in the public space they make a garden. You cannot destroy it, because now the garden has turned into a living room and a kitchen. And the original part, it's only for the night. This is where the improvisation starts for us as architects, at the point where we have to negotiate. We have a proposition to start with, but of course we negotiate one by one in all of the cases.

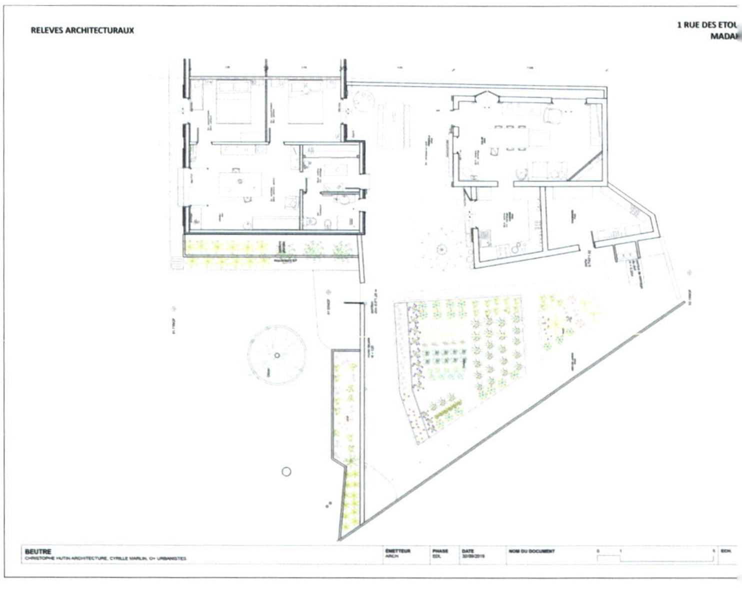

Ulrich Stock So, did you change the bathrooms and toilets?

Christophe Hutin: Yes, because they were too small and too old. It is a problem, and the people now are getting old, so they need more space and more comfort in toilets and bathrooms. Consequently, we put new bathrooms and toilets everywhere. Concerning the garden, there was a process of negotiation. All in all, what I showed you demonstrates where in the process we are right now. These are the documents we are concurrently producing with the people. They serve as a basis for transforming this neighborhood. So, if you visit Bordeaux, I recommend that you come to this place.

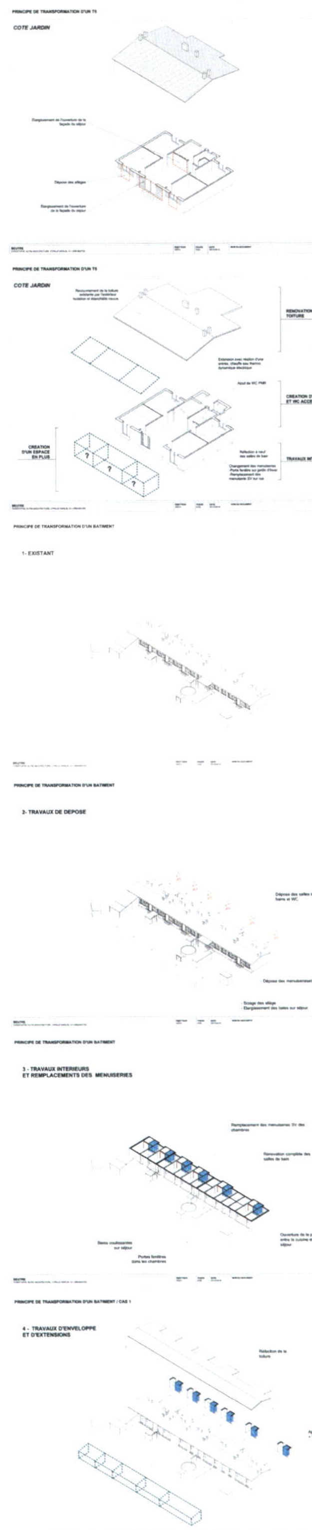

Now I'll show you this score by Udo Kasemets from 1964. This is the way he draws the music. It's very interesting because we have been having this discussion with Christopher for a long time. I'm very interested in this, in how we as architects can learn from music and can maybe bring the musical process into architecture. This score is architecture for me in terms of the way it organizes actions and systems. In a sense, this score summarizes what I have been talking about the last twenty minutes: it thematizes the way in which you can—through architecture—create a structure to welcome life and the complexity of the world. This is the goal I want to pursue in architecture.

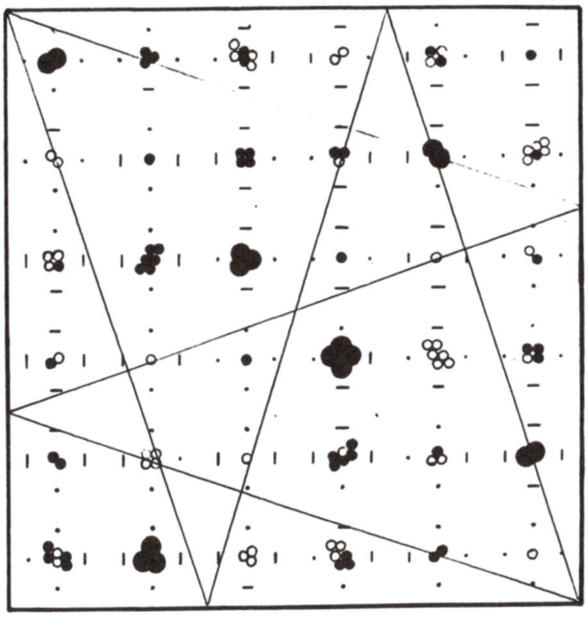

Udo Kasemets, *Timepiece for a Solo Performer* (1964)

Sometimes in architecture you have to stop early in the process to leave it to the people and their daily life, to set up a frame in a manner that enables them to bring complexity into architecture. It's a concept I was not taught when I studied the discipline in my earlier years.

The next project is a concert hall. It is next to the big buildings I talked about before. The program of the competition was to divide the building in order to create space for different functions. Again, it was a functionalist approach. One should create space for meetings, space for concerts, space for dance, space for et cetera. It's a very old structure, built thirty years ago. What I proposed was to open it, and if you want to have a meeting on the stage, you can have a meeting on the stage. It is friendlier than to be in a meeting space elsewhere. We don't have to divide the life of this building. Use it as you want. And with this proposal I won the competition. A German band once came to the concert hall, but they didn't hold the concert on the stage; they went into the audience space. It works. And also, you can open the building during the day for daily activities.

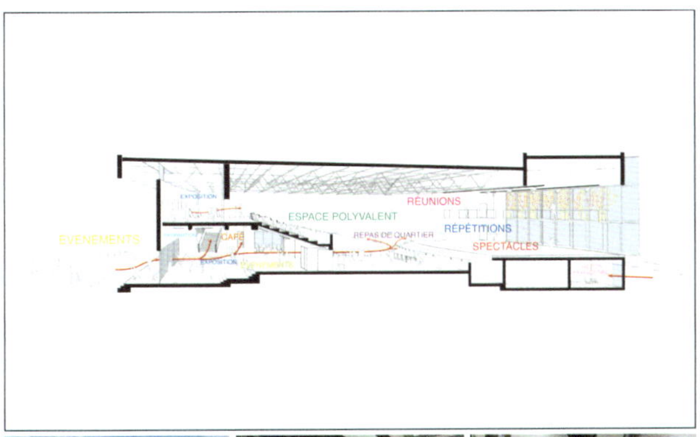

Let me come back to the basic theme of my lecture. I was taught by the architectural school to become a chef d'orchestre, a conductor. The figure of the chef d'orchestre is the best way to describe the general understanding of the architect's work. But I am very uncomfortable with being a chef d'orchestre. You are on the top and using a stick to tell people what they have to do. I don't like this. I don't want to be a chef d'orchestre, I'm sorry. I want to be a jazz man. I want to deal

with the people. And in the twentieth century, the jazz musicians brought a political issue to music: they did not want to continue to play the score of a composer. They said they wanted—as artists—to create their work themselves. Unfortunately, we didn't have this movement in architecture. Traditional architecture seeks to completely determine

how and where the people live—particularly in housing. By this I mean that, for example, the bathroom, the kitchen, and everything are today still predominantly determined by the functionalist approach. That is why we have to find new processes of making architecture where people can perform; they can use the space, and they get the freedom to enjoy their lives as they want. In fact, I just want to bring architecture back to the people. I think someone stole something from us in our daily lives.

So, in this picture, you see the inhabitants of Beutre, France, very well dressed. And this is the way we are working. You have to negotiate everything at the project. In the middle this is Marion Howa. She is in charge of the project in our team. We are not the chef d'orchestre. If we disagree with the people, we must negotiate a new way of working. You see, this is an orphanage in Soweto, and every morning in South Africa the democracy is a new work. It does have a history. It was a hard fight to get it, so the people don't want to lose it. When you do a project there,

you have to explain everything you have done every morning. And if the people don't agree, they tell you and then you have to respond. I think it's important. It's the way I work now. I learned that in Soweto. And now I want to work in this way everywhere. The people in South Africa taught me a lot of things. It's very important and it's very efficient because, in the end, in their way of doing, any architectural project is very easy to make. The performance of the people is a resource in architecture for me.

And here you see the result of the construction: all of the kids from the orphanage are performing in the space, the workers are here, the children are here, and everyone is letting the space be a part of this story and make a new story. We don't decide for others in architecture, I hope.

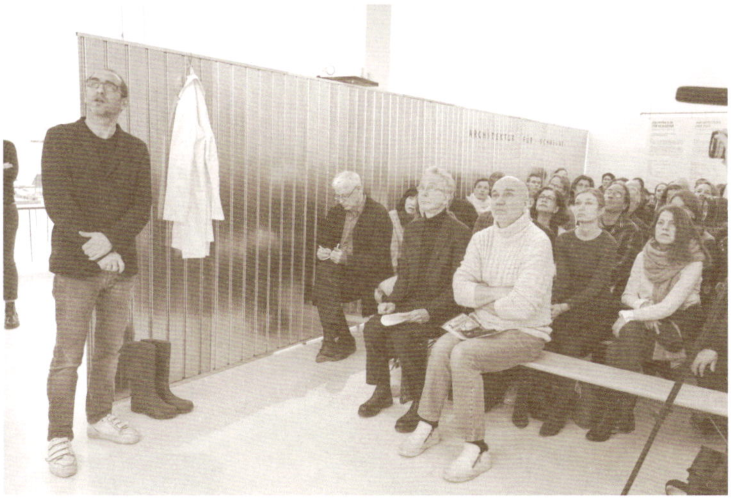

MUSSER

Christopher Dell
in Conversation with
Christophe Hutin,
Christian Lillinger,
Kathrin Pechloff,
Hans-Jürgen Commerell,
and Ulrich Stock

Christopher Dell: I want to start the discussion by focusing on performative aspects of the different formats we display within the outline of the *Dialogue Concerts*. From this perspective, it was really interesting for me to observe my playing after Christophe's lecture, and how it was influenced by his words. As I perceived it, we worked with the discursive space that Christophe had created. For me, it's a completely different way of playing. It is a different mode of contextualizing, framing, and perspectivizing what we do as musicians. In that sense, I want to start off by asking Kathrin: How was it for you to play in this setting or framing? What is the difference between performative input and a conventional concert setting?

Kathrin Pechloff: Christophe's lecture resonates. But on a deep emotional level, I guess. I didn't really think of what he said when I played. But I think I played differently because of the space Christophe had opened up. What he was talking about created a feeling of being open. But it's not in a very concrete way for me. How it was for you, Christian?

Christian Lillinger: I like this kind of environment. It is based on structures. And I really like to construct and deconstruct things. I felt inspired by Christophe's lecture. I felt even more strongly encouraged to do my work, to deconstruct and constructively play with musical material. He gave us another layer, and I added to it in my own way.

Christopher Dell: Christophe, when talking about architecture, you emphasize action and making. You take your point of departure from a theoretical concept that comprehends space as performatively produced and architecture as a practice. This concept is also connected to a certain imaginary of how to look at the world, how to read the city. What struck me the most in this context was how you elaborated on the question of transposition from imaginary to action. One of your central themes is how to open up space for anybody to do their thing. And that has an empowering effect. Christophe, when you give your lectures, you show that achieving openness in a project is a very complex task. Yet, you said that what you were trained to do by architecture education was mainly to make representational drawings. And these drawings follow a quite different concept than the one you outlined in your work. They are based on a tabula rasa thinking of space, which relies on and propels the power to convey an imaginary future. Seen in this light, the drawing has the power to project, because it shows in a figurative and imperative mode what should be built. Christophe, it has been a central point of your work to question this power and its epistemological foundations.

In a rather unique way, even though you turn traditional architecture upside down, your lecture inspired us, and it became quite understandable. How do you, when you show how you work, reflect on this showing, for example, when you give a lecture or when you create an exhibition as curator, such as the French Pavilion at the 2021 Venice Architecture Biennale? How do you show the *other* way of representing architecture and its modes of representation? How do you put it on display, and how do you conceptualize it?

Christophe Hutin
I'm talking about the trying, and sometimes we fail. We fail again and again. I'm trying to experiment with new tools for the processing of architecture. I want to show projects and not pictures. My problem is that what I'm talking about in fact is the architectural practice. I'm talking about life, and life is a question of movement. When we are discussing drawings, the drawing is completely static. For me, this is a problem, because it becomes obvious that you cannot deal with life and movement through drawings. The model, the layout, the section—all the classic representational modes of architecture—are very static. Life cannot appear in this kind of rendering or way of representing the reality. That's why for the French Pavilion at the Venice Architecture Biennale I'm making a movie. I'm creating an orchestration of moving representational fields. I'm making sequences to get into this movement. Maybe, when I'm doing architecture, I am investigating life but cannot draw it.

Christopher Dell
Your Biennale movie project will be realized and shown as a triptych. One might argue that this presents a way to render the representational mode of the movie more heterogeneous. What the triptych does is that it creates a multiperspective. When you give a talk, you seem to also mix representational layers.

Seen from a historical perspective, after the year 2000, it became trendy in some architecture circles to show only photographs of an architectural project, no drawings. Emphasis was placed on the performative aspects of architecture. This representational strategy at times hindered the reading of a project, because the photographs had a rather figurative function. It was the time of social design, which tended to stage architects as community social workers. Instead, what you have shown is exact and analytical, and you insist on that: the skill has to be shown. It is about what architects can do, which directly relates to the drawing. In this sense, I want to ask, again: How do you develop your modes of representation in relation to a genealogy of architectural experience? How do you reappropriate experience while insisting on being an architect?

Christophe Hutin
I think you're right. I'm trying to make drawings to deal with the reality of a given situation. For example, when we draw houses, you can see the furniture, you can see the way of life of the people inside. Everything is very precise. In fact, we aim at both: to be very precise, and at the same time to stay open. Drawing for me is a way of reading the reality of the situation. I'm dealing with it, but I'm not planning it. I'm drawing in order to get as precise as I can. For me, the work with photography is similar: it's a way of dealing with the reality of a situation I'm working with. In my work, the photograph, the drawings, the movie, are tools of precision. Also, I'm making a lot of tryouts. The project I was showing in the last picture of the presentation is a construction which I did with my studio. In this case we decided to make a drawing *after* the construction. Firstly, the drawing is very precise, because it is the representation of what we have done. And, yeah, it was a try. Secondly, in the end, the drawing is very beautiful, because it's not the issue of the composition but of the process.

Christopher Dell
What you have set out also implies that the time vector of architecture shifts to its reverse. Ever since the Renaissance, architecture has created drawings with a time vector that is directed toward the future. This mode of representation differentiated the architectural drawing from the painting, which, no matter whether it's abstract or representational, is about the now or the "what has been." In contrast, the architectural drawing has a completely different ontology. It is about

the "what will be." Historically, this vector has constituted the power of architecture. Its apotheosis may be found in classicism and the nineteenth century. I'm thinking of Henri Labrouste. His drawings are extremely precise; one has the feeling of being able to walk in them, yet they are obviously directed toward a future that is not in the now but somewhere else. In contrast, your work turns time around. You work with the same precision and tools as the tradition, but you turn the vector toward the "what was" and the "what is now" in order to achieve a space of negotiation. For instance, it allows you to develop the next step of a project you are doing with the inhabitants of a certain neighborhood. Through this procedure, design turns into research by means of design. How do you put that to work? Could you give an example of the interaction with the inhabitants?

Christophe Hutin — Answering this question in the light of the theme of drawing is very interesting because I think the way I'm showing the work is the process. The right wording would be to say it's a transformation. I don't have the aim to make a new form or something that doesn't exist in the present. What I'm doing, in fact, is dealing with the present, with the reality. And in my work I'm always in between two forms; I'm never in one form at the end. The final form, I don't like it. I don't like something finished.

Christopher Dell — I call this way of showing diagrammatics. By this I mean that your representations operate in a space *between* the grammar, *between* the structural elements.

Christophe Hutin — Yes, in between. The precision of the drawing allows me to transform each part of a project very precisely. To focus on and to work on it. The global form is not my question. My issue is the work with people. What I do research on in the house is the daily life of the people, their story. I can give you an example. In the project at the settlement Beutre in France, I drew each house precisely. And in one of the houses, the inhabitant is ninety-two years old; he is a Spanish man, and he is making a garden in the forest behind the military plot. This is a forbidden area. He's not allowed to go there. Nevertheless, the man has pigs and vegetables there; that is his work, and he is managing it himself. How can you determine where the house starts and where the house ends? This is a very important question. In fact, from the perspective of the man, the house is extended to the forest behind. When I'm drawing his house, I'm also drawing the forest because the pigs in the forest are part of the house. What this means is that while reading and representing a given architectural situation, you have to move with what the people are doing. In my lecture, I showed that I'm dealing with that, and how I do it, and how we are trying to transform this specific situation.

Christopher Dell — It's a very beautiful example. And it fits very well with the exhibition *Architecture for Pigs: Barn. Slaughterhouse. Shop* in which today's *Dialogue Concert* is located. This show works exactly the other way around: it presents houses for pigs, houses that were designed in the studio. Regarding this dichotomy, the theme of representation, its making and its relationship to its referent, is a central debate that we are confronted with in today's architectural discourse. Especially in actual architectural production we see a tendency to pump up representation. I am thinking of the rendering. In a representational sense, a rendering is a collage that doesn't reveal that it is a collage. Taking this aspect into account, I would argue that your work is highly political: you produce representations that are self-reflexive and critical. By this I understand representations that thematize their mediality, the fact that they are not transparent. Simply put, your drawings show that they are showing. The way you achieve this is by using diagrammatics. In diagrammatics, the relationship of the representation to its referent is neither figurative nor arbitrary, but rather structural. In the context of the political, it becomes important that through a diagrammatic way of showing—in which the nonrepresentationality of the diagrammatic space includes the thematization of showing as a practice and form of knowledge—you show the contingency of what is happening. That's the core: to show that it could have been different. Yet, far from a postmodern "anything goes," your drawings show exactly and precisely what a person who's living at a site is doing with the site and how this came about and what potentialities for future use are ingrained in the situation. I think that you operate in between by fusing precision and contingency in a very unique fashion.

Kathrin, in resonance with this theme, I want to ask you—since you studied both classical music and also improvised music—how do you see the difference between these two ways of operating? And how does the question of moving between genres resonate with you?

Kathrin Pechloff: For me, composition is very different from improvisation. Composition is about structure, about making; it's kind of mathematical. Composition is a really constructive work and improvising is letting all that go and following the intuition and being emotional. I think what is interesting for me is finding a place where both sides are connecting. You were talking about negotiation. I think this is a point which is very interesting, the negotiation between composition and improvisation, finding a new presence every time. It's always changing and developing, depending on when you play, with whom you play, what you did before, what you're thinking about, and your emotional status.

I think when we are talking about form, it's actually the same if you're constructing the form, writing it down on paper and thinking about it for weeks, or if you are improvising, which one may actually see as instantaneous composing, in a way. The way to think about the forms is the same for me, because the parameters are the same.

Christopher Dell: It's very interesting how you differentiate between the composition, which for you is very mathematical, and improvisation, which is very intuitive. However, when I hear Christian play, for example, the improvisation is even more mathematical than any composition I've ever heard. In that sense, Christian, how does it resonate for you to work in between the forms, being in between the grammar?

Christian Lillinger: I try to count all the time, actually, even if there's a rest, and force myself to structure myself all the time. And I don't believe there is an instant of emotions. Emotions might spark the knowledge, might set off what you experienced so far. I try to stretch things out by thinking about composing, about what could be the next step, and feel inspired by the composition in the way that people are doing it and so on. But Christophe, you came up with this beautiful idea to ask the people and to discuss the general question of social housing with them, right? To create a discourse, and then you try to operate collaboratively. It's about questioning hierarchies, which is a bit how we play, based on playing and constructing together. Christophe came up with the wonderful example of the conductor, who is also a dictator, in my opinion. The function of the conductor is based on money and power structures. Instead, I am interested in crossing the gap toward the possible, for every human being. When I say I try to structure myself all the time, this also means that I'm going to find a way out, and find a way to add to a given situation in a good way. You have to know when to add something, how to rearrange your furniture, or to play a different beat. Generally, you need to develop an aesthetic to create.

Christopher Dell: This aspect is connected to the question of preparing an improvisation. What Christophe and Christian are insinuating is—if I understand correctly—that improvisation is actually more work than composition. Because there is negotiation all the time, every day. You are always in the process. You have to be able to cope with the contingency of the situation and make it constructive. I think that's amazing. And it demands enormous skill. Christophe, how do you operate today if one takes into account that we still live in a functionalist era regarding building laws and economics? What is being taught in the architecture departments at universities is, as you have explained, at most times still functionalist, and this also applies to the representations. In that context, how do you operate? How do you create your own space in that environment?

Christophe Hutin That's a good question. Regarding the university, what I do is bring the students 10,000 kilometers away from school. We travel to South Africa or somewhere where we don't have the rules that are usually imposed. Also, when you go out into the world, you cannot avoid the hard type of work. It's very easy to be abstract and to think that composition is the only way to arrive at a solution. But when you deal with people, you cannot reverse time; you are obliged to deal with the complexity and with the real world in real time, where composition is not enough. You have to do more than that to solve the situation you're facing. It's not so easy. You are right, it's a thousand times more work than simply being a composer. If you take 100 houses, you can't have one solution for the 100 houses. Yet it has been done in this way until today. But this is not my vision. My vision is to make myself a little bit uncomfortable and to find another way. For example, for the Beutre project, we installed a studio in the neighborhood. And my team is living there. When we are working, we are architects to our neighborhoods. It makes a big difference in regard to the daily life of the neighborhood, because this is the way we also gain trust. To become confident with the people is very important for a project. You cannot pretend. I'm there every day, so I'm facing everyday life there.

Christopher Dell This procedure is very important. It brings back aspects of the 1950s and 1960s, and of the research method of participatory observation that one can find in ethnography, in sociology. Yet, in your work these methods are transposed to something that is conventionally called design. This movement dislocates both, the research and the design. Since the Renaissance, the studio has been regarded as the place to design, and the space is a room where rational reason is linked to the author subject, and where design is connected to universal truth. Informed by truth, the author subject draws the "beautiful" design. In your projects, however, truth is not universal; it is located outside the studio and connected to a particular situatedness. It follows another imperative: "If you want to know what to design, you have to go outside and develop the tools of how to make the fieldwork knowledgeable, in order to not end up with simplistic empiricism." Consequently, what we currently see in architecture are experiments on form that counteract the functionalist doctrine in a critical but also affirmative manner. They explore ways of combining old tools with a new way of looking, reading, and showing a given situation. One might think of your work, but also that of Atelier Bow-Wow, Lacaton & Vassal, Oda Pälmke, Bernd Kniess, Ton Matton, and others. Within the framework of this discourse, Atelier Bow-Wow coined the phrase "Architectural Ethnography" to describe this specific way of working. As an ethnographer or sociologist, you do research but you don't design. For instance, you train to become a boxer in order to investigate a boxer milieu. But you are not allowed—as a scientist—to become really involved. You become a boxer in order to produce research results for an academic space of representation. The title "Architectural Ethnography," however, signifies quite a different procedure, because you have to be constructive with the situation you are involved in or intervening in, because you are an architect. In this context, you are at the same time a designer and a researcher. That's a completely different story than ethnography as a traditional social science. Your transform while doing research, you do research in order to transform, and you also will be transformed in the process of transforming. Where you work, the place changes. Christophe, if I remember rightly, you lived in a flat in the Grand Parc housing estate when you did the construction supervision for the project at Bordeaux with Lacaton, Vassal, and Druot?

Christophe Hutin — Yes, I had a flat in that building for three years. I wanted to work and to party there and to be a part of the building.

Christopher Dell — In view of this, one can identify two main aspects for a design project. One aspect is to be there and to inhabit the site that you work on. The other aspect is to ask: If you work on site in 1:1 contexts, why do you draw? Why do you transform? Why do you design? Posing these questions implies relocating the knowledge. The functionalist perspective is based on a presumption of knowing what housing is, what the needs are, and then making a container *for* the people. In the light of the housing crisis, the planning crisis, and the rise of new life forms, the functionalist way of working seems to be getting increasingly dysfunctional. Somehow it seems as if one has to find out anew what housing is. Consequently, dwelling as a practice rises to an epistemological level. I think there are two value changes taking place here. One is the value of the knowledge that is in the dwelling. What before was without *logos*—the improvisation of the inhabitants—now appears as *the logos* of architecture. The other value change concerns economics. The explosion of rent and land value in the cities has been to a large extent created by the living forms that have established themselves as a "new urbanity." This lifestyle was responsible for an unbelievable renaissance of the city. It is obvious that it was the dwelling practice of the inhabitants of the city that created the value of the ground and not the other way around. In this sense, it is highly critical that the people who produce the value of the ground are not economically participating in the rise of value of the ground while they're dwelling—if they are not the owners of the place, which in Germany is quite rarely the case.

At this point, I'd like to bring the discussion to an end and thank you all so much for coming out and playing together with me. And we take with us the last words from Christophe to go out into the world, to confront, to be confronted.

Christophe Hutin — I was thinking when I was listening to your music that I would like to invite you to the neighborhood of Beutre to play this music for the people there. You will receive some tomatoes at the beginning, but at the end you will play for the inhabitants.

Christopher Dell — Exactly. Tomatoes at the beginning and music in the end.

Hans-Jürgen Commerell — I have a question regarding the theme of efficiency. Christophe, you work with these people, you're living there, you spend lots of time there. You do this in order to create a better architectural result, which is a surplus, as it's a societal innovation. And it is kind of a "better" architecture. It is cheaper compared to traditional architecture but has better quality, which also means that it lasts longer and works better. But architectural work is also driven by time and money. Can one say that a negative aspect of the practice is that usually the architect has to be very time efficient? How can you manage your time, and also have the means to live upon? How do you finally get paid to do very time-consuming projects, which yours are? Of course you spend more time than the usual architect. But on the other hand, you have to create a balance in order to make a living. How do you manage this? A very simple question.

Christophe Hutin — I clearly understand your question. And the owner of the house is paying me. Maybe architects are usually negotiating the money. I do not negotiate the money. But I'm very well paid to do what I do. Because I propose to the client another procedure: I say to them: "You're going to save a big amount of money with my work." Because if you use a normal system, you will spend maybe 100,000 euros per house to renovate it. If you do it my way, you're going to spend 50,000 euros. So you pay me zero, just give me the difference. 50,000 euros for 100 houses, and I am very well paid.

Hans-Jürgen Commerell — I think this is an important model to know, also so that others will understand that this work is worth doing.

Christophe Hutin — Exactly. I'm not saying that I'm more intelligent than other architects. The intelligence is the same in every person. I'm just saying that the energy and the time we spend create more intelligence than in the conventional process. And the client has to pay for that.

Hans-Jürgen Commerell — So instead of having to pay for concrete or for materials, you have to pay for the creation of an intelligent solution, and this holds great value. And this is a long-term solution.

Christophe Hutin — It also implies the responsibility of the owner to maintain the object instead of destroying it or misusing it. You can also take into account the relation that the social housing company has with the tenants. It's a cost. Social peace in society costs a lot of money. We don't solve the social question. It's a reality. You don't have to pay money to have participatory mediation, et cetera, with the aim of trying to achieve social peace. In fact, just last week I was presenting the Beutre project to the tenants, and after the presentation we had a big party. Everyone in the social housing company was dancing with the tenants. It's the first time I have seen this, no conflict.

Hans-Jürgen Commerell — One has to show that this way of working is possible. Usually it doesn't happen because the owner wants to finish the project as soon as possible. After he has quit, the owner is not responsible for the long-term cost of the problems. Whatever the materials and the maintenance, we are dealing with the social in architecture, so we have to get a better understanding of the whole time scale of efficiency, quality, and money. This is also something we have to teach and educate. It is possible, but we need to take the whole scope of collective energy and intelligence into account.

Christophe Hutin — It's more or less a work in progress. In fact, as an architect, you have to accept that you are not the master of the final form. Because you're just in this situation for a moment in time, yet the building has a very long life.

Ulrich Stock — I also have a question. You mentioned the illegal extensions in Beutre. You see them, you put them in your plans, and they persist. For instance at the site where the guy is having his pigs: Don't you encounter problems with the owners of the land or with the neighboring military site? How do you deal with that?

Christophe Hutin — It's the work I'm starting on now, from this point, because I explained the process to the people. We are going to negotiate each situation. As an architect I have the means to confirm an extension. And this confirmation is the ground on which to negotiate with the owner. I will assert my responsibility for the extension. Because I can confirm that it was done well enough to be maintained and to be legalized within the social housing company contract. But the problem is, because of the rules, if you consider the extension in this manner, the rental price will go up. Basically, the number of square meters rises. It's a big deal in terms of jurisdiction, because we have to work with the social housing company to keep the people at the same rental price per month, otherwise they can't afford to keep the apartment.

Ulrich Stock How long do you think you're going to work on this?

Christopher Dell Four years. And there is also another piece of information I didn't tell you yet: the tenants of this neighborhood will be in Venice at the Biennale, too, to discuss the project. In that sense, they will appear as peers in the visual regime of architecture.

Christopher Dell We will meet them there. Thank you all for this very incisive gathering and conversation.

Intervention
June 25, 2020

Christopher Dell (vibraphone)

Aedes Architecture Forum, Berlin

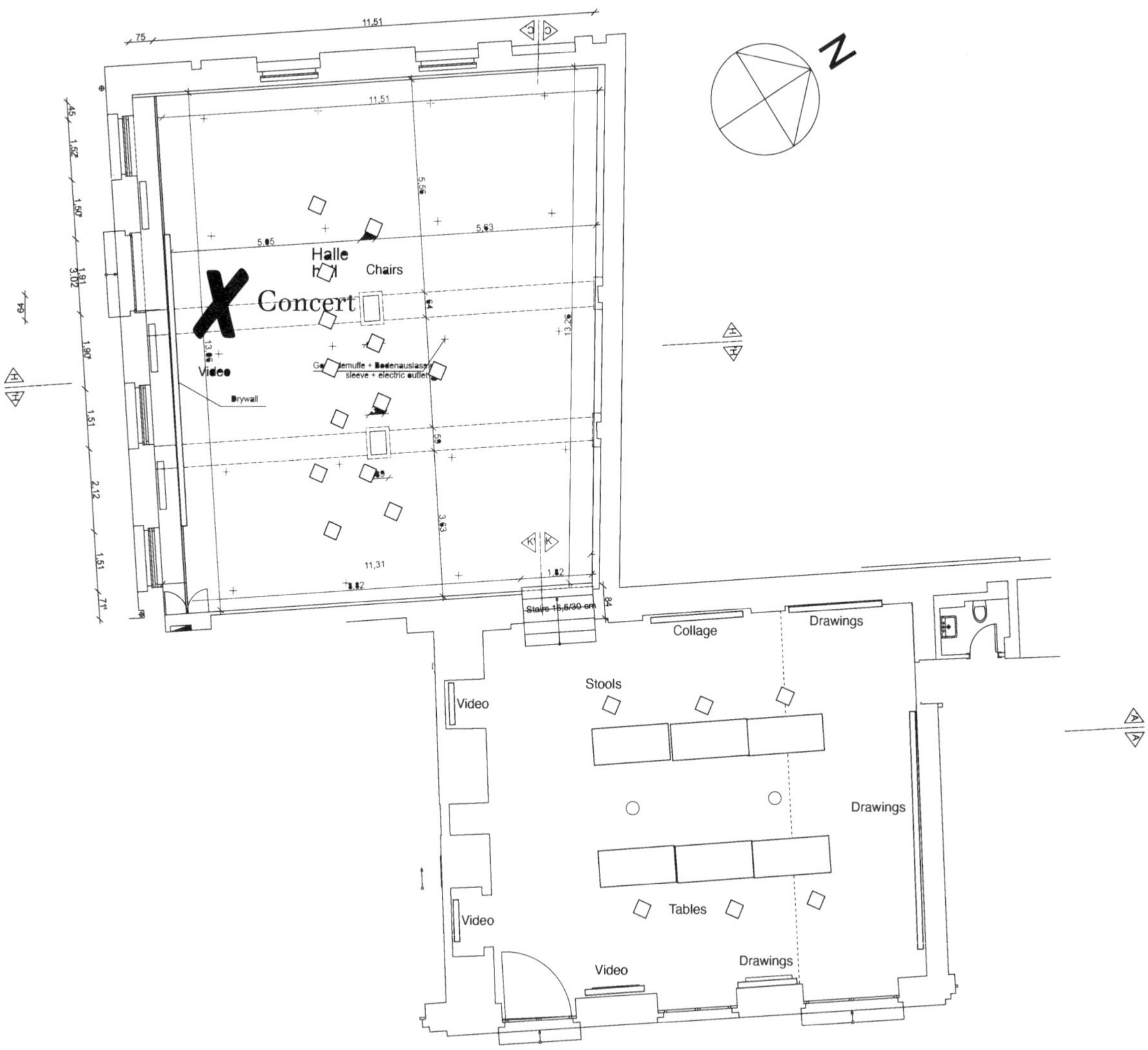

Intervention in the Aedes exhibition spaces of *Obel Award 2019: Water Garden* by Junya Ishigami & Associates (May 13 – June 25, 2020)

Betreff: Einladung
Von: Hans-Jürgen Commerell 2 <hjc@aedes-arc.de>
Datum: 18.06.20 13:35
An: Christopher Dell <cd@christopher-dell.de>, Christine Meierhofer I Aedes Architecture Forum <cm@aedes-arc.de>, "kf@aedes-arc.de Feireiss" <kf@aedes-arc.de>

Lieber Christopher,
her das erste Ergebnis zu unserem Telefonat. LG, hans-jürgen

Einladung zum Finissage - Konzert
mit Christopher Dell

Lieber Heiner yxyxy

aus Anlass des Endes der überaus erfolgreichen Ausstellung
Obel Award - The Water Garden by Junya Ishigami
laden wir am 25. Juni um 19.00Uhr sehr herzlich ein zum spontanen Aedes Dialog-Concert

Intervention!

Christopher Dell, Vibraphonist und Theoretiker, tritt in einen musikalischen Dialog mit der Ausstellung 'The Water Garden'
des japanischen Architekten Junya Ishigami. Situiert inmitten der Ausstellungsinstallationen in den Räumen des Aedes Architekturforums
nimmt das Konzert die Atmosphäre und den diskursiven Raum des dargestellten Landschaftsprojektes auf. In einer kurzen Einführung stellt Dell den verfahrens-strategischen Zusammenhang von Architektur, Raume, respektive der Landschaft und Musik her.

+Glas Wein
+ Brezel

+ ein Satz zu den Corona Regeln und das diese Einladung persönlich und nicht übertragbar ist.

xxx

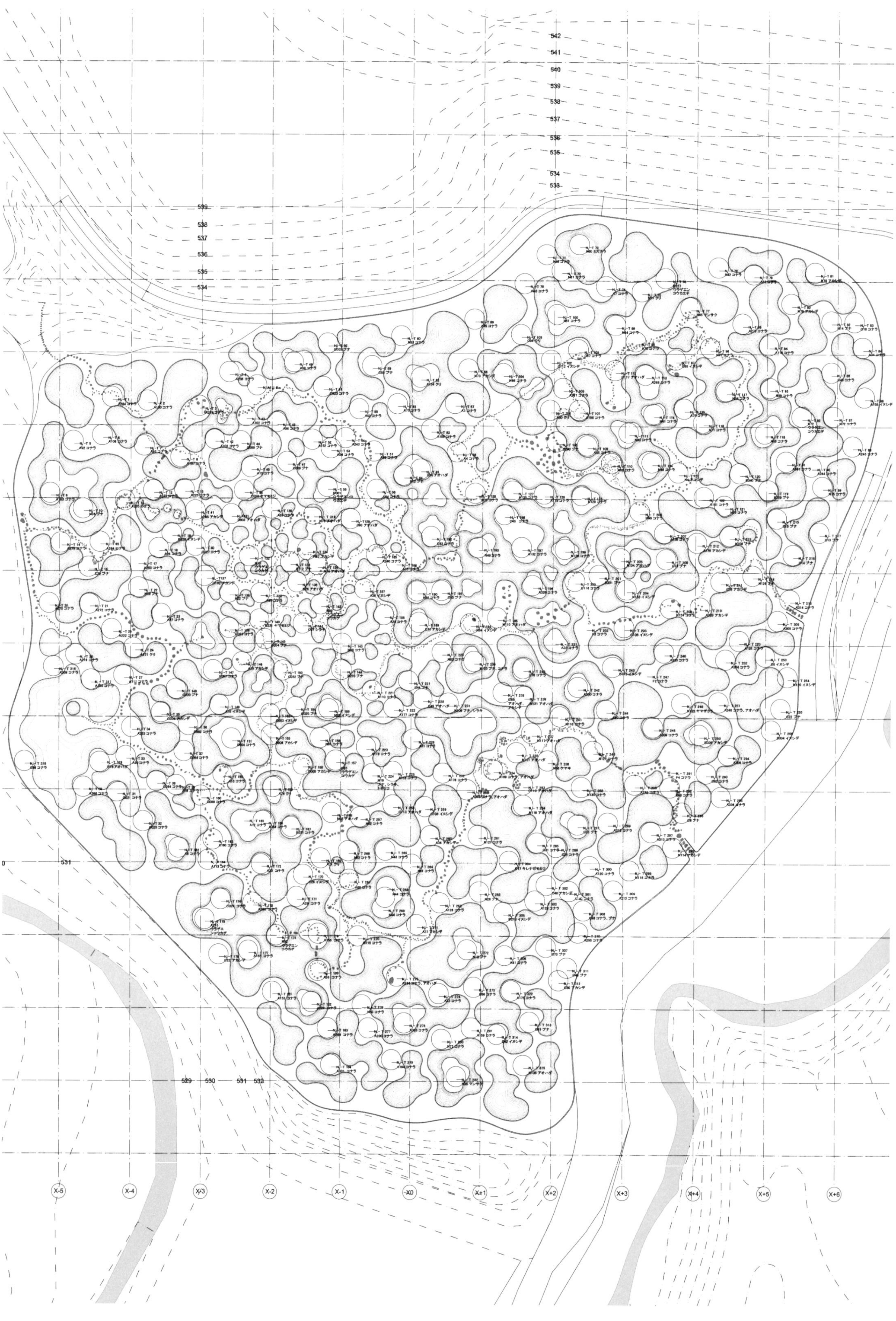
542
541
540
539
538
537
536
535
534
533
539
538
537
536
535
534
531
529
530
531
532
X-5
X-4
X-3
X-2
X-1
X0
X+1
X+2
X+3
X+4
X+5
X+6

meadow
forest

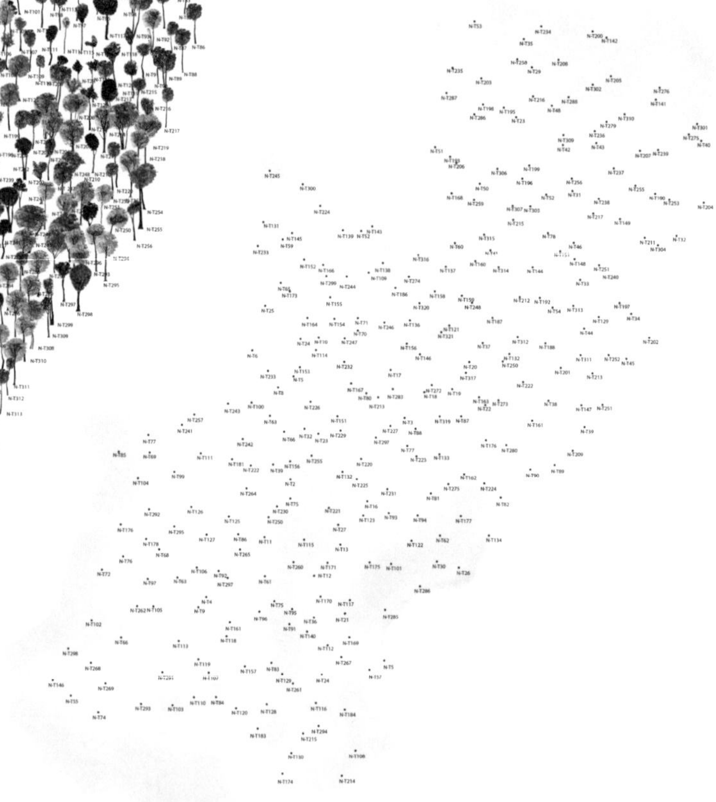

Dialogue Concert #3
Transformation
August 14, 2021

Lecture: Daniel Libeskind

Concert: Elisabeth Coudoux (cello), Christopher Dell (vibraphone), Pascal Klewer (trumpet), Christian Lillinger (drums)

Discussion: Christopher Dell, Daniel Libeskind

ANCB Network Campus, Berlin

Dialogue Concerts #3
Transformation
August 14, 2021
Daniel Libeskind

On Chamberworks: 14 Takes

1

I'm so delighted to be here. First of all, thank you, Kristin Feireiss and Hans-Jürgen Commerell. The Aedes Architecture Forum by now is a canonic institution. It's been here for forty years. And I've had the pleasure to know Kristin for so many of those decades. I think that she and Hans-Jürgen have created one of the most interesting forums for architecture anywhere in the world. And I'm especially thankful that during Covid, even with the social distancing, I'm able to see people and friends who are here; it really is so much better than the screen.

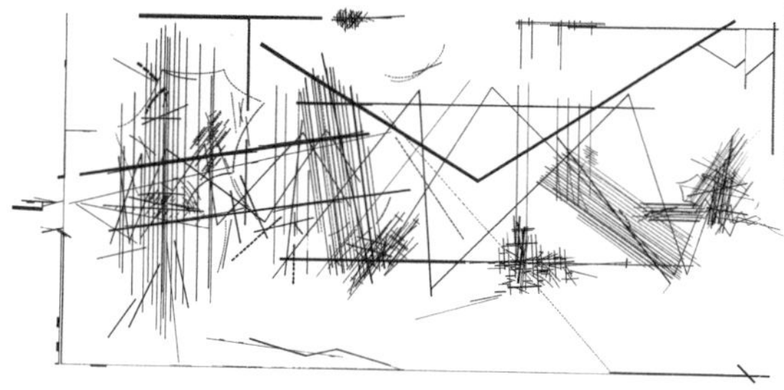

2

What can I say about *Chamberworks*?
It's hard to talk about them because they are drawings and, you know, you can't explain a drawing. There are a number of people I admire who have written about these works. Robin Evans, professor at the Architectural Association in London, who unfortunately passed away some time ago. John Hejduk, my former teacher at the Cooper Union in New York. Peter Eisenman, again, a former teacher and a very famous architect. The art historian Kurt Forster. Not to mention Aldo Rossi, a great Italian thinker and an architect. They've written their own sort of interpretations, which might be much better than what I have to say.

3

Having stated this, I want to share with you what those drawings are from my personal perspective. Why did I pursue them? Why would anybody do such a thing? Well, I'm an architect, but I've never worked for another architect. Not because I am egotistical. But I tried to work in the office of the architects I knew—and who were very famous—for one or two days. And the conclusion I drew from this experience was that it would probably be very boring to be an architect. Once you sort of start sitting at the desk, it's kind of a deadly tremor that goes through your body and you think, am I going to do this for the rest of my life? I said, "No." But what was I going to do without a job as an architect—with a wife who was willing to support me, financially and in many other ways, who allowed me to have the time? Nina's role here is very major, because how can anybody take the time to do such a thing without support?

4

And it took a long time. Think about it: if you have no commission, you have no office, you have no reason to think of imaginary buildings, because it's a futile attempt to do follies from the imagination. What would you draw as an architect? That was the problem, I said to myself. It's a little bit like the Cartesian meditations. Descartes started his thought by saying, "I don't believe in anything. I don't believe in any of the things I've been taught. I don't believe in anything that's been told to me. I'm going to start, he said, from my doubt." That's how I started. But *Chamberworks* cannot only be interpreted as a kind of Cartesian meditation. I was also inspired by Heraclitus, as the title of the work implies. The sayings of Heraclitus continue to be fascinating and as profound as anything that I can think of.

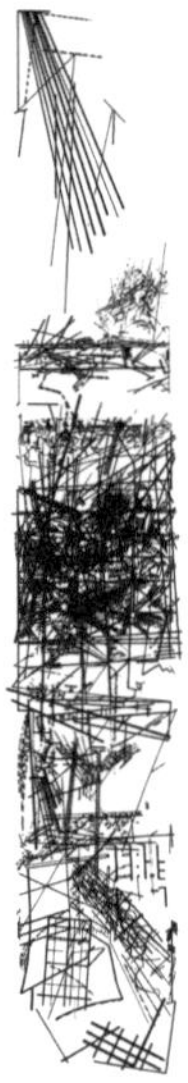

5

I sat down, and I had an idea. It was not a verbal idea, it was not an intellectual idea, it was an architectural idea. Then the question was how to compress it onto a piece of paper, which is the old model of architecture. You put something onto a piece of paper. Now you could do it on a computer screen or in a smart system. But how do you compress into that possibility all that you know which is musical about architecture, which is as fantastic in architecture as it is in the construction of a symphony, or a fugue, to be more modest? How do you create all of it without a kind of prefabricated language that is a ready-made language, without a language that is tired? It's a little bit like inviting immigrants to your board. There are borders: we don't want immigrants, we don't want anybody to interfere with our life. But if you open those borders, you're going to get all sorts of immigrants, both legal and illegal flooding through doorways. And in a metaphorical sense, those doorways were open to the immigrants that have been excluded from the architectural space of the drawing. In other words: I let into the drawing what was banned or exiled by centuries of control.

6

It is really interesting—this is just an aside—that as an artist, as a composer, you can do anything you want. So far—maybe not in Russia, but so far in the world—you could compose something in your attic, and it's not illegal. You could write a poem, you could compose a piece of music, you could paint a painting. But in architecture, it's pretty close to illegal to break the boundaries of what we consider the ordered space of architecture, of building, of

law, and also of the drawing. Consequently, when I finished these drawings, many people thought that they were not about architecture at all. They thought, this is a kind of art. But there is a difference. We have only one word called art. Everything can be art: whatever you say is art is art. But in architecture, we have at least two words: we have the word building and the word architecture. Architecture does not have to be built in order to be architecture, and a building can be built which is not a piece of architecture at all—it's just a building with no architectural value at all. This was the conceptual background of how I approached the drawings.

7

What system did I use? It was a musical system. When you play music, when you know musical notation, when you can write a piece, a score, you know that what is in the score is also what is in your ear, in your hand, in your vibrations, that you can translate it into kind of a text. The same holds true for architecture. Whatever can be drawn can be built. If you draw a line—maybe you cannot build

a line—but if you draw two parallel lines, it's a wall, especially if you fill it in between the lines. Whatever is built, even a chair or a drum, anything in this room, and anything outside, all of Berlin, all over the world, is built according to some document. Of course, a legal document, legal tender, has to be approved, just like monetary currency. But, as I explained earlier, I didn't traffic in the mandatory currency. I trafficked in pure projective creativity.

8

I put it this way: whatever is possible can be drawn. Viewed in retrospect, the drawings reveal themselves as a kind of treatise on contemporary architecture. It's not just the square, and the circle, and the triangle of the Bauhaus. It's not only what William Hogarth in his eighteenth-century treatise on art postulated: this is what art is made up of, hatched lines, crossed lines, curved lines. Rather, it goes really way back into the fact that whatever can be imagined, whatever can be represented, can be drawn in a way without even the object being there.

9

I took a step that in the realm of architecture was very radical: I created a series of drawings that didn't have a referent. There was not *a* building out there, but there were all the buildings out there, and all possible cities that I thought of. And

that's how I approached the *Chamberworks*. The term chamber here refers to different meanings. On one hand, the chamber is the *locus* where I drew them. But the chamber is also the *locus* where particle physics has been able to create new particles that show us what reality is made of. And, of course, the musical sense was neither an application nor a metaphor in the drawings; it was actually how the drawings were composed. However, it is important to note that I didn't start with a system of musical notation, but I did start with a system of musical collision with architectural drawing systems, which means lines and all sorts of things that can be drawn.

10

The drawings are systematic; they move from a large area to a very reduced horizon. There are twenty-eight of them in total, fourteen horizontal drawings and fourteen verticals. I mapped them all sort of simultaneously. They were not sequentially made. The cycle was thought as a sort of arc that contained all the drawings, even before I started drawing them. I don't think I could express how I drew them. But I can tell you anecdotally that when I read Paolo Uccello's description of the discovery of perspective in the Renaissance, I felt that it was pretty close to what I felt. Uccello ran out of his room after being locked up there for a long time and with hair sort of standing on his head. Suddenly he discovered something. That is how I felt. I was a bit of a madman. My wife could agree with that. She just nodded her head in total agreement.

11

That is what I really felt, and I still do, because I use the drawings today, I've used these drawings from the beginning of my first building, the Jewish Museum in Berlin; for every building, and every site plan, and every city plan I've ever done, I've used these drawings. How do I use them? I don't use them arbitrarily. The drawings do contain everything that I love about architecture, about cities, what can be drawn about cities, which is horizons, vedutas, plans of cities, constructions of details of cities, constructions of details of materials, how windows are made, how doors are made, how floors are constructed, how architecture is represented to a client.

12

In my view, the drawings are a mirror of architecture. But I didn't draw what is reflected in the mirror. I drew the mirror itself. What is reflected is arbitrary, just

whatever passes by the mirror. But the mirror itself doesn't change. And that's really how I conceived the *Chamberworks*.

13

The *Chamberworks* came to me through a stroke of revelation. I don't attribute them to myself, but to a lightning bolt. In this sense I did pay my homage to Heraclitus and his beautiful quotation—which I don't remember now in Greek—"the lightning bolt is what steers reality." In an Heraclitean paraphrase, the lightning bolt steers the world. It's true. In my experience, it is not about systematically sitting down and analytically discovering what is there, but about a sudden gap that opens, in which nothing shows itself, but what is. And I've read about this specific experience from my favorite artists and architects; they've had a similar experience. Kazimir Malevich had a similar experience. Marcel Duchamp had a similar experience. Le Corbusier, when he wrote "The Homage to the Right Angle," had the same experience, where he tells us that his experience with the killing of a dog gave him the idea of the right angle.

14

It's about mysticism, by all means, because drawing is a strange act. It's not a secular act, when you sit to draw and when you have nothing that you've been ordered to draw, but you're invited by the emptiness

around you to move your hand or your mind or your eye.
It is a kind of sacred thing that has been given. From the beginning of time, whoever drew something. Probably, the first drawing was made by someone in ancient times on a piece of sand. I think it's also true that Jesus's only words were written on the sand with the wind blowing across it. That is probably the first drawing, a drawing that has been erased in sand, probably a line dividing property between two competing tribes.

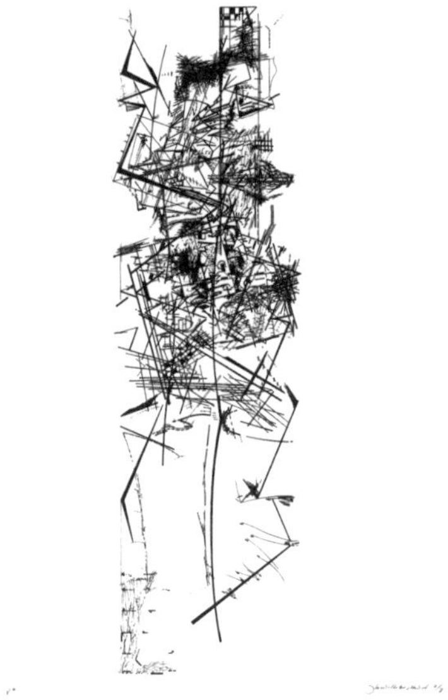

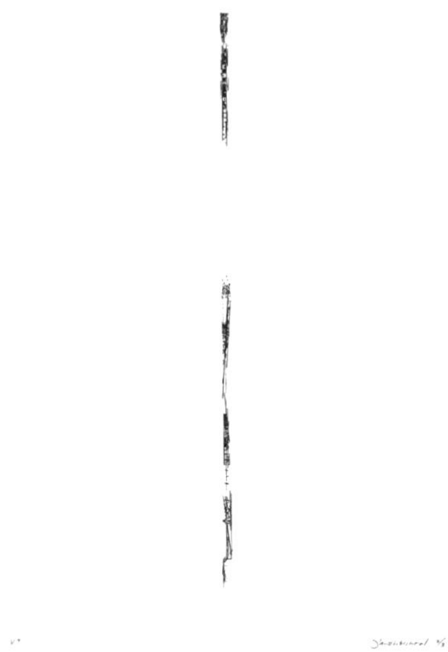

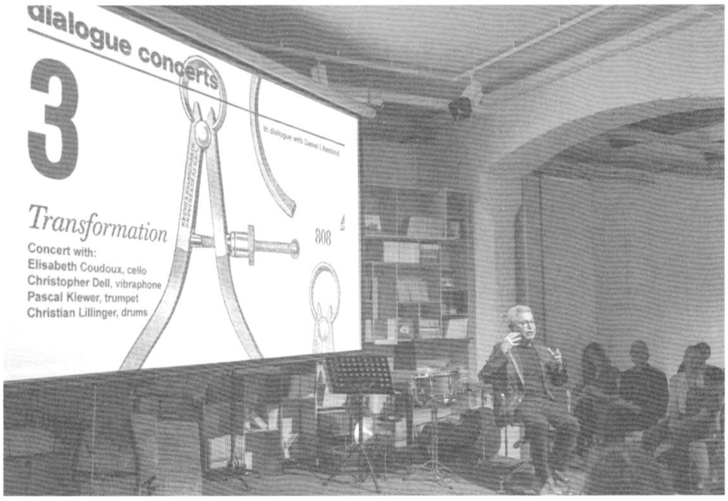
dialogue concerts
3
In dialogue with Daniel Libeskind
Transformation
808
Concert with:
Elisabeth Coudoux, cello
Christopher Dell, vibraphone
Pascal Klewer, trumpet
Christian Lillinger, drums

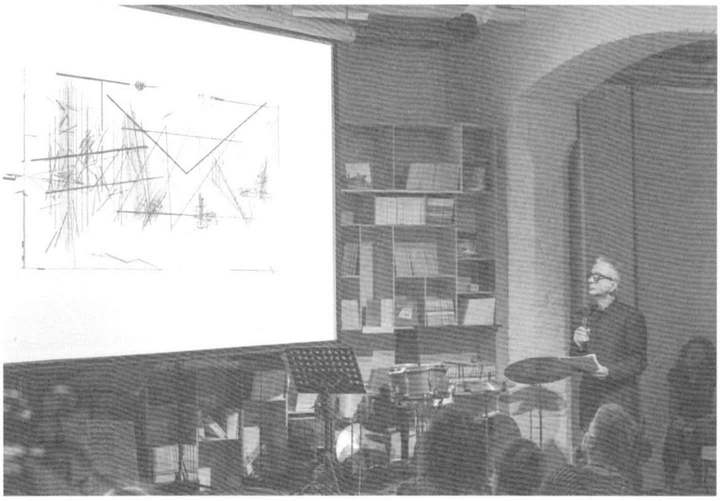

Dialogue Concerts #3
Transformation
August 14, 2021
Discussion

Christopher Dell
in Conversation with
Daniel Libeskind

Christopher Dell Thank you so much, Daniel Libeskind. I have been so strongly inspired by your work and its theme, which in my perspective is about opening the architectural imagination and the transpositional process ingrained in it. We played the *Chamberworks*, and we had a blast delving into your work. Now I'm very curious to hear from you. What were your imaginations while listening? How did our performance resonate with your work? What was sparked for you?

Daniel Libeskind I immediately thought that I have to do a new set of drawings. I was very moved. It was fantastic and very precise. I could see the drawings, even without looking at them. I could see how you interpreted the drawings in a very free, but also very disciplined way.

Christopher Dell Yes, indeed, we were very disciplined with it, very much in the sense that you explained so wonderfully in your lecture earlier today, that is, in the sense of *Chamberworks* being really a treatise.

Daniel Libeskind I'm staggered, first of all, by the musicianship of this quartet, and by the composition, and by how creative it is. You know, I have listened to a lot of contemporary music, but this is really at the very top, the apex of contemporary creativity. Congratulations.

Christopher Dell Thank you. It is very moving to hear that. We will now discuss different themes related to the *Chamberworks*, but one that struck me the most was that of embodiment. While playing the music, our bodies were sort of piloted by the *Chamberworks*. The drawings have a vector; they really have a drive. To put it this way reminds me of an anecdote that you were once telling. Glenn Gould sat at home practicing the *Goldberg Variations*, and suddenly there's a person entering the "chamber" in order to clean the house. The person turns on the vacuum cleaner. And Gould can't hear himself playing anymore. But what he realizes, while he keeps on playing, is that what Bach actually had in mind when he composed the music was a kind of topological movement, bodily movement of the fingers in space. And I always wondered, is that also something that is the trigger for you when you draw, that you move in space?

Daniel Libeskind The experience of Glenn Gould you cite is profound. I had my first revelation about architecture at my kitchen table. I lived in a very small apartment in the Bronx with my sister and my parents. And the kitchen was very small. My parents bought a very homely looking, small, brown Formica table. It's like a rectangle with big, rounded edges. And after dinner, we'd finished cleaning the dishes. I would have to do my homework. I was at Cooper Union, and I had a lot of Bauhaus teachers, refugees from Germany, like Hannes Beckmann, who was one of the top students of Wassily Kandinsky and Paul Klee. And he still taught from the notes of those masters. He showed them to us students, and at that time, I didn't read German, but it was amazing. There were corrections in the hand of Klee and Kandinsky of the exercises. To make a long story short, the exercise that I had was a classic Bauhaus exercise, namely, to draw brick courses in perspective with the precise diminishing line of mortar between the bricks, vertically and horizontally. I had a T-square. Moving the T-square on this table, it was never clear to me at what point I was on the curve. For instance, at some point I was off the perfect perpendicular by .01 degrees. I discovered the freedom to move the brick courses around the curve, so they would go in all directions—kind of like the 359 other angles that were sort of forbidden. When looking back, I always thought that had I been a little bit richer, and had my parents bought me a drafting table, I might have become a really dull architect. Because, in some way, it was the table, that kind of a really cheap table, that saved my life.

Christopher Dell — Along these lines it is all about the physical experience. And what you also imply with your example is that it's not a perfect table. It's not perfect.

Daniel Libeskind — Far from perfect.

Christopher Dell — Even far, far from perfect. There's this idea that to free yourself in your work means delving exactly into that imperfection. But this imperfection is not interpreted by you as it normally is, as something that went wrong. But as something that actually led you to a truth.

Daniel Libeskind — You're right. It's certainly a liberation to find that what is supposedly the imperfection is the most interesting part of an unknown world that lies behind the grid that has been placed there to control what the limits of your possibilities to draw are. It was a very physical, as you say, it was a visceral experience. It wasn't something premeditated. It's not somebody thinking, let's do something interesting, let's draw something which is interesting. Not at all. It was just a sudden realization that the entire atmosphere is related to architecture—everything, the table on which you draw, the kitchen, the housing project here in the city, the Bronx right behind you there, is all part of those things that you're drawing. This approach sort of translates into a different idea of what you're drawing also, because you're no longer just drawing those brick courses; you're drawing things that have been transformed there into something else.

Christopher Dell — Your vivid account leads me to the next question. You *did* study at Cooper Union. To be able to make the disciplinary transposition you undertook also entails being very disciplined. Your reflections would not have occurred to you without the discipline in which you learned your craft, in the context of the Bauhaus, the context of modernism. However, I know that a lot of times you have scolded modernism for its understanding of space as a neutral container, for example. Yet, I have the feeling that there is this longing for truth in your work, which is also a central theme of modernism. This theme was kind of ingrained in you, but then you found a different path of pursuing the truth. Does that process also resonate with your background as a musician? Did your background of playing a musical instrument influence that situation with the table?

Daniel Libeskind — Totally. Because I played the accordion, which is not an instrument known for classical music. Although today, there are many great composers who are composing classical music for accordion and symphonic orchestra. But accordion is usually associated with poor people, with folk, with gypsies, with beggars, and so on. That instrument, I think, had a big impact on my way of thinking. First of all, I played classical music, which I myself transcribed. At that time, works such as Toccata and Fugue in D Minor were not easy to find, at least not in Poland when I started playing. By listening to the music and transcribing it, I was able to perform it on an instrument, which always brings a smile to people's faces. It appears funny. Yet, I've always thought, why do people think it's funny? They don't think the clarinet is funny, they don't think the drums are funny, they don't think the vibraphone is funny, but they think the accordion is funny. And there is a criminal element in the accordion. There is a criminal dimension, somehow; I don't know why. Maybe because it has the buttons and the keys and has the bellows, and it opens in a particular way and closes in a particular way. It's just that the whole instrument has this aura about it, has illegality written all over it. But I played it very seriously, and, by the way, I just saw a letter that my sister had sent to me, written in 1959 when I arrived in New York, that I was invited to play by an association of accordionists. And I was offered a lot of money to play, and I played for only about three or four minutes. So, I said to Nina, I was far more successful financially when I was thirteen years old, fourteen years old, than I am now, because my earnings were much higher and would have remained so probably, well, who knows.

Christopher Dell: Although you played a criminal instrument.

Daniel Libeskind: Because it was a novelty when I played with famous musicians—I played with Vladimir Ashkenazy, with Itzhak Perlman. It was a bizarre thing. *The Forward*, the Yiddish newspaper, reviewed the concert, giving Ashkenazy and Perlman really no space, but they described the accordion, the bizarre appearance of a very short person, with a very large vertical instrument. In a concert that was supposed to be Haydn, and Mozart, and Beethoven playing, Rimsky-Korsakov, Bach, and so on.

But coming back to your initial question, I think this instrument has a lot to do with discipline. To play the accordion well, it's not about approximating music. Music is not an art which you can approximate; you either play it correctly, or you don't. You can't just make mistakes. You have to know which note is being played, what is the rhythm, what precise location of the particular moment it is in time. Music teaches one, as you said, incredible discipline; it's not chaotic at all. There might be chaotic moments in a Beethoven sonata, let's say, in a Liszt sonata, or what appears to be chaotic in Luigi Nono, or in your composition, but it's not chaotic at all. It's incredibly crafted with incredible tradition to it. And that's what I think about architecture: it has this incredible tradition, which, without absorbing it, you would just produce funny-looking things on a computer that look interesting for about five minutes but cannot really sustain themselves in time, in space, whether it's the space of a drawing or space in the city.

Christopher Dell: When you tell that story, especially the part about being precise, it reminds me of my childhood. What really drove me to play music is the fact that it's true. You can't lie about it. I mean, you either play it or you don't.

Daniel Libeskind: It's true. It's like sports.

Christopher Dell: Exactly. I first decided to become a football player at a young age. But after a serious injury, I had to abandon it and I switched to music, since music and sports are true.

Daniel Libeskind: They don't lie. By the way, when we say you play an instrument, we don't say you work on an instrument. You play an instrument. Which means you bring the world of playing, of freedom, to the world of music, which is amazing. We don't say you play in drawing. However, drawing has this strange etymology, because the same word in English, at least, is to draw a card from a deck, right? You draw a card, or you draw water from a well, you bring up water from it. It's a strange word, to draw, but it still has that element, like in musical play.

Christopher Dell: Absolutely. In this respect, different aspects come to my mind. One aspect is drawing as a musical practice. Since the 1960s a lot of architects, when trying to describe the meaning or *logos* of architecture, were referring to the metaphor of language. But when one refers to the metaphor of language, then one endorses a certain relation between language and meaning that puts us in a box. I always had the feeling that when you made the switch to refer architecture to music—which is also a sense-making practice—it was for you the way out of a dilemma, so to speak. Because music produces meaning in a completely different way than language in the sense that it's full of nonrepresentational aspects, yet these nonrepresentations are full of truth.

Daniel Libeskind: I didn't think about it consciously, but what you're saying is probably true. That just relating the act of drawing to music is already being in a different world. And yet, it's a world that, if you go back to the Greek texts, is all about proportions, which are musically derived, from the length of vibrating strings. In that respect, architecture is deeply musical from the very beginning. In fact, there is no real contradiction. But you're right, I think, in the sense that I was putting all of my sort of embodied will into something that had no end to it, that had no real practical application to it—it was a very different idea than drawing an imaginary building, however beautiful that imaginary building is. And I admire drawings of the nineteenth-century Beaux-Arts and all the great architects who made imaginary buildings, but I always thought that they were, in a sense, locked in. The closest genius to opening that box was probably Giovanni Battista Piranesi, who already in the eighteenth century tried to get out of the limits of architecture through drawing, but you can see that he wound up in prison. It's not by coincidence that he calls his drawings "Prisons," because he could not get out.

Christopher Dell: Absolutely. This theme leads me to the next, the theme of the nonteleological. I refer to the fact that your drawings omit the referent. However, they are no illusions; they are still connected to truth. And to make it even more complicated: while being related to music, they still exist within the discipline of architecture. I wonder how you experienced, for example, your time studying at the Architectural Association in London, discussing this radical concept—of affirmatively, and yet reflexively and critically, refraining from reaching architecture's holy grail, the building to be built—with teachers such as Richard Rogers or Alvin Boyarsky. One question is: Did they support you or not? The second is: How do you operate today? Because you also said that sometimes you don't even show the drawing to the client. The problem we have in music is the same; if you show the notation to the wrong musicians, they think it doesn't make sense.

Daniel Libeskind: It's the wrong system.

Christopher Dell: Simply because working constructively with the nonrepresentational takes discipline and a milieu, so to speak. These are the two questions: How did you go about it, then? And how do you go about it now in your architectural firm?

Daniel Libeskind: It's a great question. First of all, I neglected to mention Dalibor Vesely, a Czech philosopher, who was also my teacher when I was studying in England, who also wrote about *Chamberworks*. And he was one of the great phenomenologists of the time; he was a student of Ja Patoka and of Hans-Georg Gadamer, and so on.

Christopher Dell: And Vesely wrote a famous book on phenomenology and structure, *Architecture in the Age of Divided Representation*.

Daniel Libeskind: That's right. He wrote a book about architectural representation and structures. I was very lucky that not long after I made those drawings, someone like Alvin Boyarsky, at the Architecture Association, looked at them, and he didn't say anything negative. Instead, he said, "Would you like to publish them?" And, by the way, that set of *Chamberworks* that the Architecture Association published in 1983 was designed as a record box, in a vinyl LP format, because it was musical. It was the first of the series of box sets that they published.

Christopher Dell: The *Folio Series.*

Daniel Libeskind: Yes, the *Folio Series*, exactly. I was so lucky that Alvin Boyarsky was a visionary, as were many of the people who wrote about and supported my approach. But many people, on the other hand, particularly in the bigger public sphere, thought that it was just a waste of time, that it was not architecture. What happened to architecture? Where did architecture go to? Which is a good question. Where did it go to?

Christopher Dell: And how do you do it now in your office? Have you kind of created a media in which people know how to form, translate your drawings into building? How does it work?

Daniel Libeskind: The title of this talk is "Transformation." Of course, architecture is a very strange profession, much stranger than music, because in music, you know, you don't collapse when you see lines, and points, and triangles. And, by the way, Nina just reminded me, when I presented the Jewish Museum, in the competition, my text was written on musical paper in between the lines, and I called it "Between the Lines." I wrote the text with the Olivetti typewriter, I think Nina was typing, because I didn't know how, in between those lines. There is, from the very beginning, this sort of sense of loss and possibility.

Christopher Dell: What hits me about that story is that, traditionally, one would think that "Between the Lines" resides in the realm of art. But your rendition makes it clear that the drawing exists literally in an architectural realm as well. You managed to transgress the line of a Berlin Street with a building, a thing that in Berlin is almost impossible.

Daniel Libeskind: Well, because I was so naive. This is the problem with getting experience. It's a bad thing to gain experience. I can see it myself that I've built many buildings. And with each building, I ask myself a question: How can I forget what I know? It's very hard, because you get to be sort of trained as to what is "successful," what is accepted, what is admired. And it's more difficult to say, "I don't know anything, I am a fool." And actually, when I did the Jewish Museum, believe me, I never drew a building plan. I resisted, in five years of professional architecture education, drawing a single building, I never did, which is actually an achievement for a graduate. If I had had less visionary teachers, they would've said, "Get this person out of school. He's not drawing a plan. He's not drawing a building." But somehow, I only got one D. Can I tell you the story? This is an amazing story.

Christopher Dell: Please, go ahead.

Daniel Libeskind: I got straight As. I was summa cum laude, but I had one D. And it was in a class of a very famous engineer, Ysrael Seinuk. He just passed away a few years ago. He was one of the greatest engineers of skyscrapers in New York, whom I later encountered again when doing the project at Ground Zero. And he gave this project to the class, to design a private house, with all the systems, electricity, plumbing, everything. You've got to design the entire house, that was the assignment. Ambitious. I was thinking to myself, I'm not going to do this, because I will never build a house. Am I interested in bourgeois architecture? Am I interested in clients who want a house? I will never be in that situation. How wrong was I? I'm building my third house right now. Fourth.

I refused to follow the assignment, but I had to do something. I went to the Nervi bus terminal between Bronx and Manhattan near George Washington Bridge, and I studied the rebar, how that interesting structure by Pier Luigi Nervi was constructed, and I did an entire study of the structure. And I got a D. But everybody was laughing, because they thought, he's not really unable to draw a house, he just doesn't want to draw a house, but he did something pretty complicated. Because the calculations for the terminal are more difficult than a calculation for a two- or three-story house. All in all, I was lucky, I had great teachers. I was lucky that people didn't kick me out, that they thought it's not completely bad to do what I do.

But going back to my actual practice, sure, you have to now translate something that you know about. I didn't know anything about buildings before, because I had never built a building before the Jewish Museum, not even a small building. I didn't even draw a building, I never drew a plan, I never drew a section. And when I came to the Senate of Berlin, I remember there was a very clever engineer in the building department, very powerful. He looked at the drawings that were on display in the room. And he said, "Libeskind, come over here." There was empty piece of paper on the wall. Looking at those drawings, he said, "Go ahead, draw me the basement plan." I'll never forget that. And I said, what do you mean—"draw"? I thought about it, and I took a pen, and I drew a rectangle. And I got his approval, because initially he thought I was going to draw a kind of zigzag shape, and that would mean I failed. Because you can't build a basement like that. You've got to build a basement in some simple way. So, I passed the test. In a way, I had kind of already lost my innocence. And once you lose your innocence, you can be easily seduced by practice. And I'm glad I was because I built a lot of interesting buildings, but it's a disadvantage to know what to do, definitely. It's better not to know.

Christopher Dell: On that note, since one can be so easily seduced by practice, I want to close with a very abstract question. You once said that for you, and I quote, "exploration happens through drawing. In this sense, the drawing is not just a representational art, representative of the instruments of building, but drawing itself is a form of knowing, a form of wonder, which poses questions." What do you mean by that?

Daniel Libeskind: Well, drawing is my path. I never had any other path. I didn't apprentice myself to a stonemason like Mies. I wasn't like Le Corbusier walking around and measuring everything, and seeing, noting it down proportionately. I wasn't like Gropius going into the technological. My path to architecture was drawing: Draw! Keep drawing! Keep drawing until reality!

And I always believed in the path. I never doubted that I was an architect. People said, "Oh, you're wasting your time. Why don't you enter a competition? Why don't you do that and that and that?" But I believed that it's a path. And drawing is a very acrobatic act, because you can fall off to either side. But if you stay on that tightrope and keep drawing—and by the way, I continue to do that, even though I build buildings, which have been drawn, and I'm still drawing buildings that have not been built. To answer your question: yes, drawing itself is a form of knowing.

Christopher Dell: Daniel Libeskind, thank you so much for this very inspiring exchange.

Daniel Libeskind: Thank you. I'm really inspired by what you've done. And thanks to everybody here. Thank you.

Dialogue Concert #4
Structure
September 17, 2020

Lecture: Bernd Kniess

Concert: Christopher Dell (vibraphone), Christian Lillinger (drums), Jonas Westergaard (bass)

Discussion: Christopher Dell, Bernd Kniess, Christian Lillinger, Jonas Westergaard

Aedes Architecture Forum, Berlin

Dialogue Concerts #4
Structure
September 17, 2020
Bernd Kniess

Intro

It is September 14, 2017, a susceptibly cool autumn evening following a sunny, penultimate day of summer school. The marquee that serves as playing field and activity space offers but little protection from the cold and dampness. Like every evening, the players come together in the living room corner after the communal meal—today perhaps a little closer. Alice and Fran Edgerley talk about their work with the British architecture, design, and art collective Assemble.

The impression invokes Vitruvius. It brings to mind his narration about how everything began: with the community that assembles around the warming fire; with a language that they develop out of their desire to share experiences where showing doesn't suffice; with the knowledge that emerges from their exchanges of experiences; with an architecture that arises from their actual practices of sharing knowledge—all this in an interest to find shelter from a hostile nature.

What connects the scenes is the assemblage of people around a medium and their exchange of experiences. The symbolic dimension that produces meaning within a given order and a contextual relation

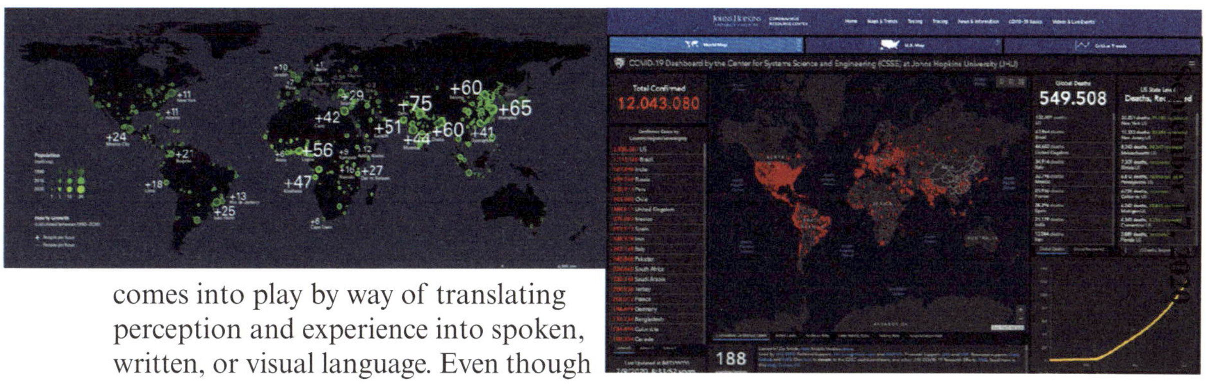

comes into play by way of translating perception and experience into spoken, written, or visual language. Even though remaining partial and contingent, this meaning provides insight into a human-made realm, which will become culture, through which humans will come to separate themselves from nature.

Staying with the myths, we could proceed with the narrative from the architectural-historical to the urban-historical perspective. Our understanding of the emergence of the city is generally based on the narration that it has been developed by agrarian societies, that the city has developed, independently and by emanating from a core, in concentric ways. Urbanist Jane Jacobs, with her hypothesis "Cities First—Rural Development Later,"[1] tried to dispel this myth. According to her, the people who originally came to places and settled down were not just hunters and gatherers, but also artisans, builders, traders, and artists. They produced things and exchanged them. It is the situation of shared labor and the exchange of its products that Jacobs identifies as the foundational quality of the city's coming into being. She argues that only through this interlocking of exchange relations among a group of cities was real development able to take place, and new forms of labor able to emerge, for instance arable farming and livestock. If we follow Jacob's theory—and there are many reasons to do so—the city builds on the exchange relations of people, goods, information, and knowledge within a fundamentally polycentric structure. Innovation proved to be the necessary impetus for its formation, and this innovation can only be explained through this dynamic liaison of assembled knowledge and agency.

Structure: The Relations of Elements and Their Agency

This leads us to the notion of structure. Christopher Dell articulated that structure describes the amount of relations between heterogeneous elements on an organizational field whose agentic mode works in such a way that transformations of one element affect the complete texture. This is what I wanted to point out in the introductory references: the city is more than its built condition. The city is produced, a sociomaterial texture that in its totality eludes tangibility.

And it is particularly the younger generation of architects, planners, and urban designers who recognize in the progress of their projects a potency unknown to them. On the one hand, this potency demonstrates the reach of both designing practice as artistic intention and knowledge borne out of experience. On the other, it leads these practitioners to become interested in the relational aspect of structures mentioned above, that is, structure's heterogeneous elements, their having-becomeness and becoming, and the question of how they "come to function."

Design that in this sense considers potencies of action in their temporal development cannot only be understood as a practice that produces knowledge. In its ambition to retrieve knowledge from practices that produce space, this design also affects these in turn. It is not a new recognition, albeit one that hasn't lost its actuality.

Let's call to mind the studies of the city that Kevin Lynch undertook in the 1950s and 1960s. The resulting work *The Image of the City*[2] serves Lynch to ground our reading of the city within a new form of observation that centers on perception. As early as the beginning of the 1970s, Lucius Burckhardt critiqued—rightly so—this approach's ignorance regarding the mediatic and conceptual frameworks. The objective image that Lynch seeks to draw is based on linguistic rules. He uses these rules to bring into play the symbolic-cultural register as a legend, without reflecting on the latter's principles. This results in a formalism proceeding from entities of the city that are reduced to the identitarian. Burckhardt, conversely, suggests reading the city as "interwoven complexes" that, while resisting transformation by design in their unity, "are easy to disturb by usually isolated single interventions, which can be conduced into unexpected directions."[3] His treatment of relational "complexes" particularly targets the organizational condition and constructedness of the city, so as to make accessible the often invisible linkages. He deliberately draws on a notion by Christopher Alexander who developed "Pattern Language"[4] with a similar intention, namely, to describe urban patterns depending on their functions. It is particularly interesting how everyday phenomena, for instance a "street corner" or "night," are deconstructed as socially constructed formations, only to then reconfigure them once more as a "net of reciprocally enriching relations."[5] We mustn't forget that these formations create complex situations. This condition of space of being interwoven and produced will never bring forth "tame" problems but instead only wicked or evil ones whose formulation itself presents a problem in its own right.[6] Adequately (en)countering this condition can only be conceived as an interdisciplinary, participatory, and multiperspectival approach.[7]

Two aspects are notable: even if more actors participate in urban-development processes today, and although planning practice has devised new protocols, little has changed in planning's dealings with the complexity and contingency of urban life. Strategies for problem-solving continue to be oriented around clearly describable problems. Simultaneously, we've seen grades of complexity with growing global interconnectedness and states of crisis that can barely be ignored, let alone undone. Think of the Lehman Brothers bankruptcy, Covid-19, or the climate emergency.

We can therefore only turn our attention to those complex questions of our time which we attend with accessible expertise and transcendence of existing (disciplinary and/or authoritarian) limits and open up new knowledge cultures that equally act out "relations between life worlds."[8] Our attention can only oblige the question of how we can continue to inhabit this world peacefully in the future. In the words of the biologist and science theoretician Donna Haraway, our task is to "make kin in lines of inventive connection as a practice of learning to live and die well with each other in a thick present."[9]

Take 3: Inhabiting

Ever since the beginning of the pandemic, Johns Hopkins University's website[10] has been documenting the global repercussions of Covid-19. Though we're familiar with the sight of relations between numbers, diagrams, maps, and lists, it evades immediate experience. Visiting the same website a year onward shows that while the numbers have changed, and perhaps also the elements and their relations, this change, however, remains abstract just like the data that is used to represent the pandemic's impact. Matters of fact that evade our perception. Yet what are the "true" stories behind this data? Events, mediated via the images and reports of the media: [infection hotspots like] Ischgl, Garmisch, Tönnies, the asparagus and strawberry harvest, applauding people and musicians on balconies, hygiene demonstrations, people on walks, conspiracy theorists like *Querdenker*innen* (lateral thinkers), and more. The never-ending stream of news washes them briefly to the surface.

Yet other stories exist that narrate how people (are forced to) reinvent themselves, how they rearrange their living conditions in unexpected situations. Stories such as that of the remeasuring of an 80-square-meter, four-room flat. Father and son share the living room in a day-night rhythm, the father for working from home, the other having returned from his studies afar to continue now as a distance learner and using the couch as a bed; two siblings persistently defend their bedrooms for their home schooling; there's the master bedroom that serves nothing else but sleeping, and so the mother who used to work in gastronomy only finds refuge in the kitchen or when sitting on the tiny balcony.[11] Let's look at the couple who after separation want to keep shared equal custody of their children, who cannot afford the second flat—which according to equality regulations must provide bedrooms for the children—and who now, under lockdown conditions, are forced to reinvent their separated lives in the existing home.[12] One research project considers the housing stories of two families who, due to a family member's dementia, create new arrangements of the home within and outside of their own flat and eventually in different places at the same time.[13] We could also tell this story by focusing on the reaches of various mobilities, for instance the wealthy employer who had tested positive upon her return from Italy but cannot do without her domestic help.[14] The virus will travel with the latter to her family and neighborhood in the favela, just as the actor who mimed Santa in a Belgian home for the elderly brought the deadly virus to twenty-six of its inhabitants who later died.[15] And there is also the dystopian vision of feverish and paranoid Paul B. Preciado who imagines how this virus would change the world for good, and therefore all couples would be forced to spend twenty-four hours a day together, whether they love each other or hate one another, or both at the same time. Those however, who had lost their love or hadn't found it in time would be damned to spend the rest of their lives alone.

His mounting fear isn't so much the thought of being ill while alone, but of dying alone.[16]

The "disturbances" that the pandemic has called forth hint not just at the urban textures with their far-reaching (global) interdependences, but also at the specific lifeworlds, the localizations and mobilities of human and more-than-human actors (including viruses), goods, capital, information, and knowledge. Albeit only briefly, these disturbances allow unusual insights into structures and modes of functioning that usually remain hidden. These transformations demonstrate how precarious and critical inhabitation itself has become as it is no longer limited to the home.

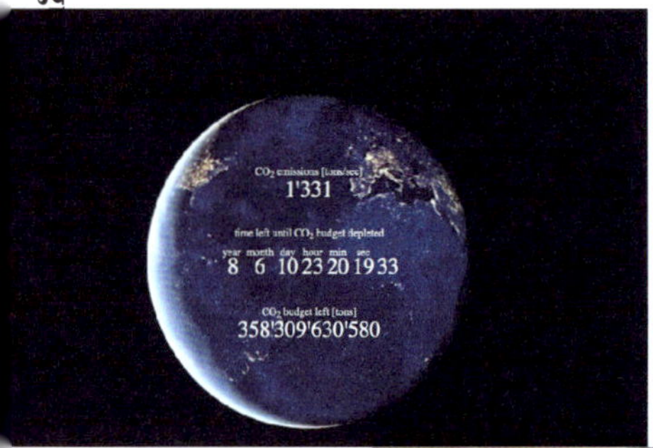

Eppur, si muove!

According to UN calculations,[17] the world's population will grow to nearly 11 billion people in the year 2100. Today there are 8 billion, when I was born there were 3 billion, and when my grandfather was born there were little more than 1.5 billion.

And yet it moves! This Italian phrase pertained to the Earth that moves around the Sun, rather than the other way around, as the former Catholic world view had it. Galileo is said to have mumbled these words as he left the inquisition tribunal, where he was forced to renounce his theory. Especially because this formula serves as a metaphor for the truth claim of the objective sciences to this day, we can only endorse Michel Serres's assessment: "The earth is moved."[18]

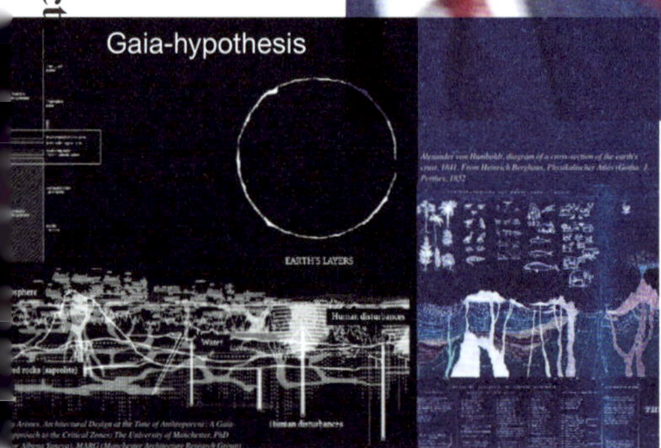

When we talk about the planet today, whose path of movement within a complex planetary system had already been proven by Galileo, we see a remembered image. It is an image, however, that we will never be able to perceive (except for a few astronauts and, more recently, wealthy space tourists). Were it our conviction that the mediated images of the "blue marble" in the black universe had created a consciousness not just for the singularity and beauty but also for the vulnerability of a planet out of its equilibrium, then today we must concur with Bruno Latour who stated that we humans have never been in agreement about the names, nature, form, and condition of the planet that we claim to inhabit.[19] What makes this planet unique is the life that exists on it, restricted to this thin layer that surrounds it.

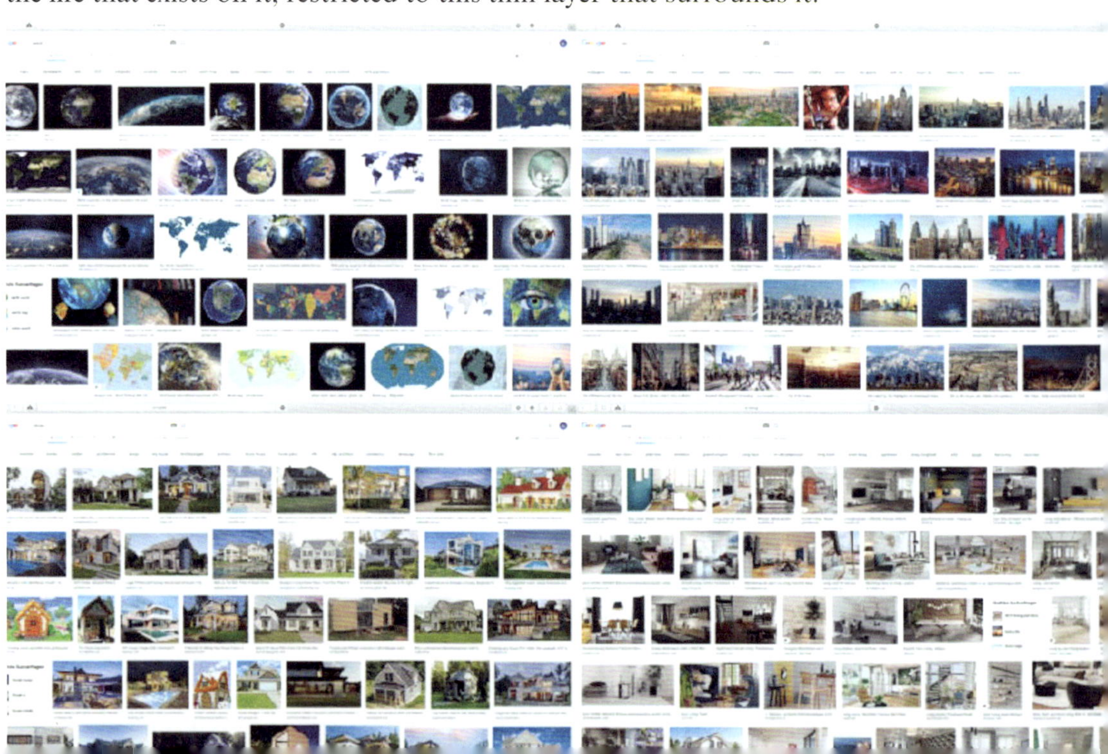

John Lovelock and Lynn Margulis discovered its mode of action in the correlation of the atmosphere and the tiny organisms that transform geology. Even if the Gaia hypothesis as a self-regulating cybernetic system remains disputed in science, the recognition stands that our living environment is being formed through processes of interacting organisms (of which we are also a part), whose activities have created this environment in the first place—and continue to do so. Today we know that the equilibrium of the exchange processes of different gases, which had been stable for billions of years and ensured our living conditions, has been seriously disturbed by our human activities.

Externalization

With the imbalance that has occurred, other certainties that were believed to be secure are also shaken up, such as the historic separation of nature versus culture which marks negatively connoted things as non-related, external, and other that distance themselves from the privileged perspective on everything unquestionably appropriated, internalized. This externalized as well as externalizing standpoint is even suitable for negating entanglements with the legacies of approaches to Western modernity whose interventions into the "system earth" have eventually led to climate emergency: that's what we call the Anthropocene today. Yet are we effectively to understand what is beginning to take shape as a crucial crisis of inhabitability as something that is external to us, although it results from a hegemonic truth regime of modern civilization which in its binary order of "hetero-patriarchal, capitalist, colonial"[20] orientation assumes the right to be THE world and subjects all other worlds to its own explanatory patterns and conditions or, worse, non-existence?[21]

The Crisis of In-Habitation: In Detail (Hamburg Case)

The housing need until 2030 is estimated to amount to 1 million flats in Germany,[22] notwithstanding the fact that the number of empty homes will rise to 3 million in the same period.[23] Flats are available but not where they are needed. Housing costs are exploding, as are building costs (for other reasons). In public debates, this is a problem that requires immediate solutions. The debated solutions include the pragmatic call to "build, build, build" and the ideological call to "socialize!" While the former is being pursued, the latter is put on the back burner in the hope that the situation will have been solved once the market is "saturated." Following the analysis that there aren't enough flats, "policy" sets concrete targets (e.g., 10,000 per year) and forms alliances (with housing entrepreneurs).[24] Tasks and responsibilities are distributed (provision of land, construction on plots). No experiments! What is being built: tried and tested buildings or even copies of existing buildings. The effects? Well, the targets are being met. What is being built is predominantly in the upscale segment; the envisioned subsidized housing falls short of meeting the "one third" target. Furthermore, the new subsidized housing by far doesn't replace the social housing stock that ceases to be subsidized. The existing housing stock that becomes available through occupancy of the new buildings cannot satisfy the anticipated affordable housing need because the rents are

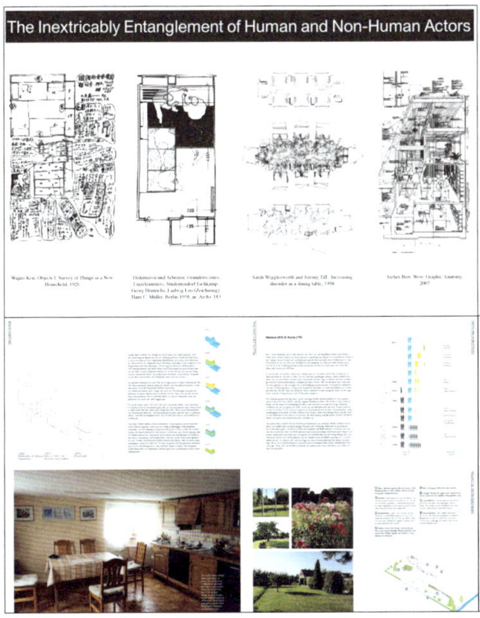

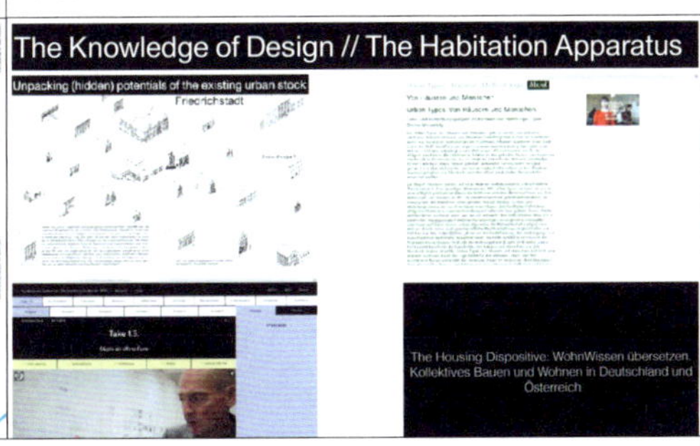

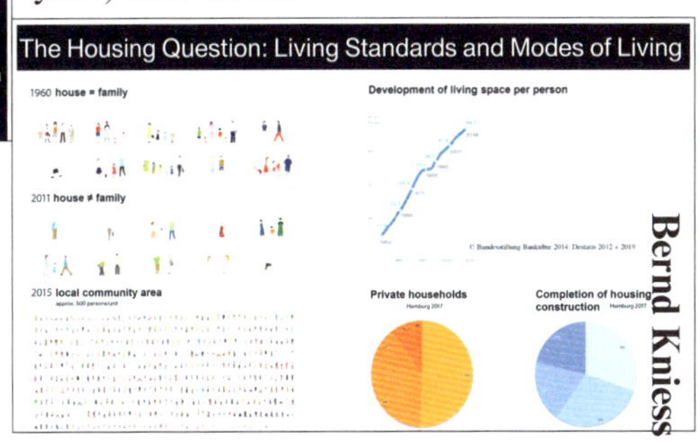

adjusted to the rent index whenever a tenant moves out. The result? The prices spiral upward uncontrollably, with locations determining affordability. The city reorganizes itself anew. The much implored "urban" diversity remains what it used to be: city marketing.

Years of reported successes of achieved dues are followed by disillusionment: "…exploding costs of living?—Rents are hiking ever faster and energy prices are getting out of hand. This will hit almost everyone hard. Governments appear to be curiously helpless."[25] However: "German property owners grew nominally richer by up to 3.3 trillion euros solely on the basis of price increases between 2011 and 2018."[26] Expansive construction activity also incurs pressure on cities to make available more and more land as designated building land, which they don't have, and this conversely results in continued land sealing to an immense extent, usage of finite resources, cost increases due to scarcity, and, finally, an unfettered CO_2 balance that further accelerates climate change.

It remains uncontested that our ways of living have changed. This transformation has an impact on our housing. The Covid housing narratives demonstrate this. And yet, the family continues to serve as a discursive frame whenever housing is a topic of policy. This is the case despite the fact that the numbers paint a different picture, to the extent that a city like Hamburg consists of 80 percent one- and two-person households, whereas the classic nuclear family makes up a meager 12 percent. Still, half of the output of new construction work continuously reproduces three- and four-bedroom homes as the ideal type of housing. Is it really surprising that our individual space consumption of housing continues to increase? In 2018, it averaged almost 47 square meters.

Equally, a detailed consideration shows that the "housing question" isn't a problem that can be grasped or even resolved from a single perspective. On the contrary, it is a highly complex matter. Henri Lefebvre had hinted at the difference between housing as a practice—which cannot be separated from urban and social space—and the house/flat as, in his terms, brutal material reality.[27] We know today that housing isn't restricted to the duality of materiality and the social practice of inhabiting. Inhabitation is a complex assemblage of interrelated economic, ecological, political, and legal factors, of processes and participating actors in places. This heterogeneous ensemble of urban discourses and institutions, architectural facilities, restricting decisions and laws, administrative measures, as well as scientific statements and philosophical, moral, and philanthropist propositions, turns housing into a *dispositif*, a net, to speak with the words of Michel Foucault, that can be spun between these elements.[28]

What remains to be studied is the meaning of these dimensions in the "professional" production of housing and the city. We would have to focus on the causes of a stated lack, perhaps changed modes of living. And wouldn't we have to consider the qualitative demands apart from the calculation of quantitative requirements?

Housing Biographies

What are we to do? A decisive step is certainly to figure out what is going on with housing practice. With our students, for instance, we are using house and housing biographies in trying to understand spatiotemporal developments, to comprehend how dwelling uses have changed over time and how this is reflected in architecture (the built environment). We reverse the architects' designing tools to turn the speculative design project into a research-based analysis. It is our concern to capture situations in the here and now and to describe them, to trace their having-becomeness, to produce knowledge about living and housing practices. Such house and housing biographies serve to trace not just transformations, but also their conditions and uses for exposing their potential trajectories.

Using the example of the harbor workers' settlement in Hamburg, we can trace how a house has grown with its inhabitants. The initial 50 square meters per house in 1935 grew step by step into 200 square meters. Although the original inhabitants have long moved out or passed away, the house or flat remains unchanged, which produces an interesting situation when it comes to a change of ownership. The new inhabitants encounter a spatial configuration that has materialized through individual use by the previous inhabitants in very specific ways. It is up to the new users to read the thus emerged space—to interpret it, expose its potentials, and transform them. This is a competence that's still underrepresented in today's architecture, which is focused on new build. Well trained to design something new from a tabula rasa situation, the architect is rarely trained in opening up existing structures in their intertextuality and in reading out their potentials and opportunities for transformation.

Representation

Christopher Dell recently pointed out that contemporary spatial theories—while addressing spatial production, relativity, and performativity, and therefore spatial uses—tend to bracket off the question of representation.[29] When we speak of the social production of space, the question arises, especially for architects and urban designers who produce space, as to how they can gain insights from how space is used for their own work. And it is precisely at this point that representation comes into play, which is necessary in order to translate experience into knowledge and to arrive at transformational knowledge.

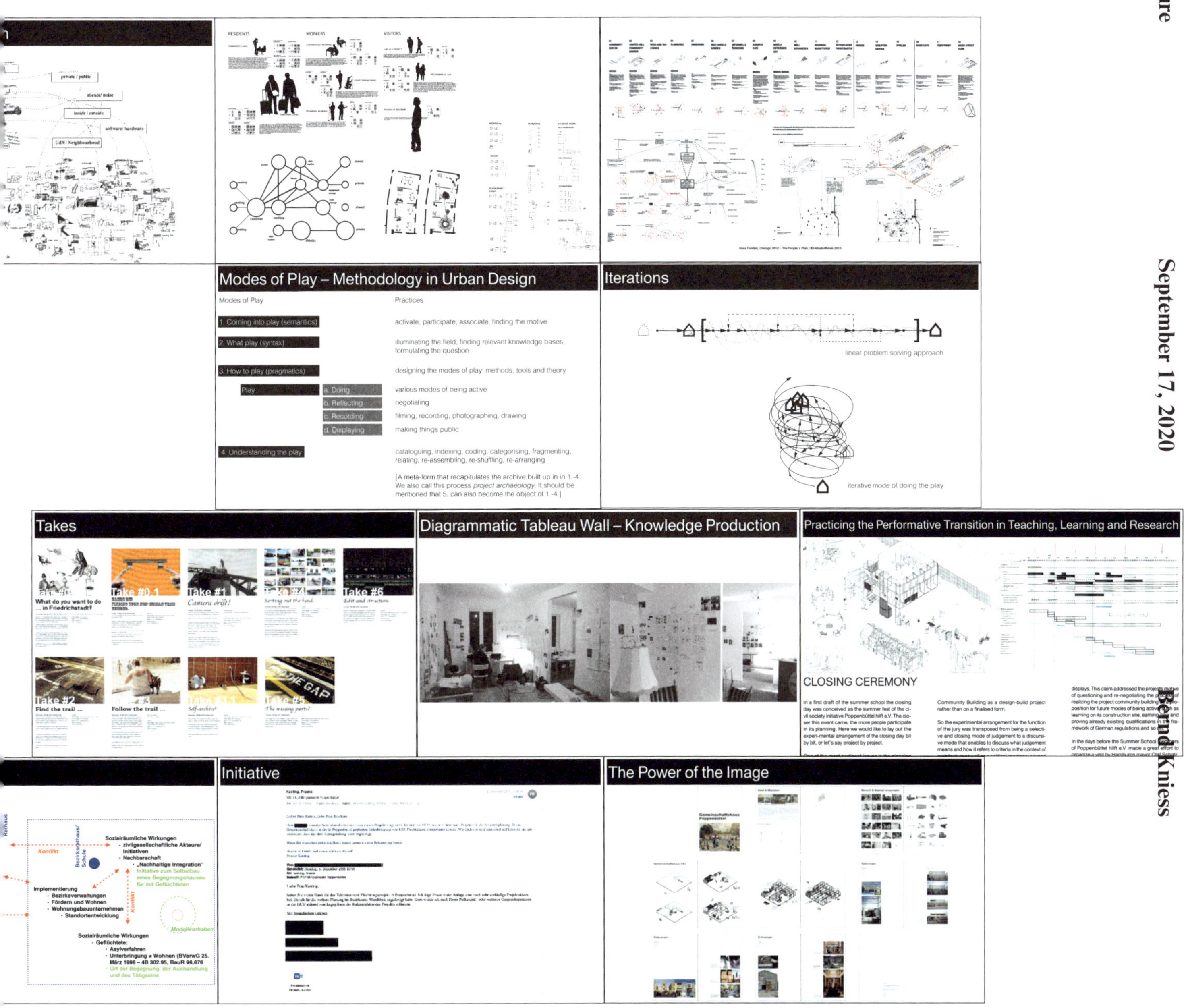

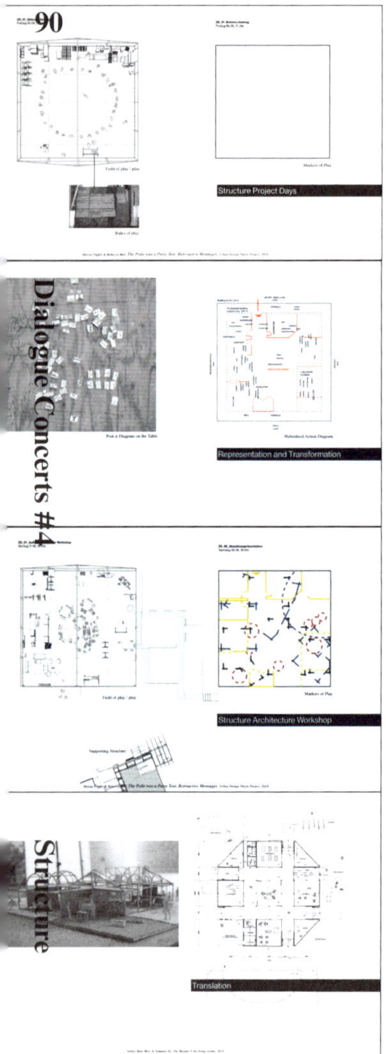

How Can This Be Achieved?

There are many ways of approaching the interdependences of the "myriad unfinished configurations of places, times, matters, meanings."[30] There are the "true stories"[31] that we seek to narrate as we are hopelessly tangled up in the patchiness of the world,[32] there are the yarn games that create patterns like stories in order to be inhabited by those who play the game,[33] and there is the opportunity to make use of working and thinking tools on our way there that diagrammatically enable us to create a new kind of relation with the unknown, to expose the invisible, to unfold the dynamic of orientation in the world.[34]

I'd like to show by way of an example how inhabitation as a relational practice, that is, the everyday practices of care and reproduction, can be located in implausible and yet real presences and simultaneously strengthen the imaginations of possible futures.[35] I thus call to mind the initially shown image: a lecture situation in the summer school course which served us as a framing for the experimental setup. It is an exceptional situation that offers an opportunity to test new forms of engagement and collaboration on the level of a

public–private–people partnership (PPPP), to use urban design as a reading of active spatial production. We seek to query the "plan" for its potentialities of knowledge production in relation to performative design capacities in the interplay of active agency and reflexive translation into the symbolic register.

"Building a Proposition for Future Activities" follows the original motif of building a community house *with* (not *for*!) refugees. As a project, it collates different formats of teaching, research, and practice. It is embedded into the geopolitical logistics of global migration and flight, at the same time tangled up with personal destinies, fears, worries, hopes, and desires, with different ideas of the "self" and the "other," with the understanding and misunderstandings that emerge from signs and meanings. The project assembles pertinent questions of social and material environments around accommodation, housing, flight, and refugees, as well as their agencies, empowerment, self-build, et cetera, in the context of an official political building program by the city, which—by naming it "Accommodation with Prospective Housing"—stresses and rates this difference in its nominal promise of a future. Situated in a local neighborhood of a wealthy district in the north of Hamburg, the project brings together a multitude of actors and actants: existing and future neighbors, refugees, students and apprentices, researchers and designers, traders, craftspeople, local and municipal politicians, administrators, developers, discourses, rules, regulations, economies, and so forth. Their roles, however, remain ambiguous.

The project comes into being when an inquiry by email reaches the president of our university. It contains a proposition for a project from a civil society initiative with preliminary information that shows certain inconsistencies in terms of content and form. The email is written in the first person singular by a representative of the initiative (whose name consists of the community's name and the verb "helps"), yet the signature of the private email address gives hints of the sender's professional position and the agential force of the state institution that comes with it. The concrete request for support through a teaching-led design planning exercise at first sight contradicts the actual idea of creating a place for encounter that involves all participants. Following the initial contact, this impression consolidates in the demand to frame the project with an image for the purpose of generating funding: a desired "rendering" is sought to anticipate what will supposedly be planned and worked out collaboratively.

With a small brochure, we seek to demonstrate a structural approach instead: the booklet shows the relations of a possible project: the local context and the background of the project, the different actors and actants, the potential development phases, and references to existing cost-efficient buildings and self-builds.

The Performative Plan

Action takes place in a marquee not far from the premises where the accommodation development will be constructed. The marquee's size corresponds with the measurements of the planned community building or meeting space. The "playing field" unfolds on its future grounds where what is being planned is tested and worked out in a performative setting. The aim is to performatively elaborate the plan as a set of instructions that builds on and integrates knowledge forms and simultaneously serves as an emerging structure and is structuring emerging activities. The experimental setup focuses on the practical trial and exploration of the desired meeting space as a community project led by "existing" and "new/future" neighbors on a one-to-one scale. The approach follows simple rules; it is structured by *takes*[36] and facilitated by Kristín Guttenberg. Various actors enter the play. We are concerned with understandings, meanings, and spatial conditions of "encountering one another." In concrete situations, these are initially negotiated, tested, and arranged in the interior space in order to eventually also relate uses and functions to the conditions of the exterior space. The real playing field, represented by a smaller-scale drawing on the table, serves as a space for negotiating and reflecting on previous experiences and helps to continuously relate and order what is at stake in new ways. The result of this kind of negotiation is translated back into the "real" space, reviewed and tested by an assembly. The thus produced space diagram is then translated into a spatial program and, in the course of the summer school, serves five teams as a basis for the transferral into architectural-spatial design models. The different knowledge forms of the neighbors, refugees, students, and apprentices who come together in the project and are facilitated by invited architects build the basis for encounters that culminate in being active.

Project Archaeology and Diagrammatics

The data emerging from this process lays the groundwork for a knowledge production with labor costs that are barely affordable for an architectural practice working under given economic conditions, but they are necessary in the attempt to develop new (and also practical) methods and procedures. The university is able to achieve this. What we envision, in postproduction, with our "project archaeology" and

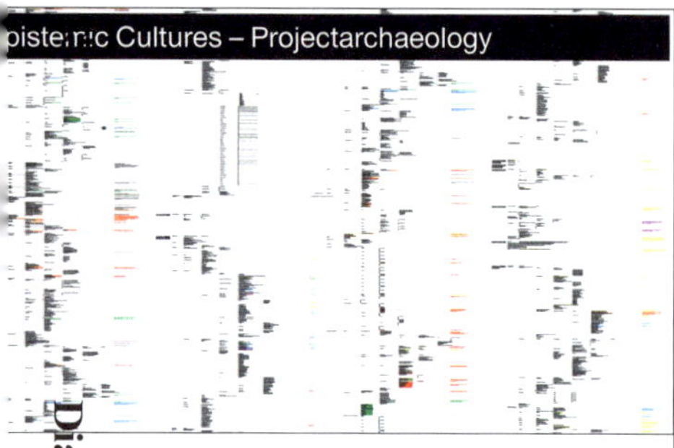

"diagrammatic approach" is to reconstruct the different situations once more, to decompose the connections—which only become visible in retrospect—in order to deduce the structure of these connections. Postproduction serves to make visible the formerly invisible, to focus on elements and enable ourselves to elaborate specific relations in order to obtain information about the structure and functioning of the texture.

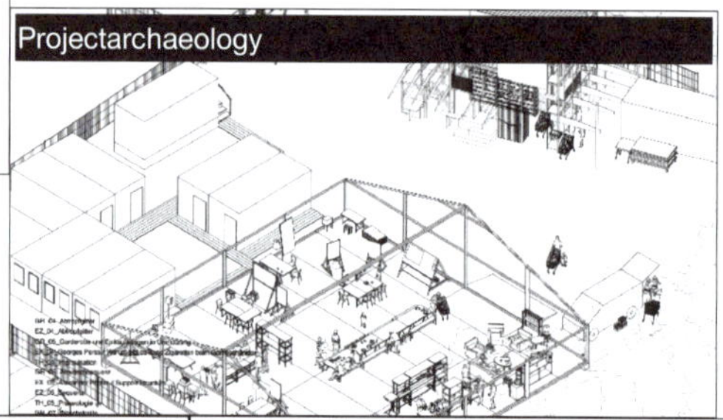

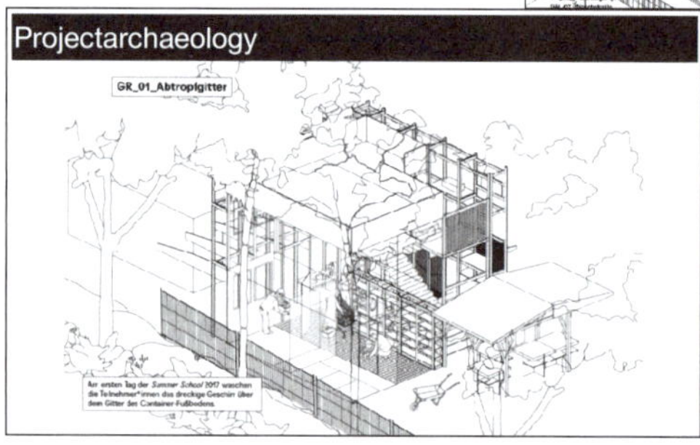

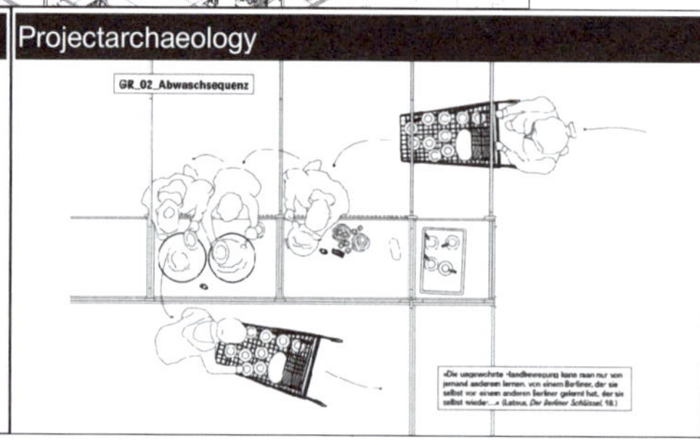

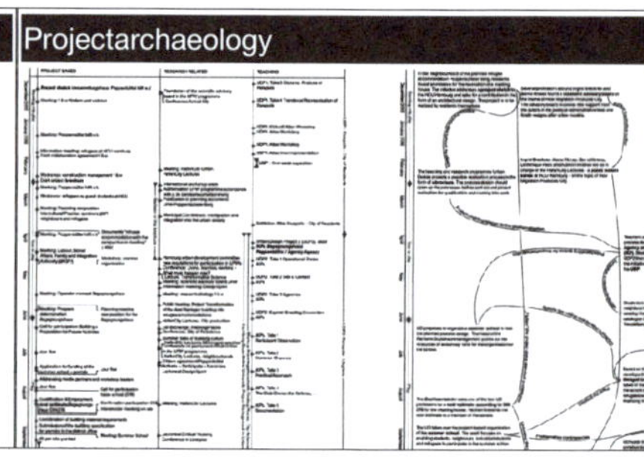

Outro

Spatial production, this much can be said in conclusion, remains a question of form. A form that behaves in a structurally open way, that is not just produced or determined by the agency of human, nonhuman, or more-than-human actors, but that simultaneously affects these—and their efficacy. This form, as something that is produced, is equally something that produces, and it structurally participates in the transformation of function in using the city. Dealing with matters of concern means to enter into a relationship *with* the location, *with* the actors, *with* their actions; to explore, make accessible, and share the different bodies and forms of knowledge in their emergence and having-becomeness, and their various materializations, in order to strengthen imaginations of possible futures and implausible presents from within contemporary collaborative knowledge and design processes.

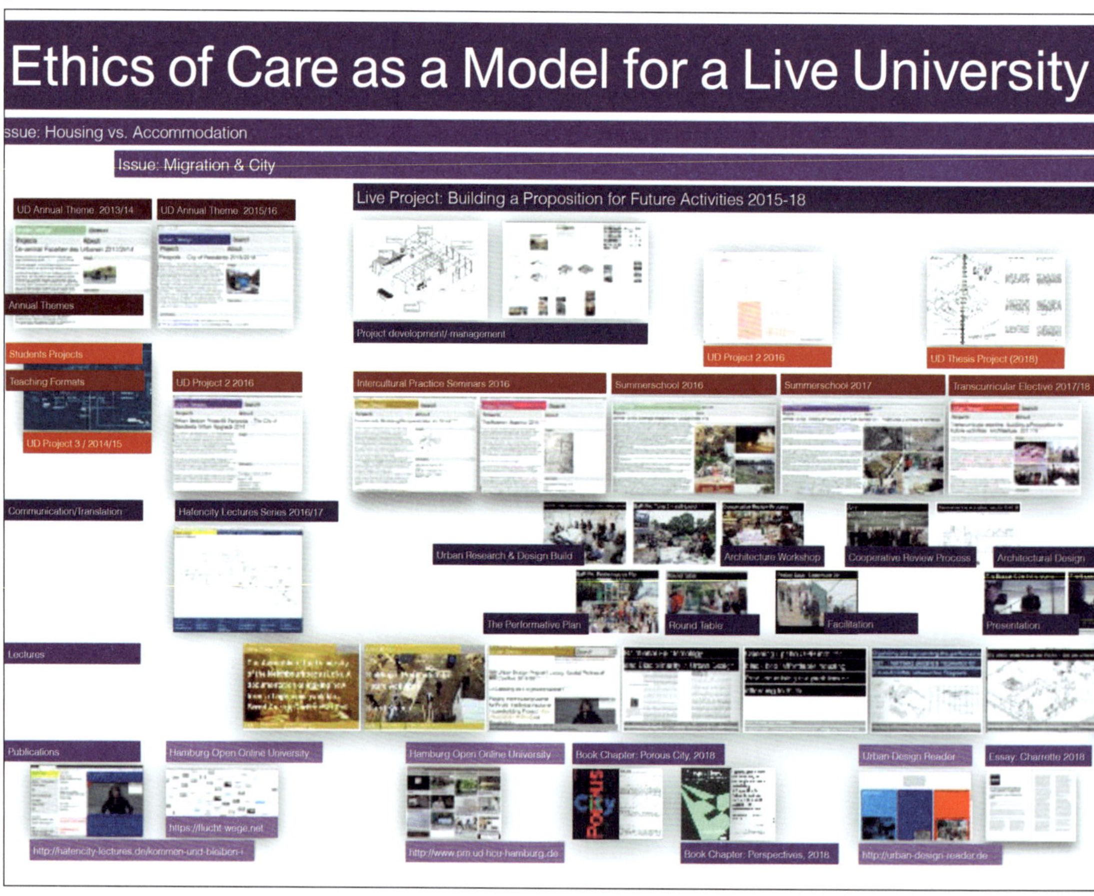

1 Jane Jacobs, *The Economy of Cities* (New York: Vintage Books, 1969), pp. 35–36.

2 Kevin Lynch, *The Image of the City* (Cambridge, MA: The MIT Press, 1960).

3 Lucius Burckhardt, "Städtebauliche Utopien: Was hindert ihre Verwirklichung?" (1970), in *Plan Europe 2000*, ed. European Cultural Foundation (The Hague: Nijhoff, 1972), https://www.lucius-burckhardt.org/Deutsch/Texte/Lucius_Burckhardt.html (all URLs accessed in July 2022).

4 Lucius Burckhardt, "Design ist unsichtbar" (1980), in *Wer plant die Planung? Architektur, Politik und Mensch*, ed. Jesko Fezer, Martin Schmitz, and Lucius Burckhardt (Berlin: Martin Schmitz Verlag, 2004), p. 188; published in English as: *Who Plans the Planning? Architecture, Politics, and Mankind*, ed. Jesko Fezer and Martin Schmitz (Basel: Birkhäuser, 2020).

5 Christopher Alexander et al., *A Pattern Language: Towns, Buildings, Construction* (1977; repr., New York: Oxford University Press, 1995), p. 484.

6 Claudia Mareis, "Horst Rittel: Bösartige Probleme in Entwurfsprozessen," in *Design als Wissenskultur: Interferenzen zwischen Design- und Wissensdiskursen seit 1960*, vol. 16 of *Studien zur visuellen Kultur* (Bielefeld: Transcript, 2011), p. 143.

7 Horst Rittel, "Zur Planungskrise" (1992), p. 53, cited in Mareis, *Design als Wissenskultur*, p. 145.

8 Karin Knorr Cetina, "Culture in Global Knowledge Societies: Knowledge Cultures and Epistemic Cultures," *Interdisciplinary Science Reviews* 32, no. 4 (2007), pp. 361–75, esp. p. 364.

9 Donna J. Haraway, *Staying with the Trouble: Making Kin in the Chthulucene* (Durham and London: Duke University Press, 2016), p. 1.

10 Johns Hopkins University, Coronavirus Resource Center, "Covid-19 Dashboard," https://coronavirus.jhu.edu/map.html.

11 Case study by students in the seminar "Urban Types 2020," Hamburg Open Online University, https://urban-types.de.

12 Case study by students in the "Urban Design Project 2020," HCU Hamburg, http://ud.hcu-hamburg.de.

13 Christine Ceci, Ingunn Moser, and Jeannette Pols, "The Shifting Arrangements We Call Home," in *Ways of Home Making in Care for Later Life*, ed. Bernike Pasveer et al., in the series *Health, Technology and Society* (Singapore: Palgrave Macmillan, 2020).

14 Augusto Paim, "Das Virus der Ungleichheit," *Nachrichtenpool Lateinamerika*, December 31, 2021, https://www.npla.de/thema/urbanes-leben/das-virus-der-ungleichheit/.

15 Sophie Barkey, "Nach Nikolausbesuch: 26 Senioren sterben an Covid-19," *Berliner Zeitung*, December 31, 2020, https://www.berliner-zeitung.de/news/nach-nikolausbesuch-26-bewohner-von-belgischem-altenheim-sterben-an-covid-19-li.129377.

16 Paul B. Preciado, "The Losers Conspiracy," *Artforum*, March 26, 2020, https://www.artforum.com/slant/paul-b-preciado-on-life-after-covid-19-82586.

17 United Nations, "World Population Prospects," https://population.un.org/wpp/.

18 Michel Serres, *The Natural Contract*, trans. Elizabeth MacArthur and William Paulson (Ann Arbor: University of Michigan Press, 1995), p. 86.

19 Bruno Latour, "Screening: Moving Earths," May 23, 2020, https://zkm.de/en/event/2020/05/screening-moving-earths.

20 Arturo Escobar, *Designs for the Pluriverse: Radical Interdependence, Autonomy, and the Making of Worlds* (Durham and London: Duke University Press, 2018), p. 67.

21 Ibid.

22 See Till Baldenius, Sebastian Kohl, and Moritz Schularick, "Die neue Wohnungsfrage: Gewinner und Verlierer des deutschen Immobilienbooms," *Leviathan* 48, no. 2 (2019), pp. 195–236, figure 1, https://pure.mpg.de/rest/items/item_3070687_1/component/file_3070688/content.

23 See the German Federal Institute for Research on Building, Urban Affairs and Spatial Development (BBSR), "Künftige Wohnungsleerstände in Deutschland: Regionale Besonderheiten und Auswirkungen," 2020, https://www.bbsr.bund.de/BBSR/DE/veroeffentlichungen/sonderveroeffentlichungen/2020/wohnungsleerstand-dl.pdf?__blob=publicationFile&v=4.

24 "Wohnungsbauprogramm des Senats Bündnis für das Wohnen," *Hamburg.de*, https://www.hamburg.de/bsw/buendnis-fuer-das-wohnen/.

25 Headline in *Hamburger Abendblatt*, December 18, 2021, p. 8.

26 Baldenius et al., "Die neue Wohnungsfrage," p. 2.

27 Henri Lefebvre, *De l'Etat*, vol. III, p. 133. For some caution, see also "Le marxisme eclate," p. 10, in Stuart Elden, *Understanding Henri Lefebvre: Theory and the Possible* (New York: Continuum, 2004), p. 190.

28 Also see Foucault's understanding of *dispositif* in: Michel Foucault, *Dispositive der Macht: Über Sexualität, Wissen und Wahrheit* (Berlin: Merve, 1978), pp. 119–20.

29 Christopher Dell, "Wohnen: Was zu zeigen wäre," in *Planung als Vektor, Skript und Sichtbarmachung: Projektarchäologie eines*

Begegnungshauses, ed. Marius Töpfer and Rebecca Wall, vol. 6 of *Everyday Urban Design* (Berlin: Botopress, 2020); Christopher Dell, *The Improvisation of Space* (Berlin: Jovis, 2019).

30 Haraway, *Staying with the Trouble*, p. 16.

31 Anna Lowenhaupt Tsing, *The Mushroom at the End of the World: On the Possibility of Life in Capitalist Ruins* (Princeton, NJ: Princeton University Press, 2021), p. vii.

32 Ibid.

33 Haraway, *Staying with the Trouble*.

34 Sybille Krämer, *Figuration, Anschauung, Erkenntnis: Grundlinien einer Diagrammatologie* (Berlin: Suhrkamp, 2016), p. 84.

35 Haraway, *Staying with the Trouble*, p. 189.

36 Bernd Kniess, Christopher Dell, and Dominique Peck, *Tom Paints the Fence* (Leipzig: Spector Books, 2022), p. 27.

Structure – The Relations of Elements and its Agency

Structure – The Relations of Elements and its Agency

»Eppur, si muove!« (Galileo 1633)
1'331

The Housing Question: Living Standards and Modes of Living

Structure – The Relations of Elements and its Agency

Dialogue Concerts #4
Structure
September 17, 2020
Discussion

Christopher Dell
in Conversation with
Bernd Kniess,
Christian Lillinger,
and Jonas Westergaard

Christopher Dell: Christian Lillinger, what does the term structure mean to you?

Christian Lillinger: To structure myself means to enter into communication with a structure. You have to visualize the structure that you have constructed in a work. A common procedure can then emerge from this, and new decisions can be made, as we have done here today during the course of our concert, for example. For me, that is structure. It means that we interconnect as actors and form the musical spatiality.

Christopher Dell: What do you mean by visualizing the structure? How can you do that?

Christian Lillinger: For example, Christopher, you provided us with a composition that contains certain patterns. And we started to take the composition apart and reread it. I read it differently than you, and Jonas, for example. And then we started talking about it, the aesthetics, how you can interpret or reinterpret it, and so on. I personally start to read it differently, and try, for example, if it says three-quarter bars, to divide it up so that it makes sense to me. I don't look at the whole composition, but at this small form, this one bar. I divide it into very small cells so that I know how to act. Further on, the beat can be interpreted or illuminated in different ways. Every time you divide the bar differently, the notes are completely different in relation to each other and in relation to the whole composition, and they also appear differently. This means that, in principle, we have to go through everything that is possible for us and seems possible in the process of practicing the structure. We do that in order to be able to activate the procedure immediately in the playing situation.

Christopher Dell: But that also means that these notes mean something different from what is usually understood by musical notes. Instead of being a given that has already been produced by an author—in music we call the author the composer—the musical space has to be activated and produced first. In principle, this aspect follows on from what Bernd Kniess mentioned in his lecture. Just as Bernd says that one can no longer externalize space in architecture, one can no longer externalize notes in music. If we behaved in this way—that is, if we said that the notes were already there, that somebody else had determined them, and that it is not our responsibility if they make sense, that we are only responsible for performing—then our music would not work. If it's badly composed, then it's badly composed by the composer, nothing can be done about it. I can't change it. In contrast, for us, the notes are an opening, a materiality of something that has to be activated in a certain way. And that leads beyond, for instance, Bruno Latour's theory on actor networks. In our playing, we are not dealing with a flat ontology. The relations are not there at our disposal. Certainly, they exist, but they are not immediately visible. They are only visible and available when we read them as such. That is, when we create and use the lenses that allow us to recognize the structure as such. By this is meant that besides ontological questions, we are also confronted with epistemological ones.

Christian Lillinger Reading is hard work. How much process can you have, can you apply, to even interpret and read something differently?

Christopher Dell This work is what has historically inscribed itself in what is generally termed as the dichotomy of nature versus culture. One works on nature, and thereby turns it into culture, through education, or whatever you want to call it. At the same time, when we play notes, action is inscribed in the body. Bernd, you said that the option of writing into the body—which is relatively obvious for us in music—is not given in architecture. Because in architecture, above all, you draw. Two questions: firstly, how do you get from drawing, which is an externalizing process, to the actions, to the making that you want to investigate as a use of an existing built structure? And secondly, how do you get back from the existing to the representation? You have touched on it, but could you go into it a little more deeply? What role does the structure play in this process?

Bernd Kniess We are dealing with two different ways of working here: on the one hand, the practice that I follow, and on the other hand, the usual practice in architectural production. Christopher just mentioned two different levels. Level one consists of the hard work, the doing. That's where the experiential knowledge comes from, which is enriched by practicing. I appropriate something so that it becomes available for my practice. Yet, this availability stays tacit; it is embedded in the doing. And the other level is: you talk about it. That is, you make your process, your practice, explicit. You share your experiences. These are two different levels in which creations relate to each other. In architectural production, as it is still mostly taught today at the university in reference to the Bauhaus model, one essentially reproduces the student–master relationship. This teaching is directed toward an experiential knowledge, the supreme discipline of design. I don't then make explicit why, how—how I arrive at something—but I have to practice it, for years and years. However, we now face a problem that concerns and is instigated by the bachelor's and master's degrees. With the Bologna Process, as a student, I simply no longer have enough time to acquire this knowledge, to internalize it so that it can be activated. On top of this deficit at the implicit level, at the explicit level not even such an essential topic as housing or dwelling is dealt with at all in the course of studies. In other words, the knowledge is implicitly and explicitly taught on a level that is far from what would be necessary to face today's obstacles.

Against the overall background of the current state of the world and the challenges it poses, we can no longer operate with this approach. What is at stake for the architect is to put oneself in relation to a situation. And that means that I have to give myself to it. It's like reading music. Only in architecture, the notes are not written on the page; we have to deal with the existing city. Where should I start? It's an insanely complex field. I have to put myself into it, have to practice my sight-reading first of all. The way we are traditionally trained or socialized, we switch off all complexity so that we can move around in the city at all, so that we are not flooded with information that has to be processed constantly. In other words, we are socialized to use filters. And we have perfected this with our earplugs, with the outsourced living functions of drinking and eating while walking and so on. We no longer perceive anything on our way through the city. This is exactly where my work at the university starts. First of all, we try to teach our students to perceive again, quite simply: to learn to see. To perceive what is there in the first place. To locate oneself in this urban being, in this structure. Through this perception, I seek to arrive at new ways of designing. Within this task it is an important condition for me to recognize the fact that I cannot perceive this Earth, this planet, in its totality. The totality of the world is an imagination. I cannot experience it myself. In this respect, I can't connect anything with this image either. That's why I think it's so important to scale things back again to our possibilities of experience in general, to make this condition the basis of the work, and to reflect on that, as you said, to be able to talk about our own experiences. This storytelling is something that has been ousted through the nature–culture dichotomy. Storytelling is said to be irrational. But now we are dealing with irrational alternative facts. But these are not the true stories reported, as for example the American anthropologist Anna Tsing has vividly shown in her book *The Mushroom at the End of the World*. Many of the so-called hard facts of capitalist progress are false stories that support political power functions.

Christopher Dell The stories that you are aiming at turn experiences into certain forms. Experience is already sedimented perception. The question is, how can we open up this experience? Bernd, you said, and I regard this as very important, that if we advocate open processes and accept complexity and contingency and so on, then a huge, at times overwhelming apparatus is created. There is a great danger that one might surrender to the muddle. But that is not what is meant here. Rather, your works aim at a constructive opening up of potentials ingrained in a given situation. Musicians do this, for example, by reducing themselves to bars when practicing. And then they iterate these bars, and work, work, work on the minimal structure. Until they have even investigated the bar from the maximum multiperspective. From this exemplificatory exploration—Bernd would say deep drilling—they derive the further procedure. If I follow Bernd, in architecture one arrives often much too quickly at the design proposal, much too quickly at the finished form. One might argue that what is missing is this minimal structure of the close-up—the ant's or the spider's perspective. Bernd, how do you actually do that with your students? How do you give them tools to write their way into this complexity?

Bernd Kniess Of course, you could say that the drawings we produce are funny compared to the conventional design; somehow a bit of architecture is drawn into the existing building, and a few people. But that's not the point. It's not at all about the individual drawings; it's basically about notations of a situation. And this notation stands in relation to another situation. And to another, and to yet another. This iterative notational work opens up a field. Certainly far from being capable of recording the entire complexity, the notation very well is able to record the range of possibilities within the complexity. One could speak of a spatial notation from which we fathom what spatial knowledge is. Spatial knowledge is a silent knowledge, like bike-riding. I know how to ride a bicycle, but I don't know how I do it. I can't explain how I ride the bicycle. I just do it. The same is the case when one asks how you live or how you drink. I can't get to the explanations. I can't get to the knowledge. I have to do it differently. We do it by describing the practices. We approach the practice by exploring how it is done. And we do this in a graphical medium in order to gain a basis for talking about practice, for reflecting on it, for making it explicit.

Christopher Dell In principle, then, the architectural drawing is precisely not the design, but instead becomes the structure for an exchange about practices and the experiences embedded in them. It is a structure for making the implicit explicit without closing the form with representation in a semiotic or rhetoric sense. Jonas, when you operate with your bass, for example, in the space of possibilities that we have just described, in this particular field, there are two levels. On the one hand, you perceive this field in order to move. On the other hand, you create the field with the sounds you play. How does that work? How do you do that at the same time?

Jonas Westergaard When I work on a piece, I also look at it from the producer's view. Who made it? How was it made? I analyze that for myself. Then I can bring in my own ideas. That's how I often do it. That is my work. I create my own spaces almost all the time. It becomes best when I do it that way. But first I check: What is the basis of the piece? And how can I formulate it in a basic form? Then I expand this basis by looking at it from different perspectives. To see many possibilities in the basic form is my goal when I learn a piece of music.

Christopher Dell Is there a certain technique that you have developed, a certain way of reading a notation, a procedure that is structurally relevant for you?

Jonas Westergaard I had a good experience the other day when I simply turned the score upside down to learn to read it the other way round. This results in melodies that are different from the original, but they are clearly related. They are not only mirrored; they also line up backward. That means that all the rhythms sound different, and the melodies sound different, but they have a clear relationship to the original form. That's one method. Then I look for things that just sound good on my bass. I search out and find what I like. For example, open strings sound stronger on the bass. The bass sounds different than when you don't use the open string sides. It also has something to do with pauses or punch. Then I try to play the piece loudly, and play it softly. I want to bring all the parameters in there. Or, as you say, Christian, I just take a bar that I modulate. Modulation is also an important method for me. I interpret modulation as remodeling a geometrical idea. In my understanding, a geometric shape can resemble a musical phrase, or a way of playing the instrument.

Christopher Dell In regard to what Jonas just described, one can argue that for the work it is important to find and work out what affects you. This ability is not static but is connected to a development. There is a history of one's own faculty of judgment, a faculty that one transforms by letting oneself be affected by something through a process of work. At the same time, one continues to write practices into the body by judging them. I understand this in the sense of aesthetics as the affective politics of permanent judgment about a state of affairs. The decisive aspect in defining the notion of affect is that it can be understood as a driver of action that oscillates between the implicit and the explicit. Neither can it be reduced to a blind emotion, nor to a transparent representation. Producing sense and intensity beyond the purely non-representational and the purely representational alike, the affective field is part of the general structural development of production relations. When we work, we are always dealing with and making constructive use of a field of affect. Christian, how do you deal with this field? How do you build fields of affect in such a way that they remain structural for you?

Christian Lillinger I see it in different ways. For example, in the case of Christopher's composition, I read the totality of fifteen bars, as I said, and I try to see it again in such a way that I can divide it into different time levels. Say, five against four, three against five. Then I have this procedure of subdivision as I described earlier. I subdivide a figure into small cells, and those again into small cells, and so on. I make myself aware of the microgrids so that I can then look beyond them. There are always two levels involved. On the one hand, it is about mastering the microstructure, but one must not forget the composition as a total form. What I aim at is zooming out and seeing the big picture at the same time. In my perspective, this is a general procedure of dealing with complexity: living together, for example, also means communicating together on different scales and levels, and so on. Obviously, there are many opinions of how to live. Dwelling is multiperspectival in that respect. How do you build form? Unfortunately, we are used to prefabricated forms today, to branding. The closed form sells well. You don't have to discuss it for long, because time is money, et cetera. Then you reach a point where it no longer works.

And it takes time. Luckily, I was able to use the phase of the pandemic to take time to spend with the trio Dell-Lillinger-Westergaard. And to work on this structure together. This opened the possibility of going deeper and thus having the chance to interpret not one-to-one but multiperspectively. As far as the out-zooming level and in-zooming level are concerned: it is the case that I perceive the action of the others on top of my own playing. For example, if Christopher's or Jonas's playing enters into a melodic movement, perhaps as a conscious shift, then I can perceive that. That is, I can also at times let go of the basic structure, without me and without us losing ourselves fundamentally. At that moment there is no right or wrong. We let the composition explode so that everything is always possible at the same time in relation to the structure. Then it becomes meta. One may call this complex, but I find it rich above all, nothing more. Usually, complexity has elitist connotations because understanding complexity takes time, and time is money. In that sense, only certain people who can invest that much time in anything can afford it.

Christopher Dell: That is a very good conclusion. The struggle for abundance has begun. So has the struggle for production relations in the sense of structural work. In this respect, I would like to sincerely thank all those who have come to this event, who have participated and helped to make it happen.

Dialogue Concert #5
Corporeality
April 20, 2021

Lecture: Christopher Dell

Concert: Chatschatur Kanajan (violin), Karen Lorenz (viola), Mathis Mayr (cello), Sarah Saviet (violin)

Discussion: Christopher Dell, Mathis Mayr, Tabea Michaelis, Ben Pohl, Sarah Saviet

Emil Berliner Studios / Zoom Conference

Under body I understand the human body on the one hand, and a thing on the other. The decisive difference between the two is clear: I can walk around a thing, but not around my body. The body isn't external to me, but the thing is. However, whereas my body is my being with and as the world, it doesn't merge with the physically experienced body. The body is a surplus. It seems to constantly avoid my reflection. Perhaps I feel its presence the strongest when I do something.

Regarding the exploration of things in general, corpus in geometry refers to any bounded three-dimensional shape. This interpretation holds the idea of the container, which took root as a general expression for naming the bodies of things. I say, "I take a walk in the city," and usually think of the city as a container "in" which one moves around. Topologically, this implication results in the provision that there is a difference between the body's internality and its externality. I take a walk in the city, leaving it as I cross the signposted urban frontier. This understanding, which initially relates to the material thing, reverberates in the understanding of living bodies. In this sense I think of the human body as an entity, sealed off from its environment—even if this contradicts the above-mentioned interpretation of corporeality.

The idea of the body as container is reflected equally in architecture and planning discourse. Two of the body's dimensions reside in this space: we speak of buildings as built structures, as bodies. Simultaneously, built structures can embody human bodies, as well as things that relate to one another and to the building. Modern urban planning sees the city as a body containing parts that come alive as functions.

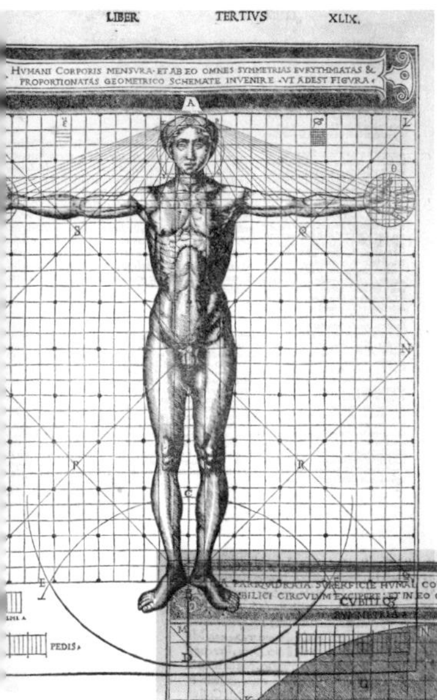

Along these lines, the relation between the human body and architecture has attracted particular interest ever since the Renaissance. Concerning the capacity to think and represent space, the rediscovery and canonization of Vitruvius's *Ten Books on Architecture* provided crucial force for a dramatic and unsettling caesura in intellectual history. Vitruvius's *Books* attest to antiquity's transfers between the human body and architecture as a form of knowledge. Not a single architectural treatise during the Renaissance has survived without reference to these transfers. Two modes of thinking spatially build their core: anthropomorphism on the one hand, which interprets the human body as a figure; and anthropometrics on the other, which implements the numerical translation of the human body into numbers (cubit, foot, hand, for instance), proportions, and geometrical bodies.

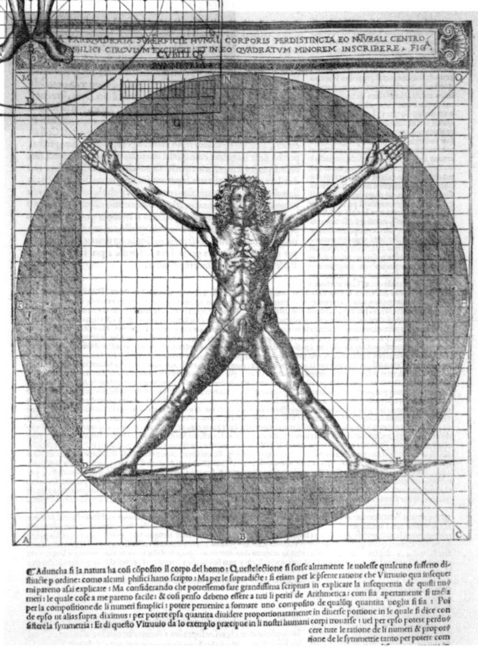

It is known that the writings of Vitruvius come without visual representations. The Renaissance however, while referring to these writings, created prominent illustrations of what the Roman architectural theorist had once defined as *homo ad quadratum* and *homo ad circulum*, namely: "Then again, in the human body the central point is naturally the navel. For if a man be placed flat on his back, with his hands and feet extended, and a pair of compasses centred at his navel, the fingers and toes of his two hands and feet will touch the circumference of a circle described therefrom. And just as the human body yields a circular outline, so too a square figure may be found from it. For if we measure the distance from the soles of the feet to the top of the head, and then apply that measure to the outstretched arms, the breadth will be found to be the same as the height, as in the case of plane surfaces which are perfectly square."[1] Such modular perception of spatial order inscribes itself into an anthropomorphically constructed production of the world that has accompanied the European spatial revolution and its practical and epistemological tensions—such as those between humanist postulations and mechanistic technology—ever since the modern era.

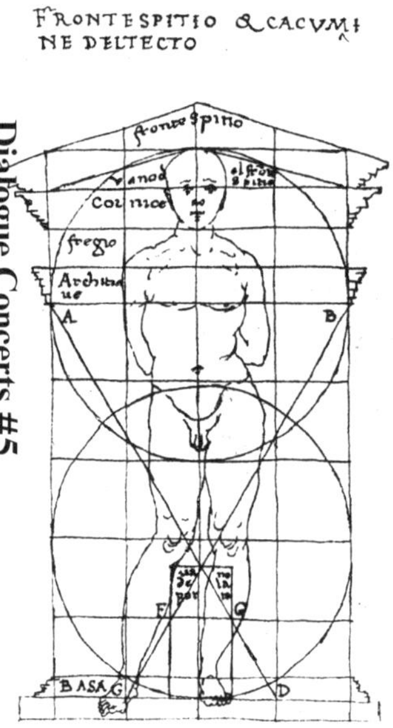

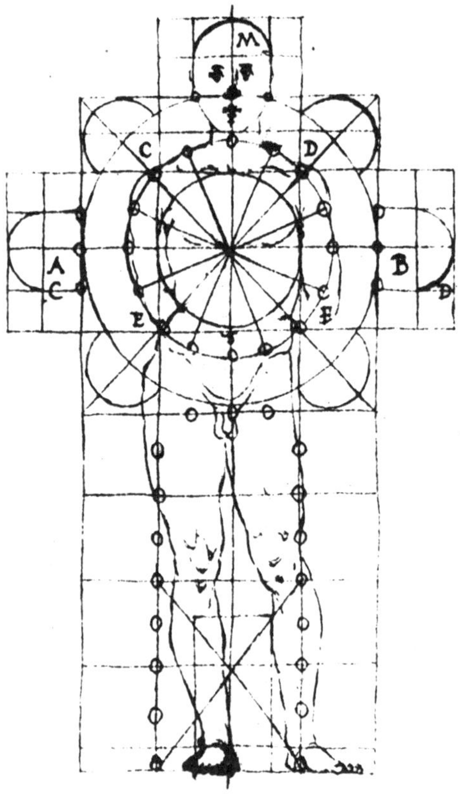

Here, I am thinking of the famous designs *church ground plan*[2] and *church facade according to the measure of man*[3] that Francesco di Giorgio Martini (ca. 1439–1501) produced in 1480–90. Here, the nave and the central building elements emerge from a geometric grid with proportionality that is oriented on the human body as drawn into the ground plan. The way in which man is inscribed into the built body points to the fact that the *epistemes* of the early Renaissance still followed mythical thinking. This thinking, Ernst Cassirer (1874–1945) emphasized, uses the human organism as a model according to which the whole of the world[4] is constructed. Here, name and thing form a unity. Consequently, forms and names of the parts of the human body can assume a predominant role in the creation of meaning in our formative understanding of the world.

Another fascinating representation produced by Martini is that of Mount Athos as human form. Here, the mountain *is* Dinocrates: a standing man who carries the ideal *polis* (city) in his left hand and a water basin in his right. One can take this drawing *pars pro toto* for the urban innovation that introduces the Renaissance into architectural discourse, namely, the idea that the ideal city has to equal the human body. While Dinocrates is considered an expert on defense fortifications, the relation between body and architecture isn't merely one of proportions but also of the political. Architecture in Martini's drawing performs the role of a guarantor and projection of a political body's sovereignty: the well-constructed city is the embodiment of the prince who governs the polity. Even more prominent in architectural discourse is the design of the ideal city of Sforzinda, published by Antonio di Pietro Averlino aka Filarete (ca. 1400–1469) in the twenty-five volumes of his *Trattato d'architettura* (Architectural Treatise). Although the Duke of Milan's name, Francesco Sforza, is inscribed into the name of Filarete's city, it is a built structure that doubles the governor's body *without* any anthropomorphic orientation. Instead, the design is aligned to the

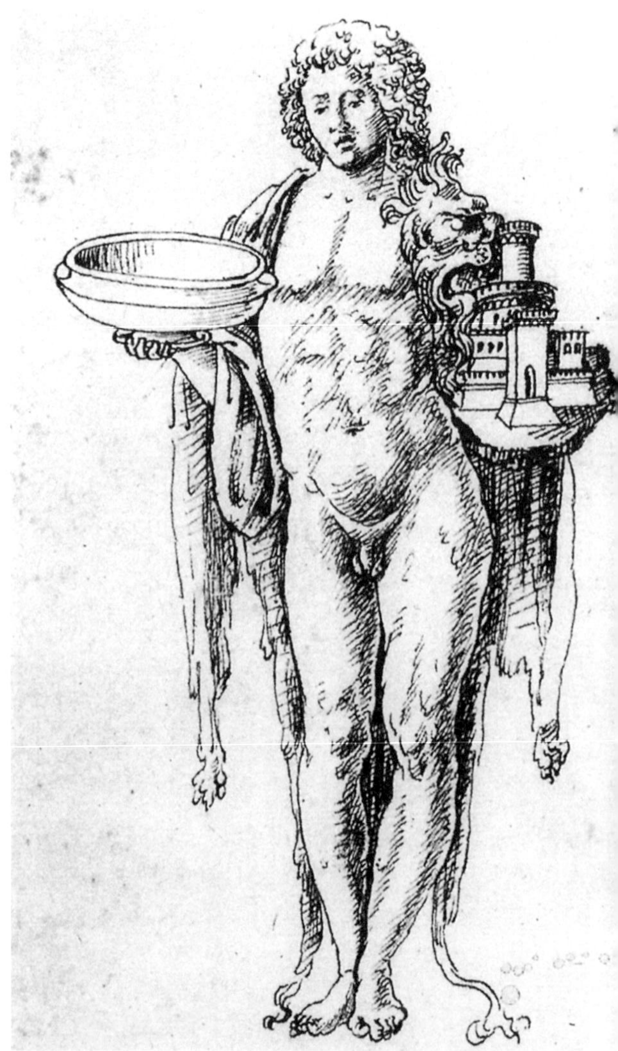

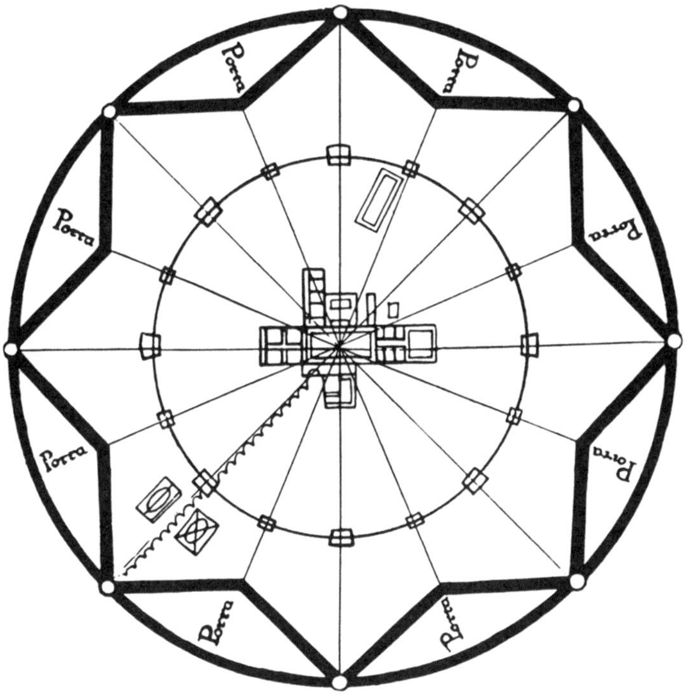

geometric forms of a concentric circle. Mathematics is employed to integrate the dwelling bodies into an order that transcends them.

What matters further in terms of architectural history are the representations contained in Cesare Cesariano's commentary on Vitruvius from 1521 that show both *homo ad quadratum* and *homo ad circulum*.[5] They conceptually stand out in that they serve as the most fine-grained support structure for proportional figures in their epoch with homotopic grid units. The surgical embedding of the human into the grid evokes the novel alliance that geometry and anthropomorphic measures, architecture and land surveying, have entertained ever since then. Governing the political body thus means not only measuring but also making these measures projectable into time and space. Both surveying or measuring and projection form the spatial-conceptual prerequisite to cutting the territory into a grid, from which later emerged both the nation-state and colonization as political modes of domination over bodies. It is the projectable grid that leads to humankind falling victim to the purview of a generalized normativity and planning politics, not only in a structuring-political sense but also concretely, physically.

We could talk about the modern corporeality of bodies: the literal inscription of the body into mathematical geometry shows that the particular was replaced and that the novelty stemmed from its mediality. While architecture in the early Middle Ages made do without drawings, *disegno* (the ability to design the whole universe[6]) advanced to become a key feature of architectural practice during the Renaissance. Meanwhile, the radical concentration on the visualization of corporeality heralds the detonating relation between word and thing. Here, we approach the harbingers of the universalizing movement that later pushes an expanding jurisdiction of a spatial norm onto all worlds, that is, across a geographically or socially bounded part of the world that holds for all humankind. Put differently: performing as an overarching scope, as a modern universality, is generally bound to regimes of representation that are capable of projecting a representational grid onto the world in a way that allows the universe to become divisible and colonizable.

Leon Battista Alberti (1404–1472) undertook the next step toward universalization by staging musical harmony as an exit from the human scale in his *De re aedificatoria* (On the Art of Building). The proportionality of buildings now followed the numerical relations of musical intervals such as sixth, quintal, or quartal. No other example demonstrates this more impressively than Alberti's design of the facade for the Palazzo Rucellai in Florence.[7] The replacement of the human scale in favor of a proportional system based on music equally summarizes the second edition of the probably most important commentary on Vitruvius in the sixteenth century. Published in 1576, it was authored by Daniele Barbaro (1513–1570). It is his system that Andrea Palladio (1508–1580) was to later transpose into his building practice, expanding proportional relationality beyond singular spatial volumes across several rooms and groups of rooms.[8]

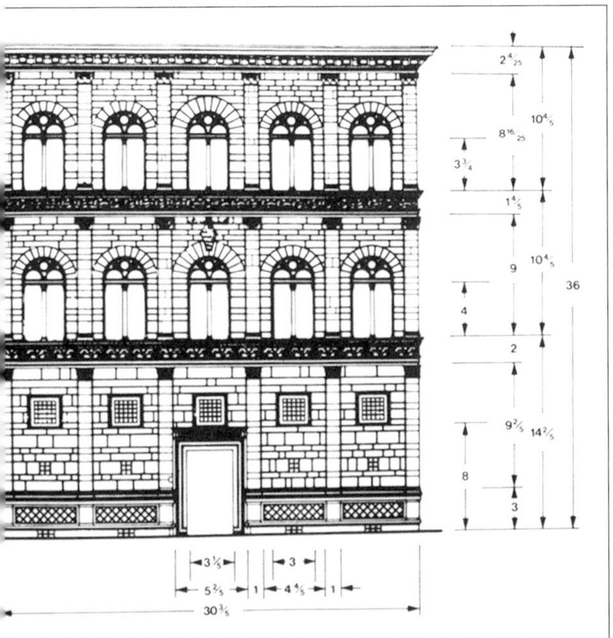

The crux is that the determination of architecture's corporeality, where translated into the register of musical harmony, paradoxically takes place via disembodiment. To be sure, this is another recourse to Greek antiquity. Because for Plato, the body is *soma*—the living creature in *Sophistes*, *zoon*, spirited body, *soma empsychon*; conversely, that which is immaterial, *asomatos*, for him remains tied to music. I remember the problem in question in *Phaidon*, which roughly goes as follows: we know that the tune of a lyre is something immaterial, invisible, *asomatos*.[9] The lyre and its strings, however, on which the tune is played and with which the latter enters the perceivable world, are bodies, *somata*, and physical, *somatoeidé.* Yet if the lyre breaks or a string rips, harmony remains present somewhere—as something corporal without a body. This recognition allows light to be shed on the following two-step logic: according to Vitruvius, only architecture is capable of carrying mathematical *truth* into the world of phenomena. Following Alberti's hypothesis, however, this effect is only possible by way of musical harmony's *asomatic*.

Even if later, with rising classicism in architecture, music receded into the background in architectural thinking and eventually was fully replaced by mathematics, it was still the musicalization of architecture during the high Renaissance that took the decisive step toward disembodiment, which created the prerequisite for the claims to normativity and universalization in modernity. Disembodiment proceeded throughout the seventeenth century with the orders of columns by Claude Perrault (1613–1688). This laid the cornerstone for the modern typology that interprets architectural proportion as dependent on cultural conventions. Leaving all column orders behind, Étienne-Louis Boullée (1728–1799), Claude-Nicolas Ledoux (1736–1806), and, later, Jean-Nicolas-Louis Durand (1760–1834) discovered Newton's natural law as a driving design in late eighteenth-century France. The work of these protagonists manifested the distancing from the human scale that the French Revolution intended by introducing the meter as a 40/1 000 000 part of the world's circumference. The final exhaustion of anthropomorphism through a pure stereometric physical geometry prepared the turning point for a performative functionalism that came to materialize in architecture with Gottfried Semper's primitive hut in the nineteenth century.

Plate 9

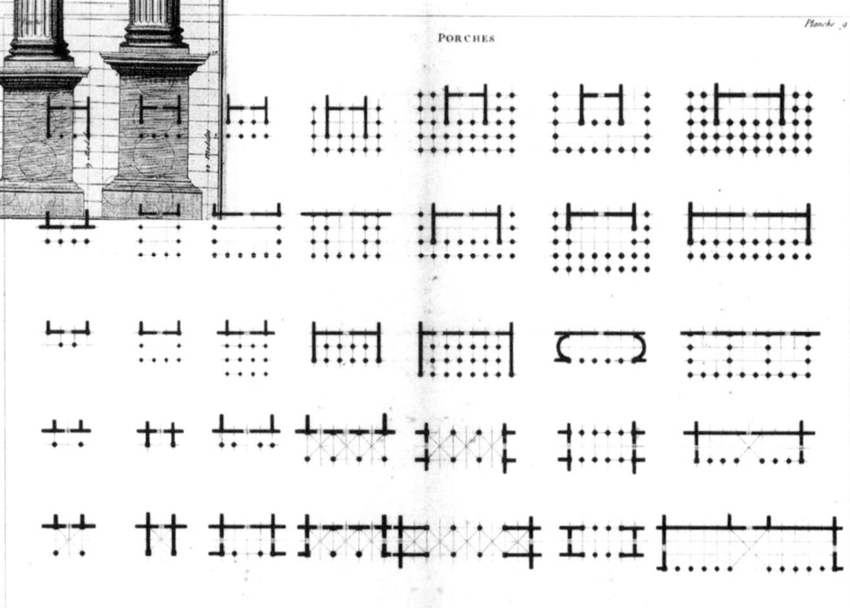

Part II. Composition in General

As is well known, Le Corbusier's theory of proportions of the Modulor (first published in 1948)[10] wove the human figure into the double square of a morphing golden ratio in the early twentieth century. The aim of this, however, was not the return of anthropomorphic architecture. Rather, architecture changed into the register of an anthropometric organization corresponding with the normed typing of prefabricated building parts. It had now become an industrial standardization that allowed a minimum amount of used units to be combined in a maximum number of variants, which Le Corbusier called "modular coordination." The modern city became a "new spectacle."[11] Introduced into contemporary music by

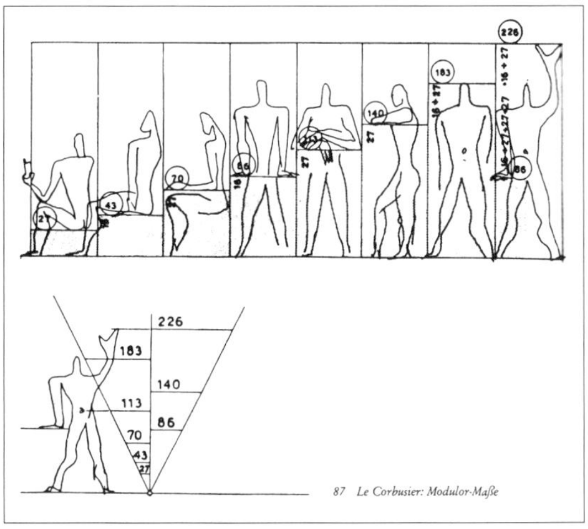

87 Le Corbusier: Modulor-Maße

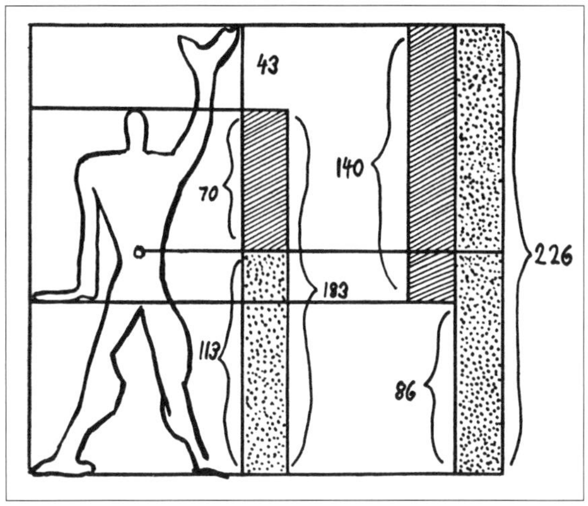

Edgard Varèse, the glissando served as a new scale accompanying the new measurements that no longer relied on the mechanical composition of Durand but were instead oriented toward "mechanic harmonization."[12] This new scale was now seen as capable of smoothing the inner turmoil of "the work of humans."[13]

The *homo ad quadratum*, in comparison, returned without the underscored grid in Ernst Neufert's *Structural Design*,[14] published as early as 1936 and likely the most influential construction design in teaching. This *homo ad quadratum* was now the housed producer, standardized and normalized in the framework of industrial mass production. This reveals not only the manifesting commodification of housing as early as the nineteenth century, but also the biopolitical implementation of the norm of housing as an apparatus of regulation. Hygiene and sanitary order, incidence of light and air circulation, dominate the discourses around the typification of dwelling space in which the surveillance and formation of the individual bodies and the biopolitical control of the population converge. Aligned with the normative structure of the nuclear family, the functionalist surveying of bodies according to floor spaces, clearance, and movement spaces serves the parallel movement of the naturalization of the habitat and the naturalization of the social, the smallest spatio-

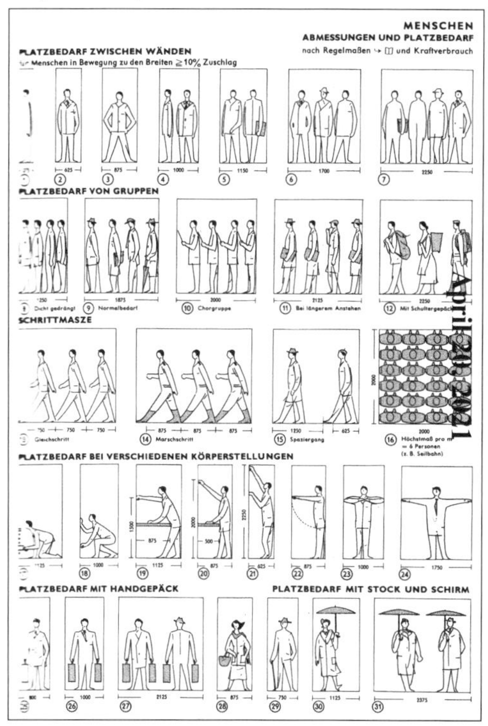

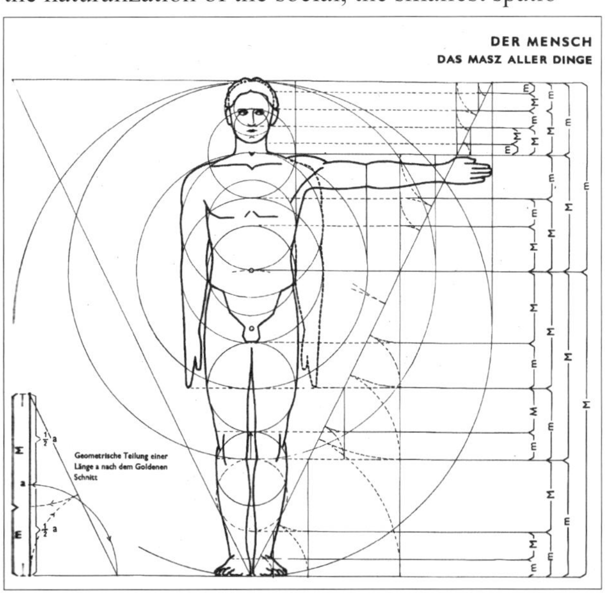

political statistic entity of which is the "household." It is fair to say that this standardization of the body is one of the decisive aspects against which the feminist movement of the 1960s and 1970s positioned the female body as a differentiating performative with their slogan "The private is political," while simultaneously fundamentally questioning the nuclear family as a normative model.

Yet what has become of corporeality today—as, no matter whether in affordable or luxury housing, the nuclear family still serves as the basic model for housing and determines the functionalist building norm of the city? Could it be recovered in a novel way? What forms of politics and societal practices would emerge from these novel kinds of corporeality? Wouldn't the diversity and heterogeneity of corporeality resurface, if use instead of function had priority? Or, how could we think the city anew if no corporeality were representative? Rather than a closure, wouldn't this constitute an opening of the political?

1 Vitruv, *De architectura libri decem / Zehn Bücher über Architektur*, ed. Curt Fensterbusch (Darmstadt: Wissenschaftliche Buchgesellschaft, 1964), 3rd book, 1st chapter, "Von den Symmetrien der Tempel." Published in English as: Vitruvius, *The Ten Books on Architecture*, trans. Morris Hicky Morgan (Cambridge, MA: Harvard University Press, 1914), "Chapter 1: On Symmetry: In Temples and in the Human Body."

2 Francesco di Giorgio Martini, *Codex Magliabechiano II.I.141*, fol. 42v, Biblioteca Nazionale, Rome (1480–90).

3 Ibid., fol. 39c.

4 Ernst Cassirer, *An Essay on Man: An Introduction to a Philosophy of Human Culture* (New Haven, CT, and London: Yale University Press, 1944). Published in German as: *Versuch über den Menschen: Einführung in eine Philosophie der Kultur* (Hamburg: Felix Meiner, 1990).

5 Cesare Cesariano, *Di Lucio Vitruvio Pollione de Architectura Libri Dece* (Como: Gotardus Ponte, 1521), fol. 49 and fol. 50.

6 Christian Gänshirt, *Werkzeuge für Ideen: Einführung ins architektonische Entwerfen* (Basel: Birkhäuser, 2007), p. 45. Published in English as: *Tools for Ideas: Introduction to Architectural Design*, trans. Michael Robinson (Basel: Birkhäuser, 2007).

7 Paul von Naredi-Rainer, *Architektur und Harmonie: Zahl, Mass und Proportion in der abendländischen Baukunst* (Cologne: DuMont, 1995), p. 147.

8 Rudolf Wittkower, *Architectural Principles in the Age of Humanism* (London: The Warburg Institute, 1949), pp. 110–24.

9 Christoph Horn and Christoph Rapp, *Wörterbuch der antiken Philosophie* (Munich: C. H. Beck, 2008), pp. 395–96, esp. p. 372.

10 Le Corbusier, *Der Modulor: Darstellung eines in Architektur und Technik allgemein anwendbaren harmonischen Maßes im menschlichen Maßstab*, vol. 1 (Stuttgart: Cotta, 1953). Volume 2 was published in 1958.

11 Ibid., p. 44.

12 Ibid., p. 54.

13 Ibid., p. 17.

14 Ernst Neufert, *Bauentwurfslehre: Grundlagen, Normen, Vorschriften über Anlage, Bau, Gestaltung, Raumbedarf, Raumbeziehungen, Maße für Gebäude, Räume, Einrichtungen, Geräte mit dem Menschen als Maß und Ziel; Handbuch für den Baufachmann, Bauherrn, Lehrenden und Lernenden; mit Tabellen* (1936; repr., Wiesbaden: Springer Vieweg, 2016). Published in English as: *Architects' Data* (London: Crosby Lockwood and Son, 1970).

Dialogue Concerts #5
Corporeality
April 20, 2021
Discussion

Christopher Dell
in Conversation with
Mathis Mayr,
Tabea Michaelis,
Ben Pohl,
and Sarah Saviet

Christopher Dell Welcome Tabea Michaelis and Ben Pohl from the architectural and urban planning studio Denkstatt Basel. The studio is concerned with contemporary urban transformation processes in urban and rural contexts on various levels in Switzerland and elsewhere. Denkstatt realizes new concepts for use following an interdisciplinary and respectful approach to existing structures. I also welcome the violinist Sarah Saviet and the cellist Mathis Mayr. They are part of Ensemble Mosaik and, as such, part of the string quartet we just heard. As musicians they dedicate themselves to an artistic practice that is based on the continuity of a musical community. Their subject matter is exploratory creativity, networking, collaboration with artists from all fields, other ensembles, with event organizers, as well as intercultural exchange as a reflection of and inspiration for global artistic concerns.

The theme of today's discussion is corporeality. My first question in this context is for Tabea and Ben. In your mode of working, for instance with the project Zentrale Pratteln, you discuss different forms of spatial use and also explore how to deal with existing building stock under the motto "Rehearsing or Practicing Dwelling." As part of this approach, you completed a project two years ago immersing yourselves on a one-to-one scale into the built structure in order to initiate co-creation, living and enjoying together, to start a conversation and to explore the built environment. What role does corporeality play for you in this context?

Ben Pohl In order to respond to your question, I would like to explain the basic situation of Zentrale Pratteln. The building is in an industrial area grown throughout the last 100 years in Pratteln, a residential community in the Liestal district of the Swiss canton of Basel-Landschaft. It holds over 6 hectares of interior floor space in the buildings, also counting the basements. What will happen here over the next few years is the transformation of the site into a residential and commercial area. We assume a very specific role within this development process, namely, the role of transitional uses. That means that we try to find uses, concerning both living and working, that the area can already accommodate as of now. To a certain extent, we have initiated this process ourselves by way of our approach to this area. What you just addressed, Christopher, is really part of a whole sequence of activations with which we attempt to bring together and enable others to physically experience planning processes and everyday life, built structure and uses. The notion of corporeality to which you refer—in relation to our summer fest that we initiated there two years ago—really concerns the question of dwelling, and it does so on various levels. This actually holds true for our overall attitude: in general, we try to understand within the territory of the everyday how communities, urban areas, and buildings can show their potential. In a first step, we try to approach the locations, not just via the plan, but by really observing and researching on site. Secondly, we provoke situations in which themes can actually be experienced physically. For instance, we charge the built structures with the possibility of moving in to live and stay overnight. This is

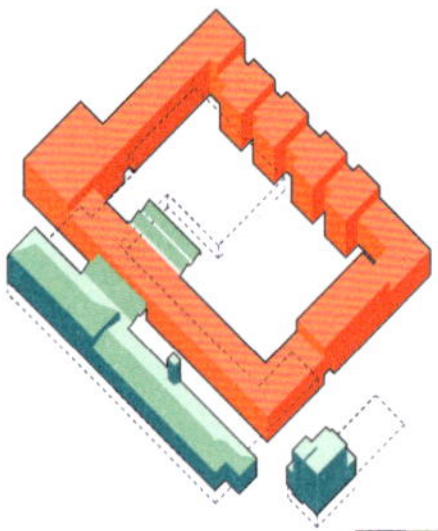

one mode in which we enable others to experience the floor plans of the hall structures, as illustrated in the image.

Another kind of activation is the living room concert. Here, we see you, Christopher, playing with your colleagues from Dell-Lillinger-Westergaard (DLW) in the middle. Corporeality here is of a kind that happens between the physical experience of spatial structures and the built

structures. It is embodied in the question: What is it that built structures can actually achieve? Corporeality can be found somewhere in between, between the actions, the actors, and the things. This charging of an area with new meaning serves to activate and put into use the existing structures with a view to finding actors. We may

well be these actors ourselves in the beginning, or there are others who join and say that they would like to test these spaces as to their potential. It is in this sense that I understand your concert. I assume that you literally sound out and test what it is that musical material and instruments

can do other than what is perhaps expected in a traditional way. Correspondingly, we actually try to explore what built structures can achieve, apart from and beyond what they have been intended for, in this case an old storage hall. We are always concerned with appropriating this unknown territory. And that always has to do with corporeality, with a presence and confrontation on site.

Christopher Dell — Looking at the photo of our concert with DLW, I now remember that especially the localization of bodies within that spatial structure had a particular impact. This is a completely different impact than what can be seen on the plan. The intensity really emerges from the one-to-one interaction with the structure. And this interaction plays an important role for you. First question: Why is that the case? Second point: you spoke of the generally known temporary use as a transitional use. Temporary use allows one to perform within particular left-over spaces, unused areas. As soon as this particular space becomes attractive, normal use takes over and the temporary use disappears. Your concept of transitional use clearly differs decisively.

Ben Pohl — The one-to-one model is extremely important because we're only capable on this level of really uncovering the potentials. The architectural drawings or the plans or the notations, by contrast, are models that remain in the architectural office, in the planning department or in some other legal paperwork of the planning context. In order to really see what this structure is capable of, what I can get from it, I have to

put it to use. This is only possible in a one-to-one model. I have to negotiate performatively with the building, together with the users, and have to find out the potentials that this location offers, and how things can be set into concerted motion again. What narrative is emerging from this? This is an exploration of the contingent, that which we can't know in advance. Certainly, we know the location and the people, but what they bring to it we can't know in advance. I'd like to give brief insight into this.

You can see a goat park on the left-hand side of the photo. They're known as *Geissen* in Switzerland, so it's a *Geissenpark*. It's located behind the built structures of Zentrale Pratteln. There's one of modernity's typical leftover spaces, an empty meadow. One day, someone approached us and asked whether he could lease these 800 square meters. He said he'd like to keep pygmy goats on it. Because he thinks it's beneficial for children for people to be friendly with animals. And we said, sure, go for it! Not a problem at all. Nobody would have even thought of planning a pygmy goat park there. How would we finance it? Where would the goats come from? Yet because we are creating a framework for making things possible, and because it is possible to lease the park and keep goats there, a different situation altogether emerges. This, in turn, plays an important role for the neighborhood, for the dialogue. The formal planning process undertaken by landscape architects and the architects of this building project later adopts these themes and acknowledges that we now have a goat park. Can't we integrate this into our further planning? That is the difficult moment: transposing the one-to-one model back into the planning level, in order to reintegrate it into the one-to-one model, and so forth. This constant movement of transposition marks the point at which the theme of transitional uses becomes relevant. This leads to the second question regarding transitional use, that is, the articulation of the learning process of using space. Transitional use doesn't mean that it's a somehow in-between phase between two clear-cut parts. Rather, it is a development process of learning within the territory. It takes place between the materiality of the buildings, the area, the location, and the people who are involved with the place, and the level of formal planning.

Christopher Dell

Speaking of learning, you imply that transitional use comes with particular epistemological questions—questions pertaining to the form of knowledge. We're also concerned with new ways of understanding and interpreting urban space. We'll get to this point in more detail later. I'd like to move on to Sarah and Mathis, as this addresses something that also plays a role for you in music, namely, the question of how corporeality is related to the spatiality of the concert on the one hand and to notation on the other. How do you describe working with notation, which, as a medium, stands between your body and the spatiality of your play on the one hand, and sound on the other? What ways of working and learning have you found? What does the space of notation in relation to your bodies mean to you?

Mathis Mayr

I really liked the way Ben just described how Denkstatt works as architects. The first analogy is of course that the composer is the architect. And the musicians are the users, in a way. Thinking about it, the real users would be the audience. However—and that's what we attempt with Ensemble Mosaik—we have the opportunity to undertake early rehearsals during which the composer, as Ben described it, can use the elements that we introduce with our instruments and our mode of play. The composer then finds out what works and what doesn't. This was surely similar in the past. We try to further integrate the musicians in having a say, depending on the piece.

Christopher Dell: The fact that you can have a say is one thing. Could you also address the question of how the piece of music spatializes? I think a lot has changed in this regard. The idea of the concert hall reached its apotheosis in Bayreuth's opera. Wagner decided—a novelty in music history—to turn off the lights in the concert hall. The audience could no longer gaze at each other, as they had done in Schinkel's or Garnier's concert halls, in order to find themselves within a bourgeois space. Wagner aimed at producing the effect of immersion by gazing at the stage into which everything drifts. This became one of Cage's themes later. Think of *4'33"*, which particularly brings to attention that we abstract from corporeality in the traditional concert hall. We repress that the medium of music happens and instead try to focus on the statement, the content of the music, independently of the fact that it is actually being played. This very repression has been critiqued steadily and intensively ever since the 1960s or 1970s. And we've witnessed a further impetus in this direction over the last ten years. The program of Ensemble Mosaik states, for instance, that their aim is to develop new concert formats in which the concerts themselves become an experimental arrangement. That's the next step after Cage and the critique of the container space. It is no longer postulated that the concert isn't a neutral space; instead, this space itself is something that's produced. How do you work in this vein? Is there anything that you have practiced or tried, for example, against the backdrop of these new conditions for concerts? Were there any experimental arrangements that offered a different mode to operate with your cello, Mathis?

Mathis Mayr: Well, I really liked our concert *time. cage* at März-Musik last Friday because the medium concert really took on a different form. The composer Manuel Rodríguez Valenzuela filmed our performance and later cut it up as a video, rearranging the snippets in totally different ways. He had really composed a piece for video. Here, the video doesn't remain in the realm of its documentary function and takes on a whole new life as a form of art.

Christopher Dell: Sarah, what is it like for you to work with the mediality of the notation and to connect it, in a sense, to your own corporeality? How do you see the relation between the notation and your body?

Sarah Saviet: There are always different steps. I start by reading the notation. Most of the time, I do so without my instrument. And already then, it somehow enters my body. I can already feel how I will play it and what kind of energy I will need for it. I then practice the piece. That's a little further afield from the physical dimension; I'd say that's rather an intellectual act. Afterward, I can really gather the physical momentum. When we played your piece *Streichquartett No. 2* (String Quartet No. 2), Christopher, for me it was really important to not stick too close to the musical score and rather to produce a physical tempo. That is to say, I'm coming into play and concentrating on the physical energy. Up and down, for me that was the strategy for physically coming into play with the piece.

Christopher Dell: Tabea and Ben, exactly what Sarah denotes as coming into play is one of your central themes. As you have mentioned already, what matters in terms of the existing building stock is working with space as something produced. It isn't possible to deal with it from within the atelier; you have to be present on site, within a specific situation that consists of contexts of action. Inscribed within these contexts is the paradox of being designers on the one hand and researchers on the other. If you are on site and want to find out something about it, you are simultaneously a part of this exploratory process. In other words: knowledge is never neutral. We're not talking about participatory observation from the 1960s or 1970s, however, which was acted out from a purely scientific perspective. Instead, you as designers make this coming into play a part of your knowledge production and work. In order to make this work, you create very specific formats. Can you perhaps elaborate on this question in the context of the Zentrale Pratteln case?

Tabea Michaelis: We have just listened to Sarah who spoke about reading the notation at first, about sensing it. I think this also pertains to our process that we set into motion from the very first moment, when we are requested by a client or when we discover a place that stands empty or isn't active anymore perhaps. We listen, so to say, or try to sense the questions this space represents. It is very important to note that this coming into play is always related to different readings and different modes of play. Of course, we also use the qualitative research methods that our interdisciplinary team offers. This means that we read the space from multiple perspectives, we listen to actors, we listen to the actants. We try to open up this dialogue in the first place—be it via activities on site, be it via walks, different guided tours, including those with local actors who have their own perspective on the object or the space. In this way, we build a narrative and our catalogue of representations and documents following different approaches, to which we can always return during the ongoing process.

In the beginning we collect a lot of voices. We start by actively gathering—until we know the question, we postpone our response in order to then create, as you just said, Christopher, the different framings and settings by explicitly bringing different users, but also the owners, neighbors, and the administration, to the table or into the space itself, before we then discuss the next steps or further approach the space. Ben, can you show these processes, using Zentrale Pratteln as an example of this format?

Ben Pohl: Zentrale Pratteln had a plan before we arrived. There was a competition, ten teams, a winner, a plan, its implementation. So we actually only have a very small foot in the door. "Activate this place." It's also called building an address. From then on, we're concerned with re-briefing the briefings that we receive from a client. You have to rewrite in them in a manner that they begin to follow your own motif for action.

Christopher Dell: Your own motif for action—that's what I find really interesting—has to be a metamotif at the beginning. There is a particular way of approaching the space. At the same time, it's exciting to hear you say that the motif for action isn't there yet, at least not with clear contours, in the beginning. You're developing your motif for action while working.

Tabea Michaelis

More specifically, the first motif for action for us always involves making the resource—space—available again. That's perhaps the basic metamotif from which we proceed.

Against the backdrop of this approach, there are different levels at which, and ways through which, a project arrives on our doorstep. It's possible that the actors themselves approach us, or that the makers ask us: What can we do with this space in the future? What potential could this space have? Yet we also act as actors ourselves and come across neighborhoods or buildings that are standing empty, for which we then actively seek users. With every project, the dialogue formats have developed further over the last twenty years with Denkstatt. That takes place on different scales; we have developed opening moments from XS to XL that really serve to enable this very first idea, this dialogue moment, to emerge. I think of the exchange box, for instance, that isn't so much about the things to be exchanged per se, but rather about the casualness of everyday encounters. Another case is the situation of a common meal where we equally create the situation for conversations to ensue. It is about this approaching one another, building trust. Who represents what, where do people come from? Drawing on the Schweizerische Bundesbahnen Werkstätte (SBB Workshop), we can show how the knowledge of so-called experts of the everyday is being integrated into the project from the very first minute of the process. We assume the role of the translator-speaker between the owner—whom you can see in the middle of the photo—and the future users.

The focus is always on the creation of a situation, of a centrality, where we either organize and observe or actively take part in the discussions. This is of immense importance on the level of the intervention. The other question pertains to the level of representation: How can the plan become communicable again in the first place? How can we negotiate what's at stake? In this sense, we also try to create new levels for access on the plane of representation. For example, we investigate how to graphically transpose or translate the knowledge of the inhabitants of a particular site and inscribe this knowledge into the plan.

We play out these permanent knowledge transformations and knowledge translations on different levels. We formulate the question, for instance: Where would the users position themselves in the area on a 1:50 scale? Where do the users identify the best location for their businesses from their perspective? We record the result and pass it on as expert knowledge to the architects. Or we show on site, on a one-to-one scale, what kinds of spaces we are dealing with here. What kinds of halls are they, standing empty, for which we can find new uses? What could an activation look like? How might the development process proceed? In the project Dietikon, we've solved this via videography. The first question was: "Dietikon, what do you do?" We invited people to the film that we had recorded over the span of eight weeks with the individual residents. We then used the screening in turn as an event to aggregate this self-recognition in a common audience. This is a small outtake from the microformats that Denkstatt developed in order to come into play with specific actors and actants.

Christopher Dell It's fascinating, Tabea, how precisely you outline that, and how minimal structures are created in order for a project to come into play, that is, setting into motion an open process and keeping it constructive. From these structures that are in themselves complex, but minimal and pertaining to specific motifs, greater elements and units can be developed at a later stage. What's decisive is that the processes keep shifting between intervention and representation, between making and showing. This enables the permanent creation of openings, but also closures. These closures are equally important. Ben and Tabea have already suggested that, when faced with design, we are dealing with a fundamental indeterminacy. And this indeterminacy today can neither be planned over, as modernity had envisaged it, nor should we simply surrender to it, as postmodernity had schemed it. Where you seek to "enter" into a situation, this indeterminacy itself advances to be a resource instead. That means that both intervening and representing are, as you have seen yourselves, related to minimal structures that have a certain corporeality and therefore a specific scale.

What matters is that you keep creating new ways to join the corporeality on a one-to-one level with the notation. First, I see a table standing in front of the actors, and on this table representations are being shifted and moved live. Then, there is the work on the wall on which you also show things at particular scales. There are posters, and there are films. You work with different medialities on different scales that play a role. How do you proceed, then? Do you determine the medialities before you come into action? Do you ask what could be best for this situation? Or do these notation formats also develop while acting, from within the interventionist analysis?

Tabea Michaelis Let's put it this way, the notations often emerge quite situatively, close to the question, tightly linked to the exchange with the object, with the space, with the building. These relations that are producing this dialogue are very important. You can see this in the shed hall, which is connected with the building itself. I think the format "rehearsing dwelling" that we ran over the summer is very closely connected to this task, to this question, and also to the shed hall; it is connected to the building itself. Meanwhile, we've certainly produced a repertoire which we know can link to universal languages. In a similar way, it is important that we operate pluralistically with our counterparts, which consist of different actors, and that we can speak different languages. Sometimes our formats quickly follow one after the other. With Studio Dietikon, for instance, we took parallel but at the same time very different approaches. For the filmic approach, we went on site with our mobile studio into the neighborhoods and invited people to have tea with us. Another example are the working sessions with the users, which we design quite systematically for us to develop with them professionally, determining throughout the process what the structure, the floor plan of the building, should look like later.

For us, the plan isn't the focus, but the process. We sometimes call ourselves process architects, simply because we actually set into motion the permanent designing of the process. And within this overall process, which from the beginning we represent as a structure, as a notation—in its milestones—we develop the smaller formats that we just showed, step by step, in a relational field of client, location, and users. We hold an overview; we know approximately when it begins and when it ends. We don't know, however, what will happen on this journey. That's not at all clear for us in the beginning, fortunately.

Christopher Dell Your descriptions are very stimulating because they illustrate what it means to build a reading machine. It addresses the paradoxical fact that the presupposition which the traditional urban design has pushed, namely, the postulate of space as a given in itself, lacks any presupposition. Within this parameter, planning either happens informally (postmodernity) or formally (modernity). Such a reduced approach is completely repealed in your work, because you firstly question fundamentally what is to be understood by space. Secondly, you don't stop at the now ubiquitous hypothesis positing that space is produced. Instead, you postulate in a next step that even if space is not given but produced, it is this very act of being produced that we need to question. And through this act of being produced, new modes of givens develop, particular situational contexts, concerted actions that aren't only indeterminate but also possess particular particularities. Yet you don't take these particularities at face value and instead question the particularities in their given modes. This creates other new structural possibilities that, in order to be able to be read, require whole new modes of reading since the old reading mode no longer suffices. What I find particularly interesting is that this in no way means that the reading techniques of architecture and urban design have become obsolete, but, on the contrary, that you are using them to inscribe them in your own way into this new reading.

Here, I'd like to come back to Sarah's and Mathis's work. A similar development took place in contemporary music over the past several decades. I speak of the embracing of more processual approaches. This means that we understand the compositions we are confronted with a lot more often in terms of processual work. Sarah, you described vividly that there are different modes by which you come into play with a notation, in which you position yourself vis-à-vis the composition in order to find a process to connect the body with the notation. Tabea and Ben spoke of the repertoire and catalogue they have developed in the course of their work with processes. Sarah and Mathis, do you have particular repertoires, particular techniques in terms of process work? Do you also have a catalogue of approaches, or of the territory that you have mastered on your instruments?

Mathis Mayr As an ensemble, we have a sort of body language that keeps evolving further and is the very precondition for composition. It's important that you aren't too sure about it. That's the challenge. Every single one of us in the ensemble has different grades of openness. An ensemble depends on not becoming specialists, because a false professionalism prevents the true being-present. My experience tells me that I have often been wrong in my presumptions about a new piece of music. We start new pieces and say: I like this, I don't like that. In the end, it has often happened that the composition changed so much over the rehearsal process, or even during the concert, that I see them completely differently afterward. There are different modes of going about it for composers to get in touch with us and make us produce something that's completely personal, physical.

I think of a composer with whom we worked and who just watched our everyday movements, how we played, how we picked up the instrument from its case and got ready. She composed the piece out of these movements. In the end, this basic, open material resulted in quite a strict piece. One could say that the piece's material consists of the respectively specific corporeality of the musicians.

Sarah Saviet I really like how you described that, Mathis. Our bodies each have a memory of the notation, which also plays into this posture and how we position ourselves toward particular notations. And sometimes I find this memory dangerous. It is always important to oppose it in order to remain open to every new piece of music. To postpone coming into play physically until later in order to have the opportunity to develop new ideas or to immerse oneself in new playing techniques or new ways of making music, really. This means that we have to be careful not to be caught in this physical memory of corporeality.

Christopher Dell Many thanks for your description. It helps to establish a center of thinking that tries to understand the physically inscribed past as a possibility rather than as a burden. Within this unscrewing of the internalized memory lies a particular ethic, especially—as you just expressed it, Sarah and Mathis—of being nonjudgmental. Or perhaps putting the prejudice aside without withdrawing from the situation, without holding oneself back—instead giving in to it, building more open structures, depending on the situation. This ethic of holding back prejudice relates to a political question. Tabea and Ben, you speak of an "other" production of space. You mentioned that you're taking apart the historical contexts of agencies consisting of locations, people, buildings, narratives, orders, organizational structures, and financial models, and then reassembling them anew. The point is, if the future is rooted in existing building stock, then this stock isn't only perceived in terms of historicization, in terms of graded buildings and so on. It is exactly at this point that architecture is tasked with interpreting the existing stock as a possibility, just as Sarah and Mathis described it in music. Yet, in contrast to music, architecture as an ethic is political charged. Can you perhaps briefly say something about this political component since it envisions a completely different mode of future urban design and a different way of living together in terms of a spatialization of politics.

Ben Pohl What I found very exciting in Sarah's and Mathis's account is this opening of the notation. To engage with it and somehow counter the quick short circuit. Normally, it would be clear; there is the notion: you can play it, straight ahead! Instead, you take such care to come into play and say, I have to keep it open. Doing so, of course, you fight against existing organizational structures. In architecture and urban development, we fight against the obligatory cost efficiency that, above all, is time efficiency, based on absolute planning standards. There is no space for an artistic opening in the first place. You permanently fight for—and this is a notion we owe to you, Christopher—safe space (*Schutzeigentum*) or spaces that serve as a form of shelter, as a safe place, a safe space in which the "other" form of development and spatial production becomes possible at all. This often has to do with ownership relations. I'm not a musician, but in music it could be the authorship of the composer, who says, you're only allowed to play it like this or you don't play it at all. And the owner principally decides pretty much everything in our field. Certainly there are different kinds of ownership: some are structurally capable of unfolding a sustained interest in the sound development of a place. Others will only hand over Excel spreadsheets. The one really political aspect, not just in terms of Jacques Rancière and his questions related to the aesthetics of the sensible, which aims to shift visibilities, is about position: we need a real change of attitude toward property rights over land and connected forms of spatial production that damage urban society. What matters is thinking of spatial production in the sense of a collectivization and establishing the city as common knowledge production, as collective production of space, as collective writing and reading rights. That's the political attitude that drives our work. Hence, the name of our small research institute format. We're concerned with reading urban space differently, but also with writing it differently. We therefore claim collective writing and reading rights for the social production of space.

In more concrete terms, for us this means opening up micro spaces within projects and formats that enable that.

Christopher Dell — That's a wonderful ending. We can summarize that the question of corporeality in the different disciplines of architecture and music relates to ethical and political questions that are in turn connected with epistemological questions, that is, questions of knowing and reading and seeing or sensing. We hope there will be many opportunities in the future to maintain these safe spaces for engaging with this "other" production of space, for enabling it, probably also fighting for it. Tabea, Ben, Sarah, and Mathis, thank you so much for joining us!

Dialogue Concert #6
Materiality
September 9, 2021

Lecture: Ton Matton

Concert: Lotte Anker (saxophone), Christopher Dell (vibraphone), Sofia Eftychidou (bass)

Discussion: Lotte Anker, Christopher Dell, Sofia Eftychidou, Francis Kéré, Ton Matton

Aedes Architecture Forum, Berlin

dialogue concerts

1

conceptual research on architecture and music

Mediality

12.12. 2019
18:30

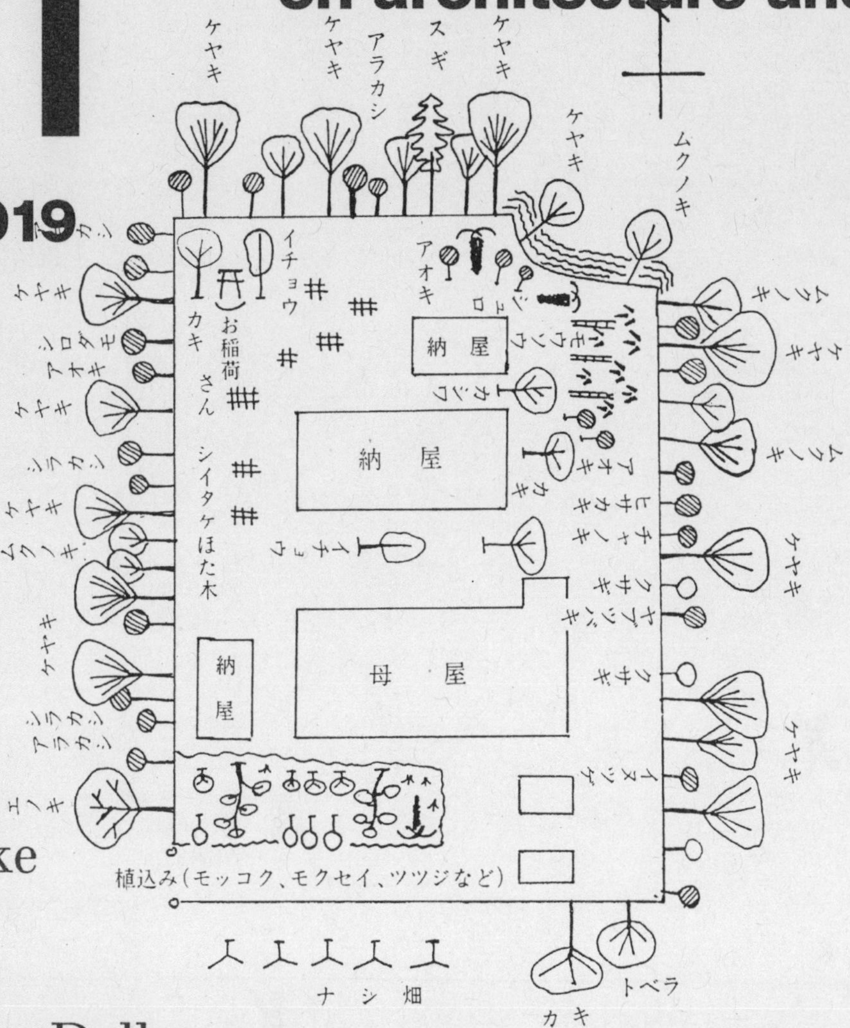

Vortrag
Oda Pälmke

Konzert
Christopher Dell,
Karen Lorenz,
Jonas Westergaard

Diskussion

Aedes Architekturforum

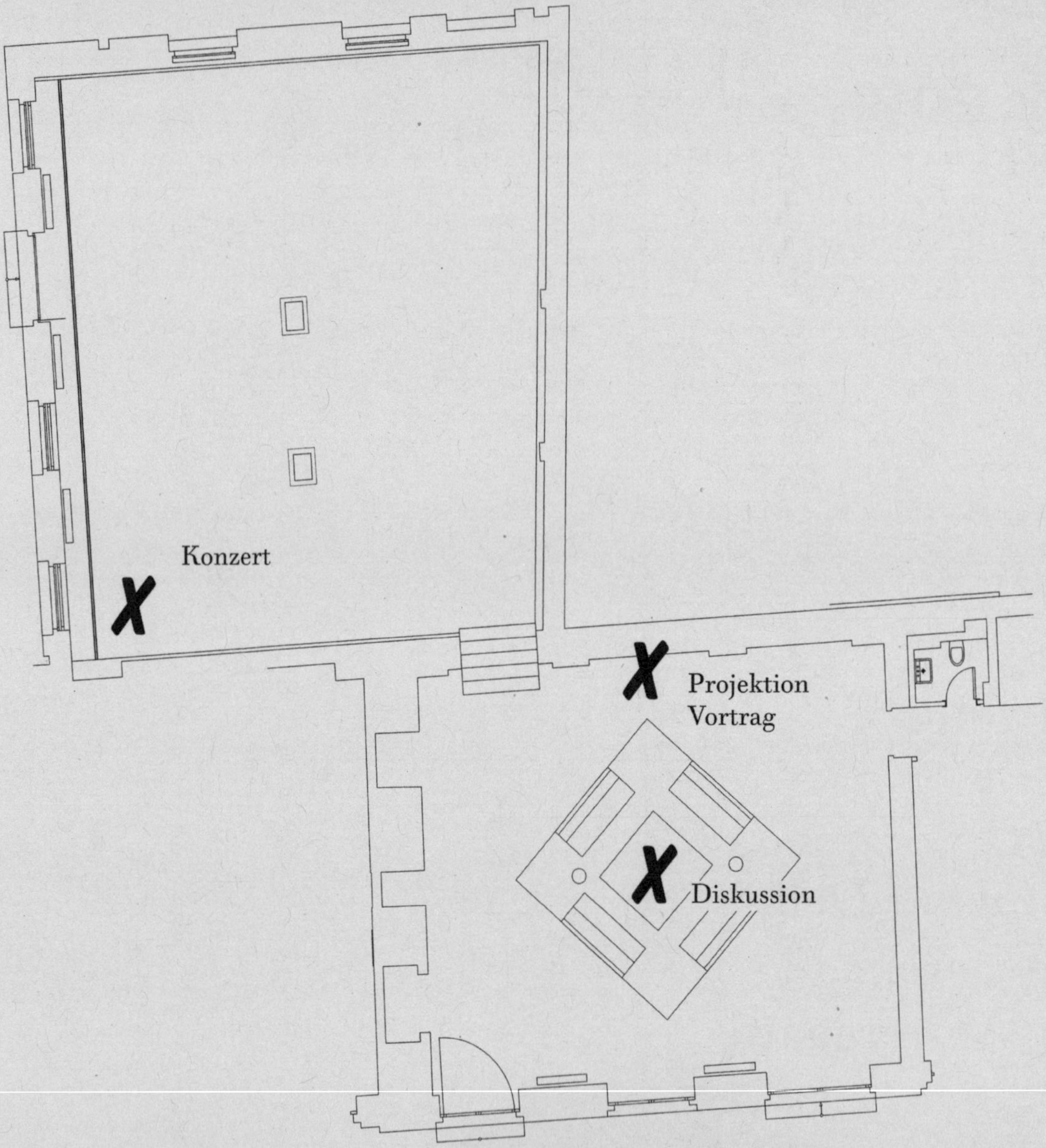

Intervention in die Ausstellung *Holzbaugeschichten – weberbrunner architekten Zürich / Berlin* im Aedes Architekturforum, 30. 11. 2019 – 9. 1. 2020

Stets ist aktuell von der Allgegenwärtigkeit und Wirkmacht der Bilder die Rede. Innerhalb dessen hat es mit den Bildern von Architektur und Musik eine besondere Bewandtnis: sie lassen sehen, was zu tun ist. Sie zeigen an, was gebaut respektive was gespielt werden soll. Indes, wie funktionieren diese Bilder des Tuns? Was zeigen sie? Wie tun sie das? Wie werden sie hergestellt? Wie zirkulieren sie? Wie navigieren sie im kategorialen Intervall zwischen Bild und Schrift?

Vor dem Bündel dieser Fragen thematisiert das erste Ereignis von *dialogue concerts* Aspekte von Medialität. Wo man sagen kann, dass Bilder als Medien über einen gegenständlich-instrumentellen Sinn verfügen, so bedeutet Medialität die undingliche Vermittlungsleistung eines Mediums zwischen Vorstellen und Darstellen. Darin erscheinen Bilder nicht nur als relata unseres Handelns sondern menschliche Praxis als prinzipiell medial, d.h. darstellungsvermittelt. Wie aber lässt diese Vermitteltheit sehen und machen? Welches Wissen enthält sie? Welche Kontexte erzeugt sie? Und anhand welcher Politik erzeugt und bestimmt sie Orte des Gemeinsamen?

dialogue concerts

Die Reihe *dialogue concerts* ist ein medienpluralistisches Format, in dem Konzerte, Vortrag, Performance und Installation gleichermaßen ihre Bedeutung finden, Austausch gefördert wird und der Diskurs entscheidend ist.

Ziel der Reihe *dialogue concerts* ist es, den verfahren-strategischen Zusammenhang von Architektur und Musik zu thematisieren und dabei die gesellschaftliche Relevanz beider Disziplinen neu sichtbar zu machen. Vor dem Hintergrund der Frage »Wie wollen wir als Stadt zusammenleben?« schließt die Reihe ein »musikalisches Raumdenken« auf, das die Stadt als kollektiven und improvisatorischen Handlungsraum neu perspektiviert und diskursiviert.

Es geht darum, neue Beziehungen zwischen den Disziplinen Architektur und Musik zu setzen, die sowohl auf thematischer, formaler als auch personeller Ebene verfolgt werden können. Das Programm der Reihe *dialogue concerts* folgt dabei dem inhaltlichen Kriterium von improvisatorischen, experimentellen und diskursiven Ansätzen und berücksichtigt Konstellationen der Interdisziplinarität ebenso wie Ebenen des Erläuterns und Thematisierens als offenes Format für Austausch und Diskurs in einem inspirierenden Raumsetting. Für eine hochgradig erlebbare Verdichtung sorgt beim ersten Ereignis das von *Holzbaugeschichten –weberbrunner architekten Zürich / Berlin* im Aedes Architekturforum gelieferte besondere Ausstellungssetting.

In raumtheoretischer Hinsicht nimmt *dialogue concerts* den Blickwinkel ein, dass der Raum, der unser Zusammenleben bestimmt relational konstituiert ist. Raum ist kein fixiertes Objekt, sondern kommt als dynamische Konstellation in die Welt, die performativ produziert wird. Vor diesem Hintergrund operiert die Ereignisserie als ein anregendes und eigendynamisches Format, in dem nicht nur das forschungsbasiertes Arbeiten mit Musik und Architektur zum Katalysator für genre- und grenzüberschreitende Diskurse und Praktiken avanciert, sondern das Verfahren des Zeigens als inhaltliche und performative Verdichtung auch das Spektrum der Rezeption und Reflexion über das Gewohnte hinaus erweitert. *dialogue concerts* legt den Fokus gleichermaßen auf die Präsenzebenen Klang, Visualität und Verräumlichung.

Durch die diskursive Überlagerung von Musik und Architektur wird auf der Ebene ihrer Strategien ein neues Wissen erzeugt und die gesellschaftliche Relevanz eines neuen Verständnisses der Improvisation von Raum aufgezeigt. Während sich einschlägige Musik und Architektur-Ausstellungen meist vor allem mit den synästhetischen Fragen »Wie klingt Architektur?« oder »Welchen Raum hat der Klang?« auseinandersetzen, thematisiert die Reihe die inneren Zusammenhänge zwischen den Gattungen Musik und Architektur. Dieses aktuelle Projekt versteht sich somit auch als Ausgangspunt für weitere disziplinübergreifende Forschungen, die in neuen Publikumsformaten Potentiale für ein zukünftiges Stadtmachen aufschließen. Im Fokus steht dabei weniger die Frage »Wie klingt Architektur?«. Interessant ist vielmehr die Meta-Sicht: Fragen des kollektiven Handelns, des seriellen Verschaltens, des motivischen Arbeitens, des Speicherns, des Collagierens, des De- und Re-Komponierens und typologischen Ordnens sind nur einige der Beispiele wirkmächtiger und strategischer Korrelate zwischen den Disziplinen von Architektur und Musik, die es vor dem Hintergrund eines Verständnisses von Raum als performativ improvisiert neu zu beleuchten gilt.

In ihrer formalen Offenheit bieten die diskursiven Konzerte sowohl für das Publikum als auch die Akteure eine kontinuierliche Auseinandersetzung von neuen Konstellationen unter verschiedenen Perspektiven an. Konzert, Vortrag und Gesprächsrunde überlagern sich in einem Format, bei dem die Herangehensweise und die Konzeption, die der Arbeit der jeweiligen Akteure der jeweiligen Konstellation zugrunde liegt, erörtert, verständlich gemacht und kontrovers diskutiert werden. Stets bleibt es das zentrale Anliegen, bestehende Sichtweisen und Repräsentationsformen zu hinterfragen, um einem möglichen, neuartigen Erkenntnisstand einen experimentellen Darstellungs- und Diskursraum zu bieten.

Insgesamt bietet die *dialogue concerts* Möglichkeiten zur Entdeckung zukunftsorientierter Wirkzusammenhänge zur Stadt als Handlung ebenso wie fortschrittlicher musikalischer Praktiken der Improvisation und der vielfältigen Zusammenhänge der in den jeweiligen Ausstellungen gezeigten architektonischen Arbeiten.

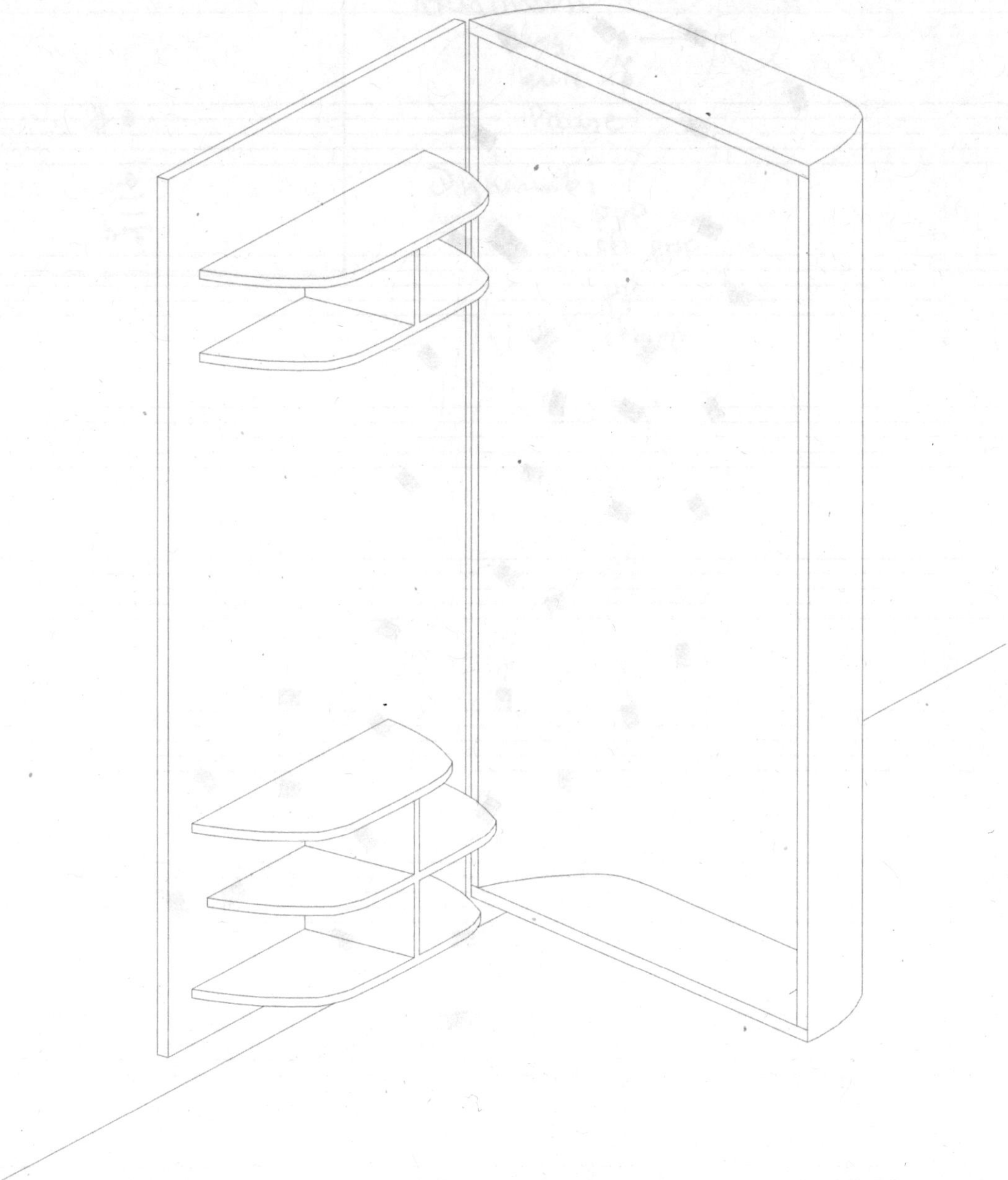

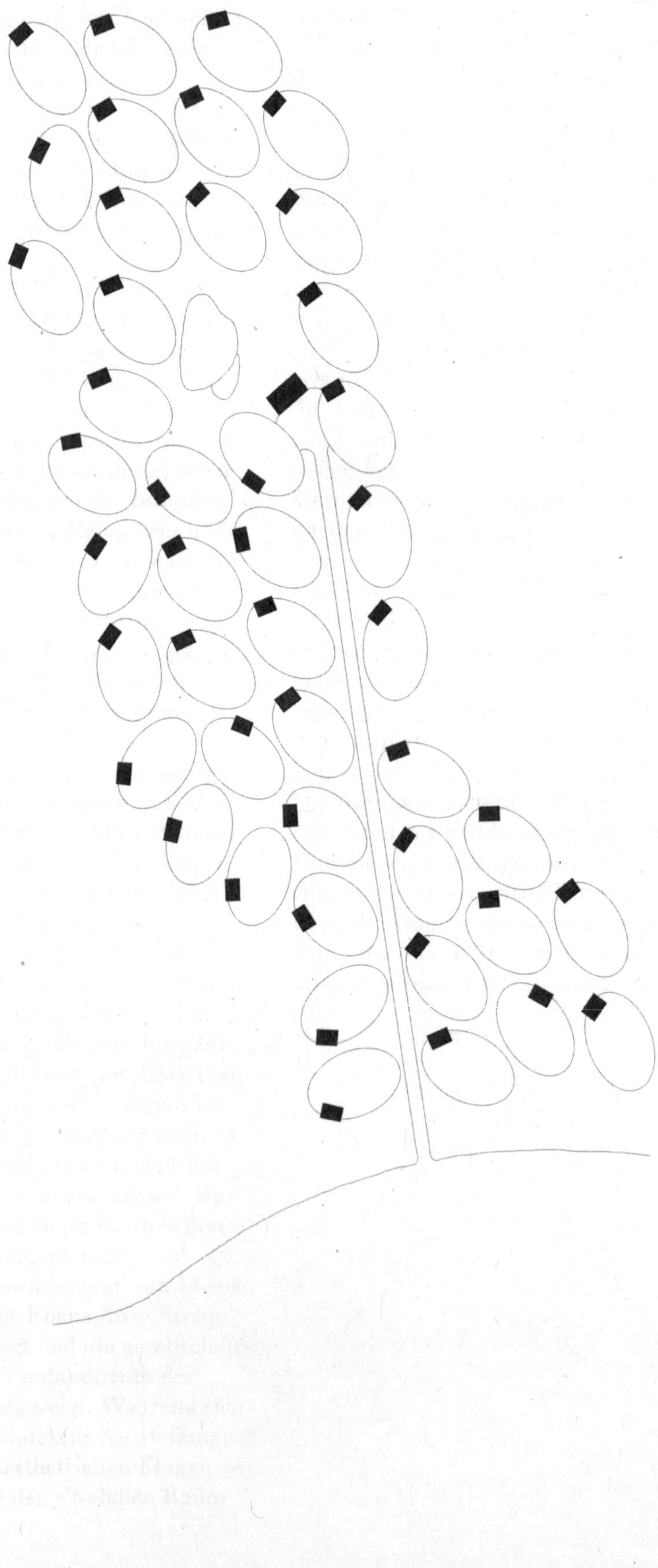

FORMBLOCK 24

[signature] 10.10.19

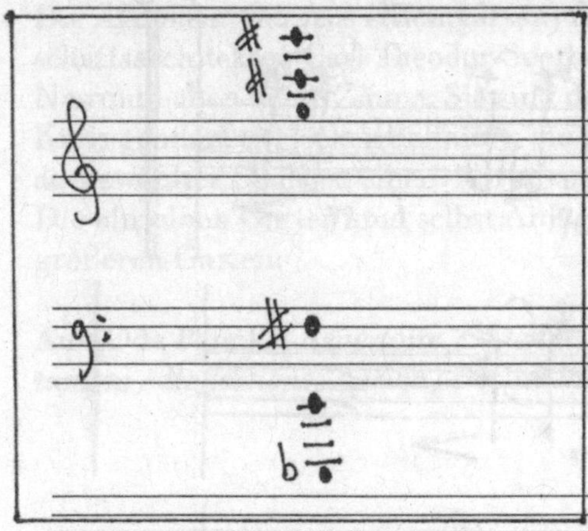

Aktionen:

lang

kurz

Pause

Dynamik:

ppp

sfz ppp

pp

sfz pp

OLEKRANON Viola Solo
für Bruno Maderna
C. Dell
1
Nr. 143, 10 Sys
Vla
senza sord
con sord

S. 3
Der von Alvar Aalto für ein Krankenzimmer entworfene halbrunde Wandschrank kann wie eine schmiegsame Ausdehnung der Wand überall im Raum hängen. Er dient dem Aufbewahren des Notwendigen. Was zuviel ist, fällt beim Öffnen heraus. In der *Dia Art Foundation NY* wird er wie ein Kunstwerk ausgestellt, offen und leer.

S. 4
Die *Allotment Gardens* (Kleingärten) des Landschaftsarchitekten Carl Theodor Soerensen in Nærum haben keine Zäune. Sie sind durch im Kreis gepflanzte Hecken definiert, die jeweils an ausgewählter Stelle zu einem Tor emporwachsen. Die einzelnen Gärten sind selbst Anlagen in einem größeren Garten.

Aus: Oda Pälmke: *Repertoire 7: Details. Betrachtungen / Reflections*, Zürich / Berlin 2019

S. 5
Christopher Dell: Formblock 24

S. 6
Christopher Dell: Olekranon

Oda Pälmke hat an der Technischen Universität und an der Hochschule der Künste Berlin Architektur studiert. Sie ist freischaffende Architektin in Berlin und Universitätsprofessorin für Raumgestalt und Entwerfen am Fachbereich Architektur fatuk der TU Kaiserlautern. In ihren Bücher Typen – Good, Bad and Ugly Houses, Ganz Gut – Quite Good Houses, Facades, Haus Ideal – The Making Of und Repertoire 1–7 untersucht sie typologisch-morphologische Qualitäten von Gebäuden und das Wesen der Gestaltfindung.

Karen Lorenz studierte Bratsche bei Rainer Kimstedt, Prof. Rohde und Barockgeige bei Christine Busch an der Udk Berlin. Daran schloss sich ein Kammermusikstudium beim Alban Berg Quartett an der Hochschule für Musik in Köln. Seit 1997 widmet sie sich verstärkt der modernen Musik vor allem im ensemble mosaik, dessen Gründungsmitglied sie ist. Karen Lorenz nahm an zahlreichen internationalen Kursen und Festivals teil und gewann 2001 mit dem Athena Quartett beim Concours de Genève den 3. Preis, sowie den Publikumspreis. Sie wirkte an vielen Rundfunkaufnahmen und CD-Produktionen (Wergo, Kairos, col legno, edition rz, NCA) mit. Konzertreisen führten sie neben zahlreichen europäischen Ländern nach Südkorea, Israel, Mexiko, Malaysia, Indonesien, Thailand und in die USA.

Jonas Westergaard studierte Kontrabassin der Solistenklasse am Rytmisk Musikkonservatorium Kopenhagen und bei Mark Dresser in New York. 2000 erhielt er den Nordic Talent Launch Award und den Jacob Gade Preis. Für sein Debütalbum im Auftrag vom DanmarksRadio erhielt er den Danish Music Award für Komposition 2009. Als Kontrabassist war er mehrmals beteiligt an Veröffentlichungen, die mit Album of The Year in Dänemark und Norwegen, und in Deutschland Preis der Deutschen Schallplattenkritik ausgezeichnet wurden. Seit 2012 lebt er in Berlin.

Christopher Dell lebt und arbeitet als Theoretiker, Musiker und Komponist in Berlin. Studium der Philosophie, Musik, Komposition und Organisationsentwicklung an den Universitäten Darmstadt, Hilversum, Rotterdam, Boston und Kaiserslautern. Er lehrt zur Zeit Städtebau und Stadterneuerung an der Universität der Künste, Berlin. Dell lehrte u. a. an Architectural Association, London und war Gastprofessor für Städtebautheorie an der HCU Hamburg und der TU München. Sein Forschungsinteresse gilt Praxen und Organisationsverläufen der zeitgenössischen Stadt. Dell ist Gründer und Leiter des ifit, Institut für Improvisationstechnologie, Berlin. Dell gilt laut Reclam Jazzlexikon als der führende Vibraphonist Europas. Dell ist und war beteiligt an zahlreichen CD-Veröffentlichungen und Tourneen weltweit. Seine Arbeit wurde mit zahlreichen Preisen ausgezeichnet, wie z. B. dem Downbeat Allstar Award, Gary Burton Award, Preis der Deutschen Schallplattenkritik, Grammy Nominierung und Musikpreis der Stadt Darmstadt.

Die Reihe **dialogue concerts: conceptual research on architecture and music** präsentiert zum 40-jährigen Jubiläum des Aedes Architekturforums ein medienpluralistisches Format, das die Erforschung des Städtischen neu in den Blick nimmt. Architektonisches Arbeiten tritt in den Dialog mit der Praxis der Musik.

Angelegt als Montage von Vortrag, Konzert und Diskussion untersucht *dialogue concerts* an sechs Veranstaltungen, wie der Stadtraum unser Miteinander bestimmt. Hier ist Stadt nicht als fixiertes Objekt definiert, sondern als dynamische und kollektive Konstellation, die performativ produziert wird.

Kuratiert vom Vibraphonisten, Komponisten und Stadttheoretiker Christopher Dell tritt *dialogue concerts* als künstlerische Aussage sowie als kritisches Dispositiv auf. Ab Dezember 2019 sind internationale Architekt*innen und Musiker*innen eingeladen, ein Jahr lang verfahrensstrategische Zusammenhänge über Disziplingrenzen hinweg zu thematisieren. Ausgehend von Fragen der Medialität, Körperlichkeit, Interaktion, Materialität, Struktur und Transformation entfaltet *dialogue concerts* einen diskursiven Raum, der die gesellschaftliche Relevanz beider Disziplinen auf neue Weise sichtbar zu machen sucht.

Konzept/Moderation: Christopher Dell
Organisatorische Projektleitung: Saori Kanemaki
Gestaltung: Helmut Völter
Controlling: Melanie Rossmann
Öffentlichkeitsarbeit: Ari Kanemaki

Das Team *dialogue concerts* dankt herzlich für die freundliche Kooperation vom Aedes Architekturforum, insbesondere von Kristin Feireiss, Hans-Jürgen Commerell, Dunya Bouchi, Tina Steiger und Mathias Schnell.

Cover: Takashi FUJI, Nobutsune SONE: *Vegetation of City Hino*, Hino 1976, S. 15

dialogue concerts

1 *Mediality* 12. 12. 2019
2 *Interaction* 6. 2. 2020, 18.30 Uhr
Vortrag: Christophe Hutin
Konzert: Christopher Dell, Christian Lillinger, Kathrin Pechloff

3 *Transformation*
4 *Materiality*
5 *Structure*
6 *Corporality*

Aedes Architecture Forum
Senatsverwaltung für Kultur und Europa be Berlin
MUSIKFONDS

Gefördert vom Musikfonds e. V. mit Projektmitteln der Beauftragten der Bundesregierung für Kultur und Medien.

dialogue concerts

2

conceptual research on architecture and music

Interaction

6. 2. 2020
18:30

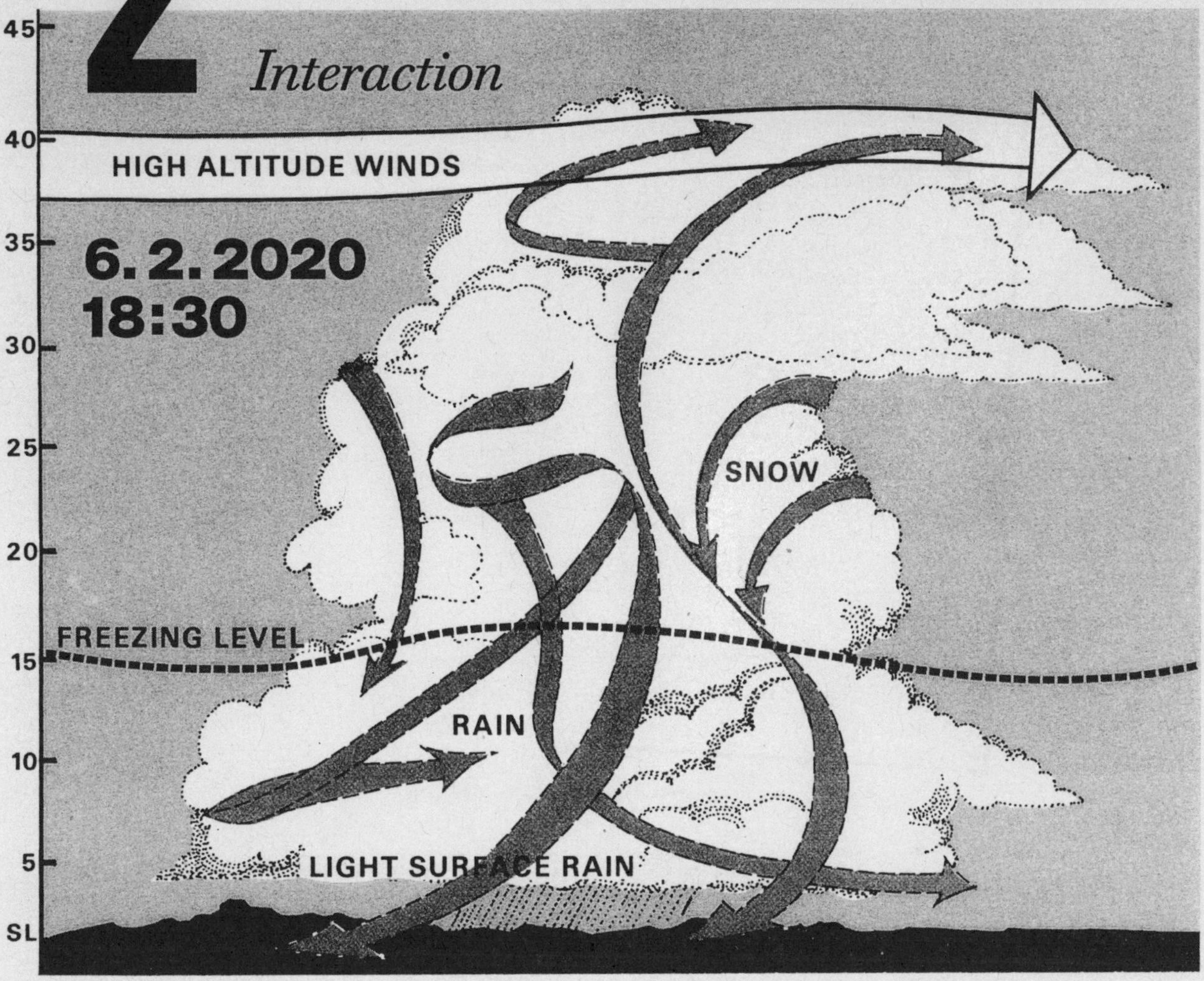

Lecture
Christophe Hutin

Concert
Christopher Dell,
Christian Lillinger,
Kathrin Pechlof

Discussion

Aedes Architekturforum

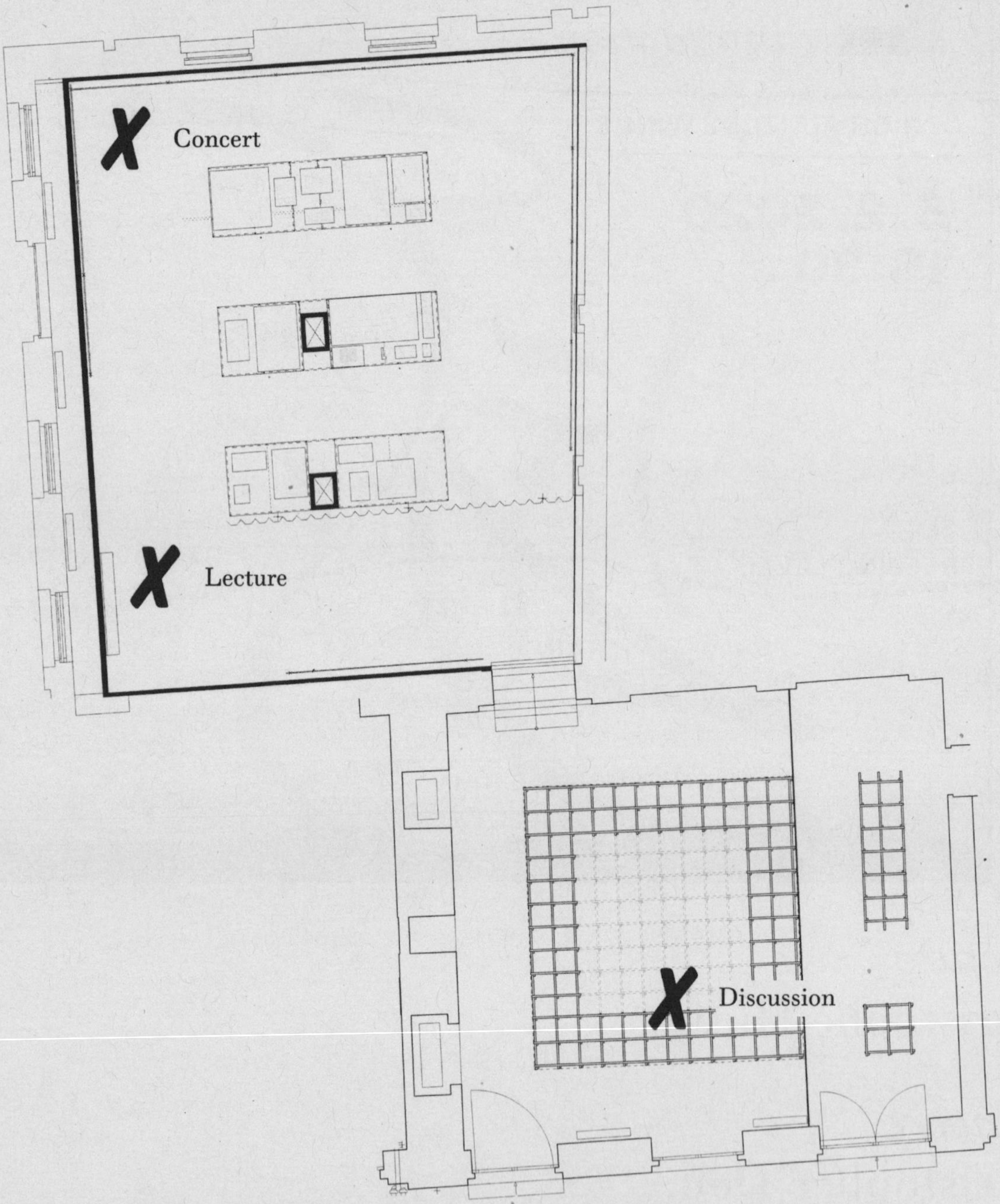

Intervention in the Aedes exhibition spaces of
Our Urban Living Room by Cobe.Copenhagen (18.1.– 29.4.)
and *Architecture for Pigs: Barn.Slaughterhouse.Shop* (18.1.– 5.3.)

Interaction

Interaction can be defined as a situation in which two or more humans or objects act in relation to each other. If "each habitat creates new patterns of individuality […] by their interaction in the close medium of the city" (Lewis Mumford), how can we regard such an interaction of humans and objects as city? And how can we show this process? Can its intricateness be tracked? Can we deal with its indeterminacy constructively? Furthermore, what does it mean that the agency of an interaction also frames, structures, or localizes humans and objects?

"It is for the architects to move beyond […] self-conscious set pieces and to devise, as in the best music scores, gaps of uncertainty in which the individual can participate" (Price 2003, 13). This commentary was given by the English architect Cedric Price in regard to his research works on flexible architecture, indeterminacy, impermanence and the fusion of action, architecture and education. While many of his projects—such as the famous *Fun Palace* or the *Potteries Thinkbelt*—remained unrealized, Price did manage to carry out important projects, among them the lesser known *Interaction Center*. Spanning from its first essential construction work in 1970 until its demolition in 1980, the building's history in itself had a performative, interaction based life. Since its realization ran short of monetary funding, the foundations, steel frame and trusses were constructed first. This basic structure could then be used for open-air community events in order to raise additional funds for the project's second phase. In phase two, cladding, fittings, finishes, services prefabricated units and log cabins were added. As was the *Fun Palace*, the *Interaction Centre* was conceived by Price as a building with a particularly short life-span. As such, its spatial key concept founded in supplying a very basic support structure, that could enable many different and unforeseen uses. Architecturally, such an openness of program was achieved by making the interior spaces functionally independent from the roof and exterior walls.

While the *Interaction Centre* building has since long been both, torn down and poorly documented, it still harbors decisive questions for contemporary design: how to create structures for open form? How to understand interaction itself as a structural component? And how to overcome the traditional dichotomy of agency vs. structure?

Against the backdrop of these questions, it is relevant to revisit the etymology of the notion of interaction. Viewed in the linguistic and semantic historical perspective, the term interaction is rather young. It was first used as a synthetic word in the 19th century (derived from the Latin inter = between and actio = action). Given that the term is so commonly used in sociological matters today, it comes rather as a surprise that the term originated in the discipline of physics. In this context, it was used to describe the relational acting and reacting of things. Driven by a desire to understand and explore the fundamentals of physics, the Irish scientist John Tyndall first used the term to describe the study of the interaction of light with matter. Through Tyndall's widely disseminated and highly influential theoretical work the word found its way into the *French Revue Scientifique* in 1872 and from there into the *supplement* of the Littré's *dictionnaire* in 1877 (Starobinski 2003, 211–212). However, it is only through the writings on modern urban society by the German sociologist Georg Simmel, at the turn of the century that the term—coined as "Wechselwirkung" (Simmel 1892, 130)—did enter the social sciences. Simmel's disciples of the Chicago School finally brought the term into the architecture and urban design discourse. Finally, in the 1970s the term "interaction" was reimported to Germany, becoming popular in psychology and sociology circles. There it came to be used as cumulative depiction of communicative group behaviour between human individuals.

Yet in the 1990s, driven by contemporary historical epistemology and the movement "science in the making", the meaning of the term interaction took yet another decisive turn. Things came back. Authors like Bruno Latour, Michel Callon and Hans-Jörg Rheinberger not only reintroduced the 19th century idea that things can inter-act. More importantly, they also insinuated that humans can inter-act with things. However, in the course of this renaissance of the acting of things a new aspect enters the center-stage: indeterminacy. Where there is interaction of humans and non-humans, one cannot expect to find a given plan or a teleological finality. As Latour vividly describes: "Interactions do not resemble a picnic where all the food is gathered on the spot by the participants, but rather a reception given by some unknown sponsors who have staged everything down to the last detail—even the place to sit might already be pre-inscribed by some attentive keeper. So, it is perfectly true to say that any given interaction seems to overflow with elements which are already in the situation coming from some other time, some other place, and generated by some other agency" (Latour 2005, 166).

When transposed to the reading of the city, the above described perspectives on interaction trigger new questions. Whereas interaction in the discourse on the urban has traditionally rather been associated with human group performance, it now proves important to consider those forms of agency that operate through concerted action of humans and non-humans as spatial configuration. Seen in this light, the city's daily becoming is neither understood as the act of a single actor, nor of a single thing or a single discourse. Rather it should be described as something that happens by virtue of the relationality of a specific urban situation, which comes about through the relation of all of them. Arising from what one could now term 'urban interaction,' the reading of the city is one that understands the latter as assemblage of heterogeneous series of agencies.

By this is meant, that forms of embodied and plural agency are essential components of any understanding of the city, even if its situations are necessarily partial. However, one might say that urban situations signify in excess of what can be said and shown, and that mode of signification is a concerted bodily interaction, a plural form of performativity. Along these lines, as has been repeatedly stressed by the 'science in the making' one has to investigate how the city's interactions operate constructively with indeterminacy. As stated above, interactions are far from being isotopic: they spill with structures, which are already part of the situation but coming from some other time, some other place and generated by some other agency.

But how at once to intervene in and represent the urban interaction, an active, deliberately sustained and trans-historical relationality, a concerted action distinct from mere disorder or non-sense? And how then do normativity and power depend on, are played out and constructed in urban interaction? If one might say that urban interactions signify an excess of what can be said, and that mode of signification is a concerted bodily action in concert, a plural form of performativity, how can one analyze it? How can one show it? How can one design it?

References

Callon, Michel, Lascoumes Pierre and Barthe Yannick. *Acting in an Uncertain World: An Essay on Technical Democracy*, trans. Graham Burchell. Cambridge, MA: MIT Press, 2009.

Jackson, Roland. *The Ascent of John Tyndal*. Oxford: Oxford University Press, 2018.

Mumford, Lewis. *The Culture of Cities*. San Diego: Harcourt Brace, 1970.

Latour, Bruno. *Reassembling the Social: An Introduction to Actor-Network-Theory*. Oxford: Oxford University Press, 2005.

Price, Cedric. *Re: CP*. Zürich: Birkhäuser, 2003.

Rheinberger, Hans-Jörg. *An Epistemology of the Concrete: Twentieth-Century Histories of Life*. Durham, NC, and London: Duke University Press, 2010.

Simmel, Georg. "Über sociale Differenzierung," in *Aufsätze 1887 bis 1890: Über sociale Differenzierung (1890); Die Probleme der Geschichtsphilosophie (1892)*, ed. Heinz-Jürgen Dahme, 109–295. Frankfurt am Main: Suhrkamp, 1989.

Starobinski, Jean. *Aktion und Reaktion*. Frankfurt am Main: Suhrkamp, 2003.

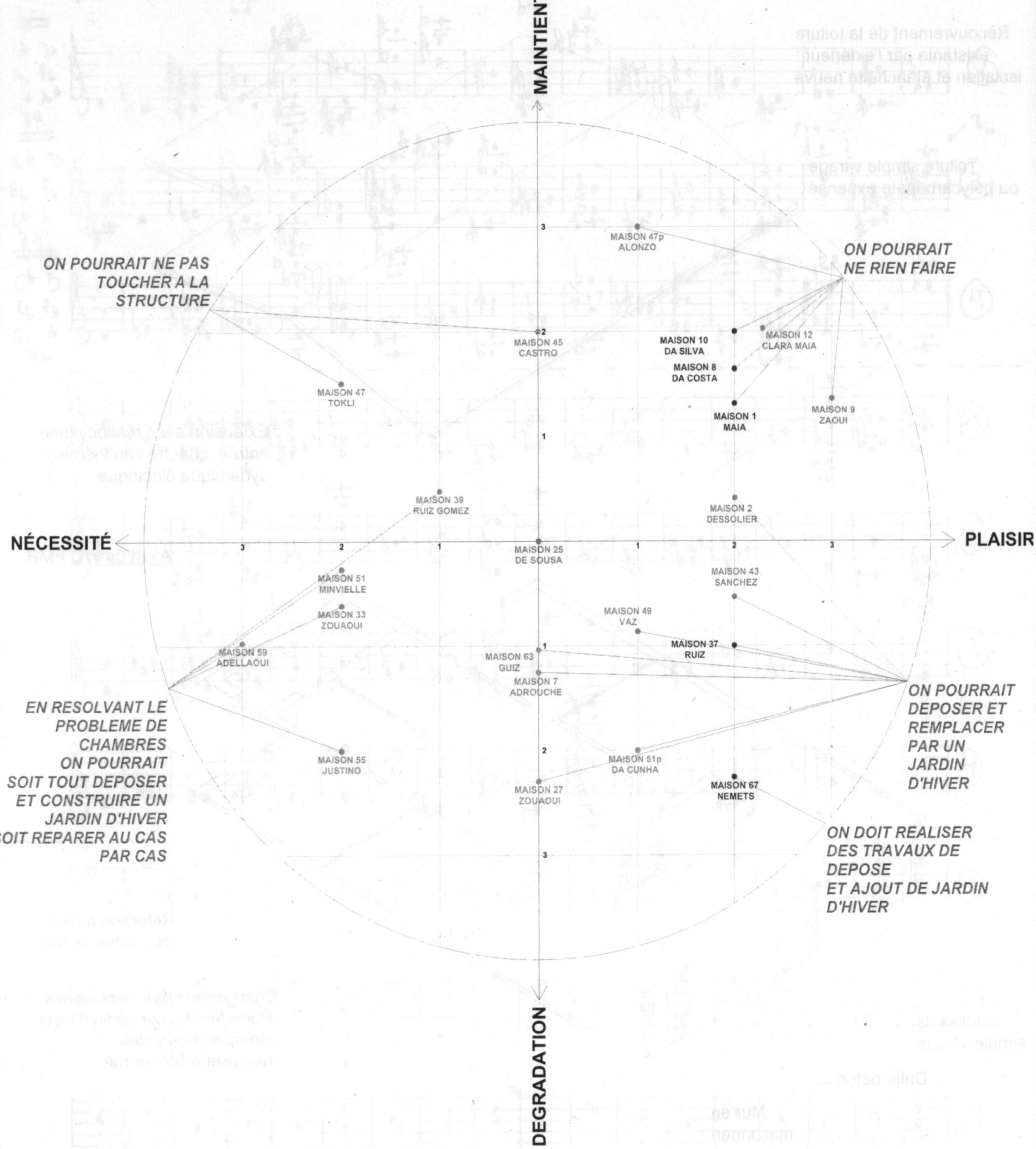
MAINTIENT
DEGRADATION
NÉCESSITÉ
PLAISIR
3
2
1
ON POURRAIT NE PAS TOUCHER A LA STRUCTURE
ON POURRAIT NE RIEN FAIRE
MAISON 47p ALONZO
MAISON 45 CASTRO
MAISON 10 DA SILVA
MAISON 12 CLARA MAIA
MAISON 8 DA COSTA
MAISON 47 TOKLI
MAISON 1 MAIA
MAISON 9 ZAOUI
MAISON 39 RUIZ GOMEZ
MAISON 2 DESSOLIER
MAISON 25 DE SOUSA
MAISON 43 SANCHEZ
MAISON 51 MINVIELLE
MAISON 33 ZOUAOUI
MAISON 49 VAZ
MAISON 37 RUIZ
MAISON 59 ADELLAOUI
MAISON 63 GUIZ
MAISON 7 ADROUCHE
ON POURRAIT DEPOSER ET REMPLACER PAR UN JARDIN D'HIVER
EN RESOLVANT LE PROBLEME DE CHAMBRES ON POURRAIT SOIT TOUT DEPOSER ET CONSTRUIRE UN JARDIN D'HIVER SOIT REPARER AU CAS PAR CAS
MAISON 55 JUSTINO
MAISON 51p DA CUNHA
MAISON 27 ZOUAOUI
MAISON 67 NEMETS
ON DOIT REALISER DES TRAVAUX DE DEPOSE ET AJOUT DE JARDIN D'HIVER

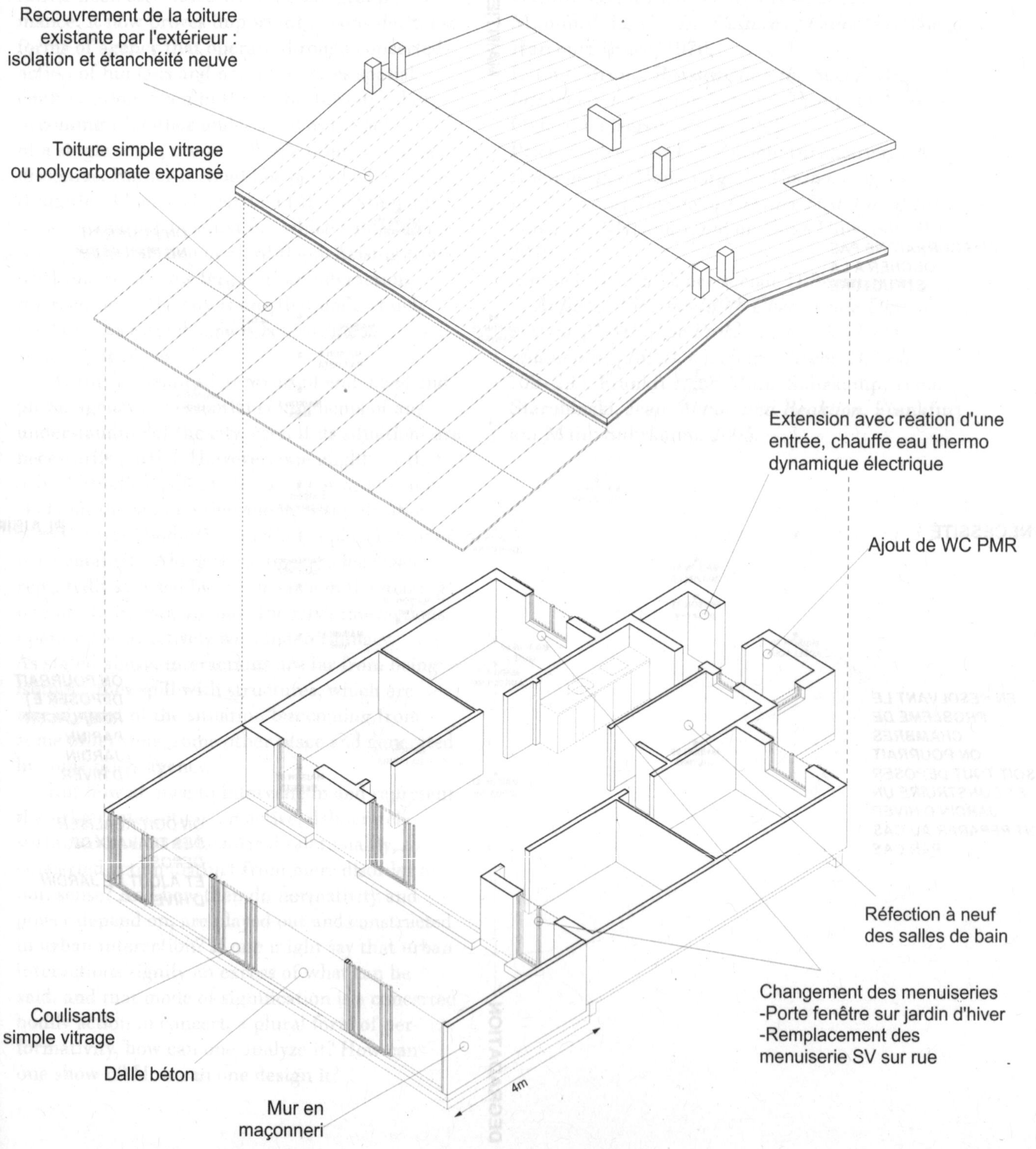
Recouvrement de la toiture
existante par l'extérieur :
isolation et étanchéité neuve
Toiture simple vitrage
ou polycarbonate expansé
Extension avec réation d'une
entrée, chauffe eau thermo
dynamique électrique
Ajout de WC PMR
Réfection à neuf
des salles de bain
Changement des menuiseries
-Porte fenêtre sur jardin d'hiver
-Remplacement des
menuiserie SV sur rue
Coulisants
simple vitrage
Dalle béton
Mur en
maçonneri
4m

short notes only
mp throughout
FORMBLOCK 30 b) 1 bar ≈ 112–96
C D
Eb Fb
Gb A A#
H
C# D
Eb Fb
G# A#
B#
C# D
Eb Fb
G# A
B#
C# D
Eb Fb
G A
Bb
C#
Bb
8va
FORM: ||: ① – ② – ③ – ④ – ③ – ② – ① :||

♩ = 100 approx.

Topology für Harfe solo

play freely

für Kathrin Pechlof

Christopher Dell

S. 3
Christophe Hutin: Beutre. Projet architectural et paysager. Diagramme sur les types de projets d'extensions (detail)

S. 4
Christophe Hutin: Beutre. Projet architectural et paysager. Principe de transformation d'un T5 (detail)

S. 5.
Christopher Dell: Formblock 30 b

S. 6
Christopher Dell: Topology für Harfe solo

Christophe Hutin is an architect and lecturer-researcher at the Bordeaux National School of Architecture. Graduating in 2003, he studied for several months and documented the townships and squatter camps in Soweto near Johannesburg. This experience gave rise to the publication of the book "Learning from Soweto, Construct freely" at Éditions Acte Sud, co-written with Patrice Goulet. From there he developed recognized expertise on housing issues in South Africa which led him in particular to design and organize since 2008 the annual EUNIC international architecture studio events supported by the European cultural institutes of South Africa in Johannesburg. These are workshops and exchanges between architects, residents, teachers and students on issues of contemporary urban development in critical sites (informal housing, squat, etc.) Specializing in sustainable architecture based on the construction economy, he has carried out numerous projects in the field of housing but also public cultural facilities. Several achievements bear witness to this research carried out in particular in collaboration with the architects Lacaton and Vassal (urban study of 50,000 dwellings, project to transform buildings G, H, I in the large park in Bordeaux). With them he won the European Union prize, the Mies Van Der Rohe prize in 2019. Christophe Hutin has been appointed ccurator of the French pavilion at the Venice 2020 bienniale of architecture around his project: "communities at work."

Christian Lillinger is German Avantgarde-Musician, drummer and composer. In 2019 he released his project "open form for society."
In 2018 he established his own label Plaist, which has already released four albums. In 2017 Lillinger was awarded the SWR Jazzpreis. He was the artist in residence in the Marktgräfle Hof in Basel for eight months by the Stiftung Bartels Foundation in 2016. The same year the German broadcaster 3SAT released Gegen den Beat a documentary about Christian directed by Jan Bäumer. In 2014 Christian Lillinger founded the quartet Amok Amor with Peter Evans on trumpet, Wanja Slavin on saxophone and Petter Eldh on bass. The band released their self-titled debut on Boomslang in 2015 and We Know Not What We Do in 2017 on the Swiss label Intakt. Between 2012 and 2013 Christian sat on the board of the Union for German Jazzmusicians (Union Deutscher Jazzmusiker) and he received a composition scholarship from the City of Berlin. 2008 saw the foundation of Christian Lillinger's Grund, which allowed him to realise his own composition. So far three albumshave been released through the labels Clean Feed (First Reason in 2009 and Second Reason in 2012) as well as Pirouet (Grund in 2015).

The concert performer, improviser and composer **Kathrin Pechlof** is one of a very small number of harpists who integrate the sound of the harp into contemporary jazz and improvised music. After studying the classical harp in Munich and jazz composition and improvisation in Cologne she chooses her very own path, disregarding any conventional stylistic categories. Her vision of a synthesis between improvised and composed music attracted international attention after the release of Imaginarium, the debut CD of her trio with Robert Landfermann and Christian Weidner on the Munich Pirouet label in 2013, as well as the following album Toward The Unknown, released 2018 again on Pirouet. Apart from the almost 10 years lasting work with her trio she was invited all over the years to collaborate with numerous renowned musicians and she is lucky to perform with many protagonists of Germany´s and European jazz scene at prestigious clubs and festivals. Her work has been documented in numerous radio, TV, and CD productions. Together with Christian Weidner she was co-curator of the Serious Series, an concert series for contemporary jazz and improvised music in Berlin from 2013 to 2019. Since 2016 is doing cultural policy work with IG Jazz Berlin, a syndicate representing the interest of the berlin jazz scene. Currently she is a fellow of the Àrvore Foundation. Kathrin Pechlof lives in Berlin.

Christopher Dell works in Berlin as a theorist in urban design and architecture, as musician, composer and as artist. Since 2000, Dell has been head of the Institute for Improvisationtechnology in Berlin. He held professorships in Urban Design Theory at the HafenCity Universität Hamburg and the Technical University Munich. At the moment he teaches Urban Design and Urban Renewal at the University of Fine Arts, Berlin. The Reclam Jazzlexikon hails him as one of Europe's leading vibraphonists. Dell has recorded numerous CDs and toured worldwide. His work was honored with several awards e.g. the Downbeat Allstar Award, the Award of the "Deutsche Schallplattenkritik," the JazzArt-Award – Music of the 21st Century, the Musicprize of the City of Darmstadt, German Jazz Prize and a Grammy-Nomination. He received composition awards, fundings and commissions from, among others, Goethe Institute, Deutscher Musikrat, Musikfonds, Beauftragte der Bundesregierung für Kultur und Medien, Senatsverwaltung für Kultur und Europa, Berlin and WDR Cologne. He has published numerous CDs, articles, and books.

On the occasion of Aedes Architecture Forum's 40th anniversary, the series **dialogue concerts: conceptual research on architecture and music** presents a pluralistic media format, re-envisioning urban research. Architectural practice will enter into a dialogue with musical praxis.

Designed as a montage of lectures, concerts and discussions *dialogue concerts* is a series of events that will examine the interplay of urban space and communal life. Set up as an experimental interdisciplinary format, the *dialogue concerts* series is comprised of 6 events from December 2019 through December 2020. In this context, the city is not defined as a fixed object, but as a dynamic and collective constellation that is performatively produced.

Curated by the vibraphonist, composer and urban theoretician Christopher Dell, *dialogue concerts* is presented as artistic statement and critical dispositif. International architects and musicians are invited to address aspects of procedural strategies across disciplines in a series of six *dialogue concerts*. Taking questions of mediality, corporality, interaction, materiality, structure and transformation as starting points, *dialogue concerts* creates a discursive space seeking to illustrate the societal relevance of both disciplines in a new way.

dialogue concerts is organized by Christopher Dell in cooperation with the Aedes Architecture Forum, funded by the Senate Department for Culture and Europe and the Musikfonds e. V. with project funds from the Federal Government Commissioner for Culture and the Media.

Concept/Moderation: Christopher Dell
Project Management: Saori Kanemaki
Graphic Design: Helmut Völter
Controlling: Melanie Rossmann
Public Relations: Ari Kanemaki

The Team of *dialogue concerts* would like to thank everybody at Aedes Architecture Forum for the friendly cooperation, especially Kristin Feireiss, Hans Jürgen Commerell, Tina Steiger, Dunya Bouchi and Mathias Schnell.

Cover: Cessna Pilot Center: *Professional Manual of Flight*, 1975, S. 18–37

dialogue concerts

1	*Mediality*	12. 12. 2019
2	*Interaction*	6. 2. 2020
3	*Transformation*	20. 3., 18:30 Uhr Vortrag: Daniel Libeskind Konzert: Christopher Dell, Elisabeth Coudoux, Pascal Klewer, Christian Lillinger
4	*Materiality*	
5	*Structure*	
6	*Corporality*	

Aedes Architecture Forum
enw
ifit Institut für Improvisationstechnologie
Senatsverwaltung für Kultur und Europa | be Berlin
MUSIKFONDS
Gefördert vom Musikfonds e. V. mit Projektmitteln der Beauftragten der Bundesregierung für Kultur und Medien.

dialogue concerts

3

conceptual research on architecture and music

Transformation

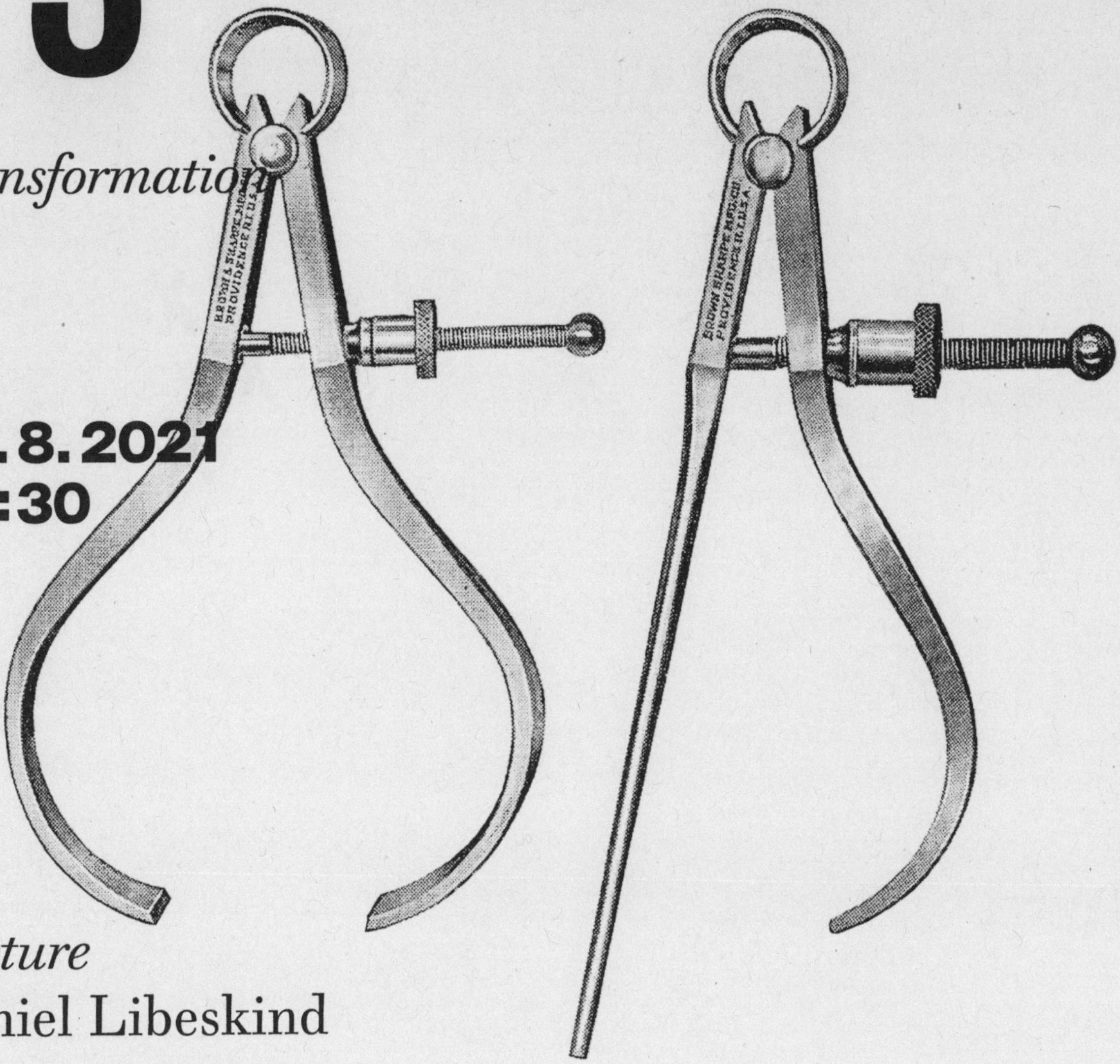

14. 8. 2021
18:30

Lecture
Daniel Libeskind

Concert
Elisabeth Coudoux,
Christopher Dell,
Pascal Klewer,
Christian Lillinger

Discussion

Aedes Architecture Forum

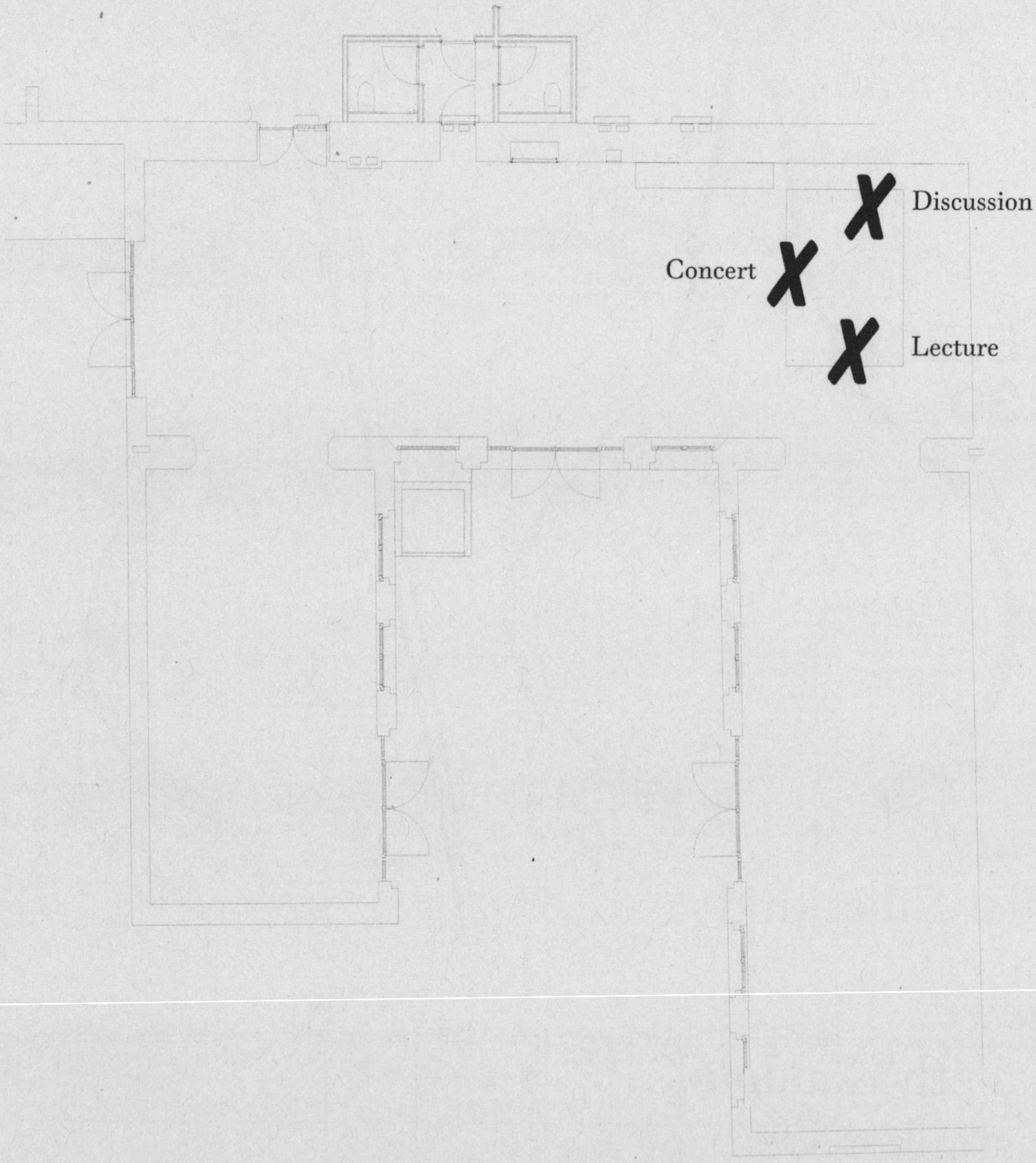

Discussion
Concert
Lecture

Transformation

What is form? A form can be a sensual shape—a *morphé*—as well as an *idea*, or an *eidos*, or what today is considered mental content.

Trans-formation means to give new form to that which had already been formed. In other words: to give form to the passage of shapes and ideas from the now to the not yet. A task more important than ever, as urban processes defined by change and indeterminacy are major forces shaping the world today. How can we understand these processes, which seem now beyond the grasp of our traditional way of thinking? What questions are being asked? And what makes architecture and music so fascinating in this context?

I

In the second half of the 19th century the French researcher Etienne-Jules Marey designed and built notating machines that could register and graph the physiological processes of the body through mechanical sensors. The most famous of these, the *sphymograph*, could draw the curve of blood pressure transformations evoked by a pumping heart—in real time. Delivering notations of streams of bodily processes, the machine's writing graph allowed insight into and generated an entirely new form of knowledge. It produced a notation that made visible and calculable the invisible: the internal qualities of the human circulatory system.

The efficiency of the notation procedure led Marey to redefine scientific writing as an inscription process, thereby emphasizing the importance of written visualization in the production of scientific knowledge in general. Astonishingly, Marey did so by methodologically correlating musical notation and scientific graphical systems. Musical notation became the central reference point for the visualization strategy of his experimental writing machines. Marey's treatise *Du movement dans les fonctions de la vie* from 1868 drew on the assumption that musical notation is universal (readable and understandable everywhere in the world independent from language) and a system that can denote complex movements that no language can describe. (Marey 1868, 93)

II

In the same manner that music can be related to science in the form of visualization, it can also be related to architecture. Not only do music and architectural notation—through variation, modulation and invention—elegantly move across forms, they also have the capacity to let transformation take place across categories. For instance both, a translation of a geometric formula into the material state of an architectural drawing or model, or a making over of a musical concept into the performance by players, let a mental *idea* become sensual shape. But this does not mean, that the origin of the shape is the idea. Quite on the contrary, the geometrical as well as the musical concept are grounded in a *praxis*. In other words, they have—and historically have had—to be activated in order to take place. One can claim that in a strange way the geometrical as well as the musical concept are ideal entities that are also historical. While containing an ideal core, they accrete sedimentations in their transmission, their delivery to the present and future, which transforms their shape.

By this is meant that the practical historical sedimentation of sense through reactivation interplays with the creation of new sense within the situation of a present sense. All of which according to the German phenomenologist Edmund Husserl is connected to the capacity of notating. During the process of transformational re-activation of an idea, the notation is the medium that guarantees a persistence and thereby the objectivity of the idea. In his reflections on *The Origin of Geometry* Husserl writes: "The important function of written, documenting linguistic expression is that it makes communications possible without immediate or mediate personal address; it is, so to speak, communication become virtual." (Husserl 1989, 164). The core argument of Husserl is, that writing and the activation of the writing in new contexts and histories, an *idea*—such as a geometrical formula—is transformed, while staying the same. The argument sheds light on Husserl's use of the term sedimentation in the context of the production or activation of a geometrical formula's self-evidence by anyone who reads its notation: "the writing-down effects a transformation of the original mode of being of the meaning-structure, [e.g.,] within the geometrical sphere of self-evidence, of the geometrical structure which is put into words. It becomes sedimented, so to speak." (ibid., 164) What is at stake is that through sedimentation and through becoming working matter, the meaning structures transform enduringly through time. (ibid., 171) In this context, the question of the methodological and disciplinary status of notation posed by Marey reappears. I argue that it is under the lens of music—this time allied to geometry—that the notations of science reveal themselves as knowledge form that is constituted by its visual organization. Such a reading allows a correlation of layers of scientific data, which raise questions about their relationality, to identify reoccurring patterns that could not be identified without notation and to show the richness of data as moving stream. In sum, it is the methodological reference to music that opens an access to the emergence of knowledge as epistemological act of transformation that appears through, and always beyond notation.

III

It is along these lines that the architect Daniel Libeskind refers to Husserl when he aims to show the close techno-historical connection of graphical methods and the practice of measurement. What Libeskind continuously draws attention to, is that and how the historical genealogy of geometry is being grounded in the operation of land-surveying and in the politics and economics of the partition of the spatial. Paradoxically however, and in this way Libeskind transgresses the theses of Husserl, the architect hyperboles the very being ingrained in the operational of the primordiality of geometrical reflection. He interprets it as a function that guarantees the opening of the geometry to the contingent. *Dis*closing experience of direct encounter through any act of objectification propels an *in*cluding void. By being represented, the spatiality of an encounter—as a genealogical trace of the primary horizon of geometry—creates exactly the void that allows a re-insertion itself, in any project of objectivating closure. Libeskind argues that the transposition of experience to representation always takes place through structural relationality. What one experiences as the ordering of an initial encounter of a situation is not a posteriori fixation of formless matter. Rather, one pre-reflexively experiences structures that are constantly transposed to the realm of representation, where they then can give rise to description and inscription. Far from simply superimposing hierarchies or the reduction to mere figuration, a geometrical drawing therefore constitutes a trajectory which "transposes content into operation and at the same time displaces descriptive geometry to the structural." (Libeskind 1991, 15) This emphasizes the temporality of transforming an object into operation, a process which "is not arbitrary and yet is not predetermined either." (ibid.) Libeskind's statement offers an understanding of his early notational works such as *Micromegas* or *Chamberworks* as endeavors to free the architectural drawing from its ontology of a teleological blueprint. Instead, the architect practically and materially reconnects the sublime presence of the drawing to "a very ancient tradition of coordination of mathematics, of drawing as a musical order and a musical medium." (Libeskind 1997, 29) To this end, the drawings should be understood as a new type of visual organization. For Libeskind „an architectural drawing is as much a prospective unfolding of future possibilities as it is a recovery of a particular history, to whose intentions it testifies and whose limits it always challenges. In any case, a drawing is more than the shadow of an object, more than a pile of lines, more than a resignation to the inertia of convention." (Libeskind 1991, 15)

IV

Somehow, the dualism of form versus matter, of *morphé* versus *hyle* collapses here: matter gains agency in the interplay of transformational procedures. In this perspective, architecture and music become reading machines of immanence in the truest sense: an architectural drawing is blind but makes us see, a musical notation is deaf but makes us hear. Consequently, to draw the city, to perform a musical piece suggests the immersion in an open process of change. Those who aim at being confronted with concrete situations and the transformational possibility of yet another recursive take, have to go out and dare to intervene in and represent them.

References

Husserl, Edmund. "The Origin of Geometry (1936/1954)" in Derrida, Jacques. *Edmund Husserl's Origin of Geometry: An Introduction*, transl. John P. Leavey. Lincoln and London: University of Nebraska Press, 1989 (1962).

Libeskind, Daniel. *Counterdesign.* New York: Rizzoli, 1991.

Libeskind, Daniel. "Chamberworks" in Szyszkowitz, Michael. *Architecture Music.* Graz: Haus der Architektur, 1997.

Marey, Etienne Jules. *Du movement dans les fonctions de la vie.* Paris, 1868.

FERNBLOCK 31 b)
CD 8-3-2020
1
0'00''
1'30''
choose (one) note
2
1:00 min
pppp
3
1:30 min.
p < f > pp < ff > p < f > pp < ff > p < f > p < ff
center tone material
FB 31 a) + b)
4
0:40 min.
1:20 min
5
ppp
ff
fff

NOEM für Violoncello und Trompete in C

pp. 3, 4
Daniel Libeskind: Chamber Works: Architectural Meditations on Themes from Heraclitus

p. 5
Christopher Dell: Formblock 31 b

p. 6
Christopher Dell: Noem für Violoncello und Trompete in C

Elisabeth Coudoux is a german cellist at the crossroads of different musical genres: free improvisation, experimental music, new contemporary music and Jazz. Based on classical studies she graduated with a jazz degree with Frank Gratkowski and Prof. Dieter Manderscheid at Cologne music university. Besides her own projects (like *Emißatett* she composes for) she is part of a lot of ensembles and temporary projects with Signe Emmelruth, Peter Evans, Hanne de Backer, Wilbert de Joode, Paal Nillesen Love, Steve Swell, Xavier Charles, Gunda Gottschalk, Pascal Niggenkemper, Felicie Bazelaire, Achim Kaufmann, Biliana Voutchkova, Kathrin Pechlov, Kaja Drachsler, Philip Gropper etc. and plays cello in interdisciplinary projects with dancers, visual artists, poets and performers. Elisabeth is member of *IMPAKT*, a collective for free improvisation in cologne.

Christopher Dell works in Berlin as a theorist in urban design and architecture, as musician, composer and as artist. Since 2000, Dell has been head of the Institute for Improvisationtechnology in Berlin. He held professorships in Urban Design Theory at the HafenCity Universität Hamburg and the Technical University Munich. At the moment he teaches Urban Design and Urban Renewal at the University of Fine Arts, Berlin. The Reclam Jazzlexikon hails him as one of Europe's leading vibraphonists. Dell has recorded numerous CDs and toured worldwide. His work was honored with several awards. e.g. the Downbeat Allstar Award, the Award of the Deutsche Schallplattenkritik, the JazzArt-Award—Music of the 21st Century, the Musicprize of the City of Darmstadt, German Jazz Prize and a Grammy-Nomination. He has published numerous CDs, articles, and books.

Pascal Klewer (born 1997) studied jazz trumpet under Niels Klein, Andy Haderer and Jürgen Friedrich at the Musikhochschule Köln. He was a part of the Bundesjazzorchester 2018–19 and leads several ensembles (f. e. *Evan Parker is my Hero*, *Bräumer/Klewer/Eftychidou*, *Pascal Klewer Bigband*, *MOZAH*), as well as working as a sideman with *Shaikh9* and the *Aurora Octet*. Since 2019 he curates in Cologne the successful concert series *Pascal Klewer Bigband meets*, pairing avantgardistic soloists with the bigband and Klewer's compositions, f. e. Peter Brötzmann, Evan Parker and Christopher Dell. He is a finalist of the Neuer Deutscher Jazzpreis 2020 for composition, curates the 222 festival and leads in June 2020 a project of the WDR Bigband. Concerts have led him through large parts of Europe, Israel, USA, Canada, Bolivia and China.

An international figure in architecture and urban design, **Daniel Libeskind** is renowned for his ability to evoke cultural memory in buildings. Informed by a deep commitment to music, philosophy, literature, and poetry, Mr. Libeskind aims to create architecture that is resonant, unique and sustainable. In 1989, Mr. Libeskind won the international competition to build the Jewish Museum in Berlin. A series of influential museum commissions followed. In 2003, Studio Libeskind won another historic competition to create a master plan for the rebuilding of the World Trade Center in Lower Manhattan. As Principal Design Architect for Studio Libeskind, Mr. Libeskind speaks widely on the art of architecture in universities and professional summits. His architecture and ideas have been the subject of many articles and exhibitions, influencing the field of architecture and the development of cities and culture. Mr. Libeskind lives in New York with his wife and business partner, Nina Libeskind.

Christian Lillinger is German Avantgarde-Musician, drummer and composer. In 2019 he released his project open form for society. In 2018 he established his own label *PLAIST*, which has already released four albums. In 2017, he was awarded the SWR Jazzpreis and the artist in residence in the Marktgräfle Hof in Basel by the Stiftung Bartels Foundation in 2016. The German broadcaster 3sat released *Gegen den Beat: Christian Lillinger und die JazzBaltica*, directed by Jan Bäumer. In 2014 Christian Lillinger founded the quartet *Amok Amor* with Peter Evans (tr) Wanja Slavin (sax) and Petter Eldh (bass). Between 2012 and 2013 Christian sat on the board of Union Deutscher Jazzmusiker and he received a composition scholarship from the City of Berlin. 2008 saw the foundation of Christian Lillinger's *Grund*, which allowed him to realise his own composition.

On the occasion of Aedes Architecture Forum's 40th anniversary, the series **dialogue concerts: conceptual research on architecture and music** presents a pluralistic media format, re-envisioning urban research. Architectural practice will enter into a dialogue with musical praxis.

Designed as a montage of lectures, concerts and discussions *dialogue concerts* is a series of events that will examine the interplay of urban space and communal life. Set up as an experimental interdisciplinary format, the *dialogue concerts* series is comprised of 6 events from December 2019 through December 2021. In this context, the city is not defined as a fixed object, but as a dynamic and collective constellation that is performatively produced.

Curated by the vibraphonist, composer and urban theoretician Christopher Dell, *dialogue concerts* is presented as artistic statement and critical dispositif. International architects and musicians are invited to address aspects of procedural strategies across disciplines in a series of six *dialogue concerts.* Taking questions of mediality, corporality, interaction, materiality, structure and transformation as starting points, *dialogue concerts* creates a discursive space seeking to illustrate the societal relevance of both disciplines in a new way.

dialogue concerts is organized by Christopher Dell in cooperation with the Aedes Architecture Forum, funded by the Senate Department for Culture and Europe and the Musikfonds e. V. with project funds from the Federal Government Commissioner for Culture and the Media.

Concept / Moderation: Christopher Dell
Project Management: Saori Kanemaki
Graphic Design: Helmut Völter
Controlling: Melanie Rossmann
Public Relations: Ari Kanemaki

The Team of *dialogue concerts* would like to thank everybody at Aedes Architecture Forum for the friendly cooperation, especially Kristin Feireiss, Hans Jürgen Commerell, Tina Steiger, Dunya Bouchi and Mathias Schnell. Thanks to Tchoban Foundation for supplying the scans of Daniel Libeskind Chamberworks.

Cover: Brown & Sharpe: *Machinery and Tools: Catalog No. 139*, 1929, p. 525
pp. 3, 4: image courtesy of Daniel Libeskind, scan courtesy of the Tchoban Foundation

dialogue concerts

1	*Mediality*	12. 12. 2019
2	*Interaction*	6. 2. 2020
3	*Transformation*	14. 8. 2021
4	*Structure*	17. 9. 2020
5	*Corporality*	20. 4. 2021
6	*Materiality*	9. 9. 2021, 18:30 Lecture: Ton Maton Concert: Christopher Dell, Lotte Anker, Sofia Eftychidou

Aedes
Architecture Forum
enw
ifit Institut für Improvisationstechnologie
Senatsverwaltung für Kultur und Europa | be Berlin
MUSIKFONDS
Gefördert vom Musikfonds e. V. mit Projektmitteln der Beauftragten der Bundesregierung für Kultur und Medien.

dialogue concerts

4

conceptual research on architecture and music

Structure

17. 9. 2020
18:30

Vortrag
Bernd Kniess

Konzert
Christopher Dell,
Christian Lillinger,
Jonas Westergaard

Diskussion

Aedes Architekturforum

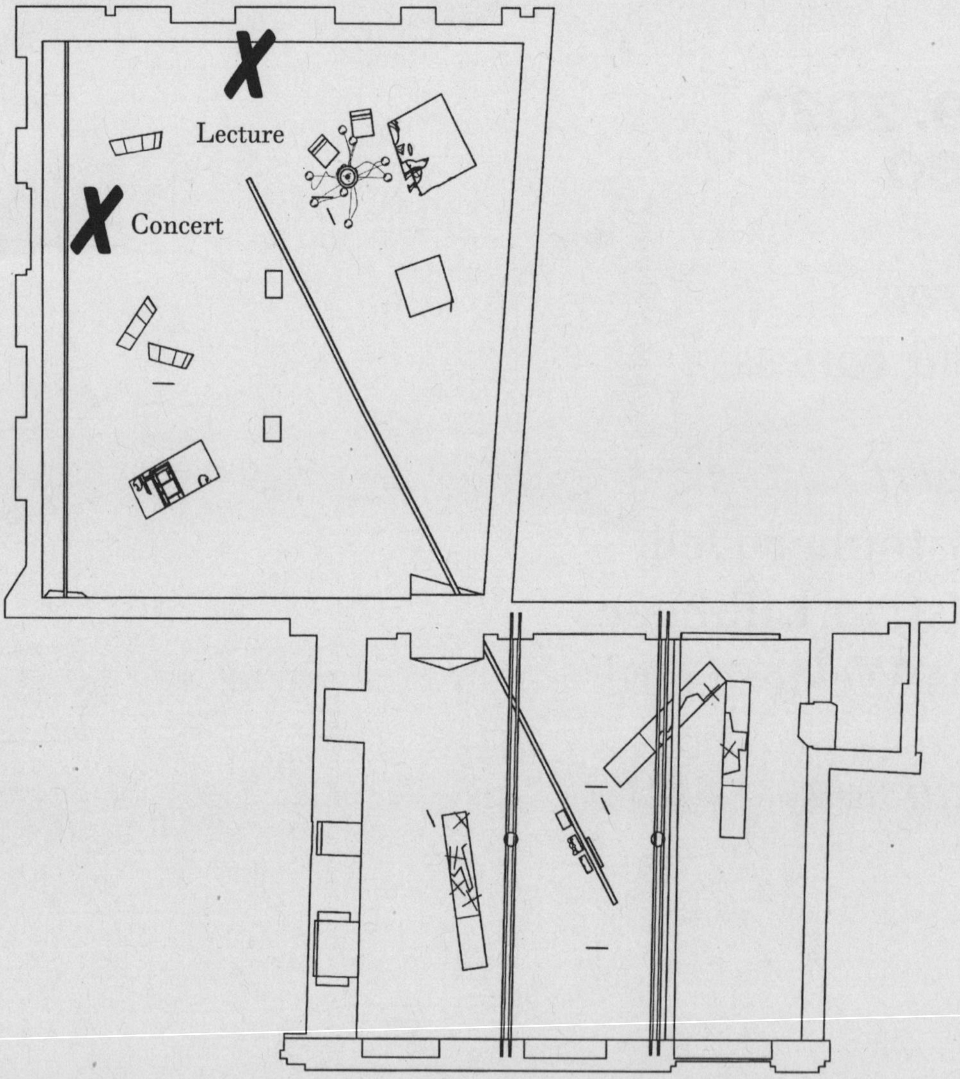

Intervention in die Ausstellung *Omer Abel – Architektonische Experimente in Material und Form* im Aedes Architekturforum, 29.8.–22.10.2020

Structure

In den 1950er Jahren erscheint in Europa eine neue ideologische Strömung, die sich anschickt, jegliche Weisen der Formgebung zu revolutionieren und Musik wie Architektur für immer zu verändern. Inspiriert durch die Entdeckungen der Linguistik und der Anthropologie zu Invarianten der Struktur von Sprache und Kultur, wendet der Strukturalismus Struktur auf die Formgebung an. In Absetzbewegung zu Funktionalismus und Formalismus, die Form von einem Außen her bestimmt hatten und von diesem Gerüst gefangen schienen, sucht der Strukturalismus neue künstlerische Ansätze und Ausdrucksformen zu finden, indem er Form von ihrem Innern her denkt.

Der Begriff »Struktur« meint von nun an die Menge von Relationen, welche Elemente eines organisationalen Feldes miteinander verknüpfen. Eine strukturelle Relation zwischen unterschiedlichen Elementen ist dann so bestimmt, dass aus der Veränderung eines Elements die entsprechende Veränderung des anderen Elements resultiert. Z.B. kann in der Musik ein Motiv in Bezug auf die Form des Werks als strukturelles Element gelten, in der Architektur etwa eine Nutzung im Bezug auf die Akteurskonstellation einer Gebäude-Straßensituation.

Fasziniert ist der Strukturalismus von der Autonomie des Verfahrens und der Methode, die nur auf die innere Relationalität des Werks abhebt. Struktur bedeutet ihm – in der Musik ebenso wie in der Architektur – das neuartige und überraschende Verfahren einer Matrix an Kombinationen und Verschaltungen, in denen sich jeweilige parametrische Bestimmungen zum Ton oder zu einer Gruppe von Tönen respektive einem Gebäude oder einer Gruppe von Gebäuden herausbilden.

Ebenso bahnbrechend ist dem strukturellen Verfahren das Gebundensein des Arbeitens an die radikale Dekomposition. Das meint nichts anderes, als dass die Arbeit alle Voraussetzungen und Gegebenheiten auf Null setzt. In der Musik verlangt dies, alle Phänomene auf ihre abstrakten Parameter wie etwa Dynamik, Tonhöhe, Klangfarbe oder Tempo zu reduzieren. Die strukturalistische Architektur hingegen widersetzt sich formalistischen und funktionalitischen Konventionen, in dem sie die Gegebenheiten bestimmter räumlicher Situationen auf typologische Raster und Parameter wie bauliche Dichte, Nutzungen, Formen und Akteure und bauliche Regelwerke wie etwa baugesetzliche Normen zurückführt.

Ob Musik oder Architektur, in beiden Disziplinen entspringt der Nullpunktsetzung die Option zur Re-Kombinatorik sowie zum Neu-Versammeln. In aller wünschenswerter Klarheit hat die serielle Verfahrensweise der musikalischen Spätmoderne deutlich gemacht, wie Parameter seriell in Reihen diagrammatisch notiert und katalogisiert werden, um sie dann in unterschiedlichen Formen zusammenzusetzen. Dergleichen geschieht in den seriell-strukturellen Studien der Architektur der 1950er und 1960er Jahre, die stets auf das Prinzipielle des Raumzusammensetzens abheben. Man denke an Hermann Hertzbergers berühmte Untersuchung zu Übergangsräumen zwischen privat und öffentlich, die er 1959 in der niederländischen Zeitschrift *Forum* publiziert. Es handelt sich um die photographische Studie von verschiedenen Kombinationen gestapelter Streichholzschachteln. Von der Grundlage räumlicher Zellen ausgehend, reicht die seriell angeordnete Reihe vom geschlossenen Block bis zur mäandernden Textur. Der Experimentalaufbau zeigt einerseits, wie sich durch die Neuordnung einfacher Standardelemente Übergangszonen zwischen privat und öffentlich schaffen lassen. Andererseits fragt sie in räumlicher Hinsicht, ob nicht in solchen Übergangszonen Flächen der Gemeinschaft entstehen, die die parametrische Dichotomie von privat vs. öffentlich neu beleuchten; beispielhaft für eine solche nicht-hierarchische Verschaltung von Räumen ist der 1960–1962 vollzogene Ausbau der Firma LinMij in Amsterdam. Auf dem Dach der Wäschefabrik aus dem Anfang des 20. Jahrhunderts verortet, waren die neu errichteten Nähateliers als erste Phase einer das Gebäude überwuchernden strukturellen Erweiterung gedacht, zu der es jedoch nie kam. Hertzbergers Entwurf nutzte eine Fertigteilkonstruktion um Raumkonfigurationen zu schaffen, die unterschiedliche Nutzungen oder Programme aufnehmen können. Formal konzipiert der Entwurf die Erweiterung indes als abgeschlossene Einheit, so als ob Elemente, erst wenn sie autonom seien, unterschiedliche Funktionen erfüllen könnten.

Konsequent weitergedacht kehrt eine solche Verstärkung der Relationalität um, was Leon Battista Alberti einst in der Renaissance für die Stadt ersann: Die Stadt sollte wie ein Haus funktionieren. Dem Strukturalismus hingegen soll das Haus wie eine Stadt funktionieren. Dessen wohl bekanntestes Beispiel ist der Campus Dahlem der Freien Universität Berlin, entworfen von Candilis-Josic-Woods. Was diesen Gebäudetyp auszeichnet ist »eine spezifische Überlagerung von Mustern und Gebrauch und die Desintegration durch diese Vermischung.« (Smithson, 1974) Wer den Entwurf von Candilis-Josic-Woods betrachtet, sieht zunächst einen Grundriss mit einem regelmäßigen Raster. Beim näheren Hinsehen zeigt sich jedoch eine komplexere Schichtung und Verschiebung dieses Rasters, die auf der Grundlage der allgemeinen Ordnung eine differenzierte Wechselbeziehung zwischen den Bereichen des Gebäudes entfaltet. Dies geschieht beispielsweise durch die Schaffung von gerasterten Zonen, deren Abmessungen durch den Abstand ihrer Mittellinien von den zentralen Durchwegungsachsen des Gebäudes bestimmt werden. Gegenläufig zum Funktionalismus sucht der Entwurf starre Trennungen und Hierarchien zwischen den universitären Disziplinen aufzuheben und die Universität zu einer Plattform für einen gerechten und demokratischen Wissensaustausch zu machen. Wie man weiß, fanden besonders die flexiblen Verschaltstrukturen der Raumeinheiten des Entwurfs keine Umsetzung – das Gebäude blieb Passagenwerk. Gleichwohl sahen die Architekten die hier entworfene Mischung von Linienführung (tracés) und offenen Räumen (espaces ouverts) als universelle Fragestellung der Form, die über das spezifische Projekt sehr wohl hinausreicht: »Dieses Schema ist ein Versuch, strukturierende Prinzipien zu erschließen die auf die Organisation der gebauten Umwelt anzuwenden sind.« (Candilis, Josic, Woods, 1964)

Ein wirkmächtiges Beispiel der musikalischen Arbeit an und mit der Struktur ist Pierre Boulez' Werk *Structures I* für zwei Klaviere aus dem Jahr 1952. Alle kompositorische Arbeit geht hier vom vorsortierten Materialkatalog aus, der die Parameter Tonhöhe, Tondauer, Anschlagsart und Intensität in Reihen gliedert. Darüber hinaus strukturiert der Katalog auch die Reihenfolge der Reihen in einer Metastruktur. Der Verschaltmatrix von zwei Ziffernquadraten ordnet Boulez etwa die Tonhöhenreihe in Grundgestalt, Krebs, Umkehrung und Krebsumkehrung zu. Ziffernquadrat 1 enthält die Grundreihe in seiner ersten Quer- und Längsachse, dann folgen die Transpositionen der Reihe, die sich immer in ihrer Position an der Grundreihe orientieren. Gleiches unternimmt Ziffernquadrat 2 mit der Reihenumkehrung. Ziffernquadrat 1 gilt für die Tonhöhen von Klavier 1, die Reihenfolge der Reihennutzung aber folgt Ziffernquadrat 2. Für die Tondauern verfährt Boulez genau umgekehrt, während er die Lautstärkenreihen aus den Diagonalen der Ziffernquadrate ableitet. Dem Regelwerk erwächst so die Komposition Werk als abgeschlossene Form.

Der Komponist, der einen Ausweg aus der Serialität in die offene Form kannte, war Bruno Maderna. Wesentlich an Madernas Musik ist, dass sie innerhalb der Tonhöhenreihenbildung nicht bei der Fixierung der Ziffern auf die absoluten Tonhöhen stehen blieb. Wie sich an seinen umfangreichen, den Partituren vorausgehenden Studien ablesen lässt, bezog Maderna auch die Relation zwischen den Tonhöhenelementen in die Reihenkonstruktion ein. Dementsprechend beinhalten etwa Madernas Reihenkataloge zu *Improvvisazione 1*, komponiert von 1951–1952, spezifische Fluss-Diagramme, die geordnet in zwölf Zeilen eine Tonhöhenklasse mit 1 = A, 2 = B, 3 = Bb bis 12 = G# darstellen. Chronologisch von links nach rechts gelesen und mit einer Linienziehung verbunden, projizieren die zwölf Spalten eine dynamische Folge von Zeitpunkten. Weit entfernt, Serien nur auf die Verortung von Punkten entsprechenden Positionen der Matrix zu reduzieren, entwirft Maderna eine prozesshafte Topologie, die auch auf die Bestimmung der Linien zwischen den Positionen zurückgreift. Was Maderna hier gelingt, ist, geschlossene Serialität zugunsten einer neuen Technik serieller Permutation zu überwinden, die die Identität der Originalserie gewissermaßen auslöscht. Auch Madernas Formgebung rekurriert auf das verbindende Element einer Serie. Beim Erstellen der musikalischen Oberfläche jedoch kommt er zu besonderen diagrammatischen Katalogen, die jegliche Systeme sprengen. Man hat es hier mit einem neuen Konzept des Kontrapunkts und der Harmonie zu tun, die jetzt nicht mehr von der Überlagerung verschiedener kontrapunktischer Schichten (z. B. mehrerer Serien) oder der Vertikalisierung von Seriensegmenten herrührt, sondern vielmehr direkt aus der Permutationen der Serie hervorgeht. Am besten exemplifiziert ist diese Technik wohl in Madernas späten Werken, etwa *Ausstrahlung* (1971) und *Biogramma* (1972). Als offene Formen nehmen sie in jeder Aufführung eine neue Gestalt an – ohne indes auf Struktur zu verzichten. Madernas Werke fordern uns zur Frage auf: wie lässt sich heute das Unabgegoltene am »Verschalten« und am »ins Funktionieren kommen« von Strukturen denken?

Literatur

Georges Candilis, Alexis Josic, Shadrach Woods: »Berlin Free University«, in: *Le Carré Bleu* no. 1, 1964

Alison Smithson: »How to recognize and read mat-building«, in: *Architectural Design* no. 9, 1974

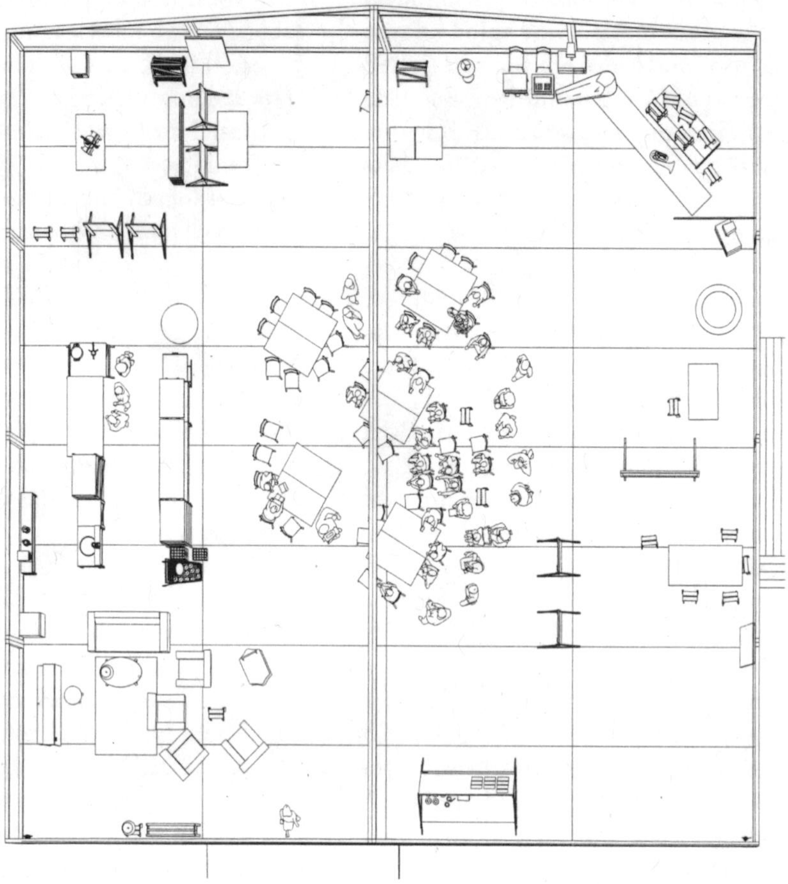

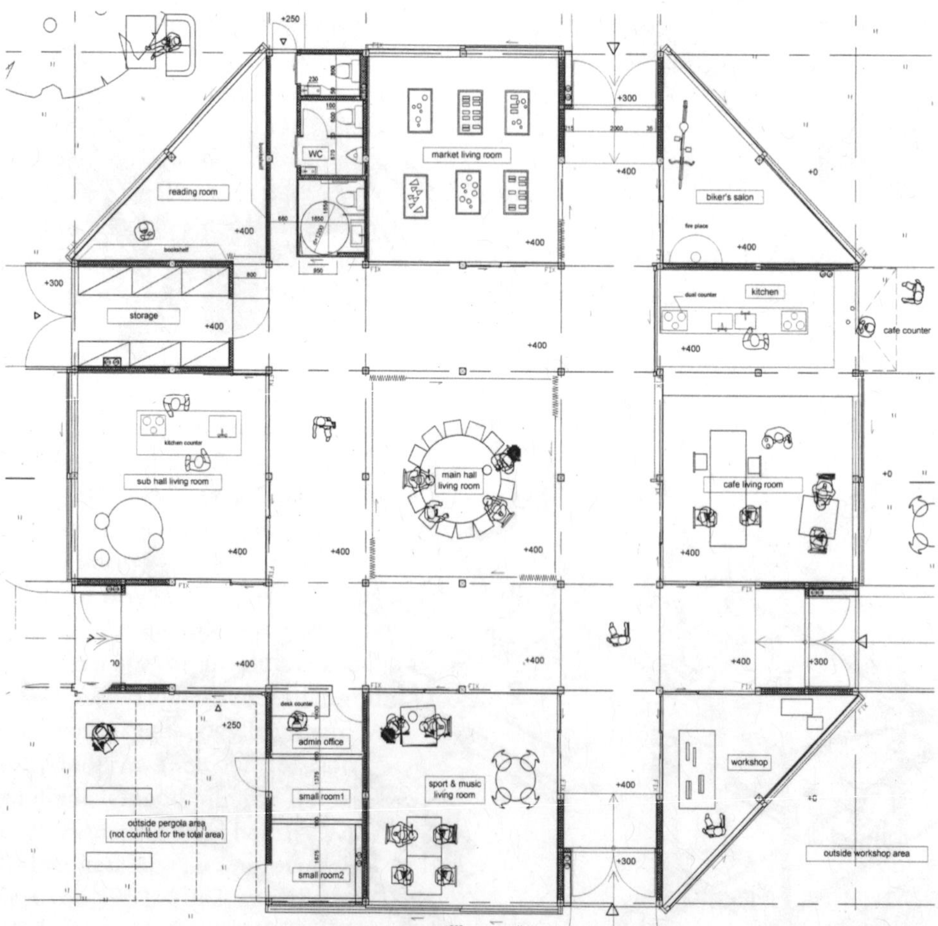

reading room
storage
WC
market living room
biker's salon
fire place
kitchen
dual counter
cafe counter
kitchen counter
sub hall living room
main hall living room
cafe living room
desk counter
admin office
small room1
small room2
sport & music living room
workshop
outside pergola area (not counted for the total area)
outside workshop area

INTERVALLSTRUKTUR:
60 = 3+3
60 = 12 × 5
60 = 3 × 20
60 = 6 × 10
33 = 5 + 7,5 + 3 + 4 + 0,5 + 1 + 4,5 + 1 + 3,5 + 3
MODES
CHORDS
REIHEN
MELODY
30 Akkorde (Anschläge) aus einer Gruppe von 6 Akkorden à 7 TÖNE
6x7=42
BASS aus einer Gruppe von 5 x 2 basierend auf A und Eb → 30 ANSCHLÄGE
MELODIE aus 60 Tönen

struktur 60

Rot

60 Töne: ein Melodiebogen aus 60 Tönen bis Doppelstrich

Intervallstruktur: Zwischensumme von 60 ist diesselbe wie von 33
33 setzt sich zusammen aus Quint 5+ grosse Sepitm 7,5+ kleine Terz 3+ Quart 4+
kleine Sekund 0,5+ grosse Sekund 1+ Tritonus 4,5+ grosse Sekund 1+ grosse Terz 3,5+ kleine Terz 3
Oktavierungen sind möglich

Blau

Bass besteht aus 5 Tönen in 2 Tonarten (A und Eb), 30 Töne bis Doppelstrich

Gelb

Akkorde sind aus einem Fond von 6 Akkorden
30 Anschläge bis Doppelstrich, Variation in der Anordnung

Grossstruktur:

1. Thema 15 Takte
2. Spiegelung des Themas 15 takte
3. Krebs der Spiegelung 15 Takte
4. Krebs des Themas 15 Takte

4x 15= 60
Thema Reprise(Melodie um ein sechzehntel verschoben)

S. 3
oben: *Building a Proposition for Future Activities, Closing Ceremony*, Rebecca Wall, Beyza Gürdogan, Research and Teaching Programme Urban Design, HCU Hamburg (2017)

unten: »Abwaschen«, aus: Rebecca Wall, Marius Töpfer: *Everyday Urban Design 6, Planung als Vektor, Skript und Sichtbarmachung. Projektarchäologie eines Begegnungshauses*, Berlin 2020, S. 96–97

S. 4
oben: »Auftakt Architektur-Workshop, Montag, 11.9.2017, 10:00 Uhr«, aus: Rebecca Wall, Marius Töpfer: *Everyday Urban Design 6, Planung als Vektor, Skript und Sichtbarmachung. Projektarchäologie eines Begegnungshauses*, Berlin 2020, S. 55

unten: Atelier Bow-Wow & Tamutso Ito, *The Bazaar × the Living Rooms* (2018)

S. 5
Christopher Dell: Melodie mit 60 Tönen (2001)

S. 6
Christopher Dell: Strukturmatrix zu Melodie mit 60 Tönen (2001)

Bernd Kniess ist Architekt und Stadtplaner. Seit 2008 ist er Professor für Urban Design an der HafenCity Universität Hamburg, verantwortlich für den Aufbau und die Leitung des interdisziplinären Masterprogramms Urban Design und die Durchführung von Realexperimenten in der Verbindung von Lehre, Forschung und Praxis wie bspw. der Universität der Nachbarschaften (2008–14), dem Begegnungshaus Poppenbüttel (2015–18), der Zukunftstadt Friedrichstadt (2016–22). Im Rahmen der Forschungsinitiative »Low-Budget-Urbanity« initiierte er das Projekt »Baumarkt 2.0. Praktiken und Materialitäten des urbanen Selbstbaus und der Sparsamkeit«.

Weitere Stationen seiner Tätigkeiten im Rahmen von Gastprofessuren sind BU Wuppertal, Tokyo Institute of Technology, University of the Witwatersrand Johannesburg, Cairo University, Escola da Cidade und USP in São Paolo. Derzeit hat er die Graham Willis Gastprofessur in Sheffield inne. Er ist Mitglied der Nordrhein-Westfälischen Akademie der Wissenschaften und der Künste.

Christopher Dell lebt und arbeitet als Theoretiker, Musiker und Komponist in Berlin. Studium der Philosophie, Musik, Komposition und Organisationsentwicklung an den Universitäten Darmstadt, Hilversum, Rotterdam, Boston und Kaiserslautern. Er lehrte Architekturtheorie u. a. an der Universität der Künste, Berlin und der Architectural Association, London und war Gastprofessor für Stadttheorie an der HCU Hamburg und der TU München. Sein Forschungsinteresse gilt Praxen und Organisationsverläufen der zeitgenössischen Stadt. Dell ist Gründer und Leiter des ifit, Institut für Improvisationstechnologie, Berlin. Dell gilt laut Reclam Jazzlexikon als der führende Vibraphonist Europas. Dell ist und war beteiligt an zahlreichen CD-Veröffentlichungen und Tourneen weltweit. Seine Arbeit wurde mit zahlreichen Preisen ausgezeichnet, wie z. B. dem Downbeat Allstar Award, Gary Burton Award, Preis der Deutschen Schallplattenkritik, Grammy Nominierung und Musikpreis der Stadt Darmstadt.

Christian Lillinger beginnt im Alter von 13 Jahren mit dem Schlagzeugspiel. Bereits als 16-Jähriger wird er 2000 an der Hochschule für Musik Carl Maria von Weber Dresden zugelassen und studiert dort bis 2004 bei Günter Baby Sommer und Michael Griener. Im Jahr 2000 ist Lillinger Preisträger des Internationalen Improvisationswettbewerb Leipzig. Seit 2002 besteht die intensive Zusammenarbeit im Trio HyperactiveKid (Philipp Gropper, Ronny Graupe, Christian Lillinger). 2008 folgt die Gründung der eigenen Band Christian Lillingers GRUND, mit der er intensiv seine eigenen Kompositionen umsetzt. Mit dieser Formation erscheint am 19. Januar 2018 *COR* auf dem von ihm gegründeten Label PLAIST. Er erhält 2013 ein Kompositionsstipendium der Stadt Berlin. 2016 erscheint der Dokumentarfilm *Gegen den Beat* von Regisseur Jan Bäumer auf 3SAT. 2017 wird Lillinger mit dem SWR Jazzpreis gekürt. Bis heute ist er auf etwa 80 Tonträgern zu hören. 2018 gründete er sein eigenes Label PLAIST, das bereits vier Produktionen vorzuweisen hat.

Jonas Westergaard aus Kopenhagen studierte am Rytmisk Musikkonservatorium. Seit den 1990er-Jahren arbeitet er in der dänischen und deutschen Jazz- und Improvisationsszene u. a. mit Christopher Dell, Benjamin Koppel, Christian Lillinger, Henrik Walsdorff, Marc Schmolling, im Trio Spoom (mit Ronny Graupe und Christian Lillinger), ferner mit Michael Wollny sowie den Formationen Delirium (u. a. mit Mikko Innanen) und Field (mit Oliver Steidle, Ronny Graupe und Uli Kempendorff). Im Bereich des Jazz war Westergaard zwischen 1997 und 2012 an 33 Aufnahmesessions beteiligt, außer den Genannten auch mit Jakob Bro, George Garzone, Søren Kjærgaard, Jesper Løvdal, Hans Ulrik, Petter Wettre und Jesper Zeuthen. Nachdem ihm 2006 ein Spezialpreis des Danmarks Radio verliehen worden war, nahm er mit einem Nonett das Album *Helgoland* (2008) mit Eigenkompositionen auf.

Die Reihe **dialogue concerts: conceptual research on architecture and music** präsentiert zum 40-jährigen Jubiläum des Aedes Architekturforums ein medienpluralistisches Format, das die Erforschung des Städtischen neu in den Blick nimmt. Architektonisches Arbeiten tritt in den Dialog mit der Praxis der Musik.

Angelegt als Montage von Vortrag, Konzert und Diskussion untersucht *dialogue concerts* an sechs Veranstaltungen, wie der Stadtraum unser Miteinander bestimmt. Hier ist Stadt nicht als fixiertes Objekt definiert, sondern als dynamische und kollektive Konstellation, die performativ produziert wird.

Kuratiert vom Vibraphonisten, Komponisten und Stadttheoretiker Christopher Dell tritt *dialogue concerts* als künstlerische Aussage sowie als kritisches Dispositiv auf. Ab Dezember 2019 sind internationale Architekt*innen und Musiker*innen eingeladen, ein Jahr lang verfahrensstrategische Zusammenhänge über Disziplingrenzen hinweg zu thematisieren. Ausgehend von Fragen der Medialität, Körperlichkeit, Interaktion, Materialität, Struktur und Transformation entfaltet *dialogue concerts* einen diskursiven Raum, der die gesellschaftliche Relevanz beider Disziplinen auf neue Weise sichtbar zu machen sucht.

Konzept/Moderation: Christopher Dell
Organisatorische Projektleitung: Saori Kanemaki
Gestaltung: Helmut Völter
Controlling: Melanie Rossmann
Öffentlichkeitsarbeit: Ari Kanemaki

Das Team *dialogue concerts* dankt dem Aedes Architekturforum herzlich für die freundliche Kooperation, besonderer Dank geht an Kristin Feireiss, Hans-Jürgen Commerell, Christine Meierhofer, Mathias Schnell und Dunya Bouchi.

Cover: Walter Klauser, *Die Entwicklung der Raum-Auffassung beim Kinde. Eine Untersuchung anhand von Kinder-Zeichnungen* [Dissertation], Zürich 1916, S. 100

dialogue concerts

1 *Mediality* 12. 12. 2019
2 *Interaction* 6. 2. 2020
3 *Transformation*
4 *Structure* 17. 9. 2020
5 *Corporality* 11. 12. 2020, 18.30 Uhr
Vortrag: Tabea Michaelis, Ben Pohl, Denkstatt sàrl
Konzert: Christopher Dell, N. N.
6 *Materiality*

Aedes Architecture Forum
enw
ifit Institut für Improvisationstechnologie
Senatsverwaltung für Kultur und Europa | be Berlin
MUSIKFONDS
Gefördert vom Musikfonds e. V. mit Projektmitteln der Beauftragten der Bundesregierung für Kultur und Medien.

dialogue concerts

5

conceptual research on architecture and music

Corporeality

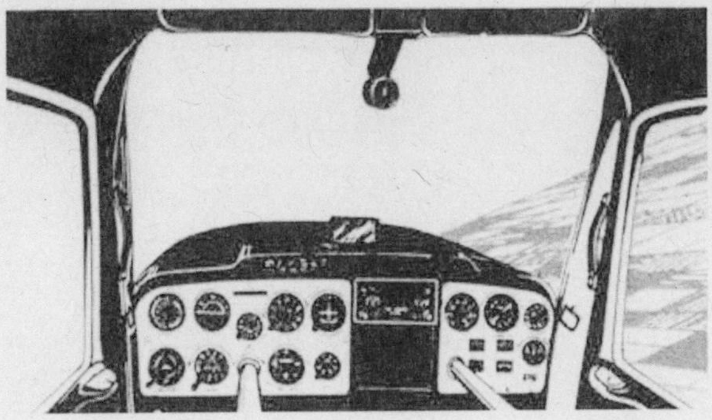

20. 4. 2021
18:30

Vortrag
Christopher Dell

Konzert
Chatschatur Kanajan
Karen Lorenz
Mathis Mayr
Sarah Saviet

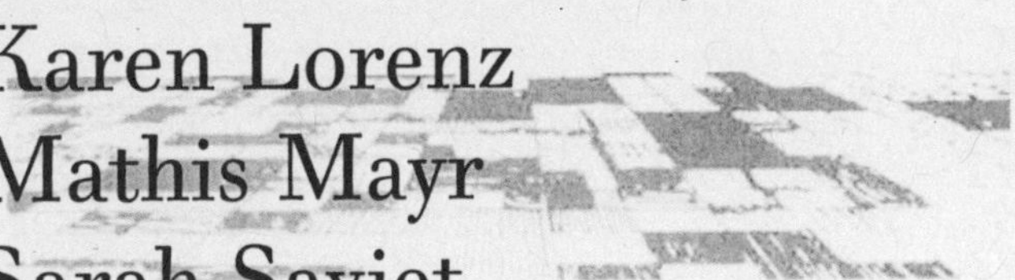

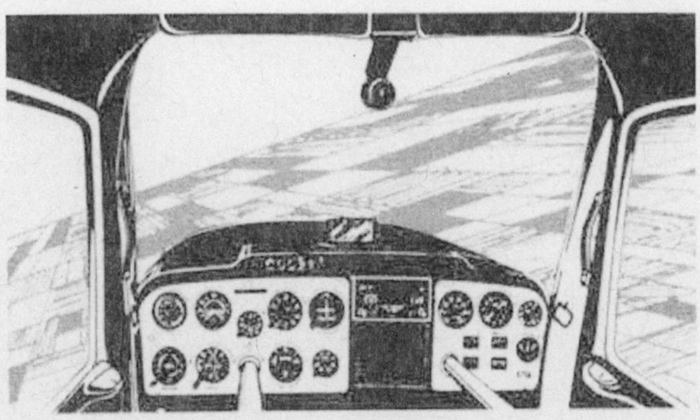

Diskussion
denkstatt sàrl

Aedes Architekturforum

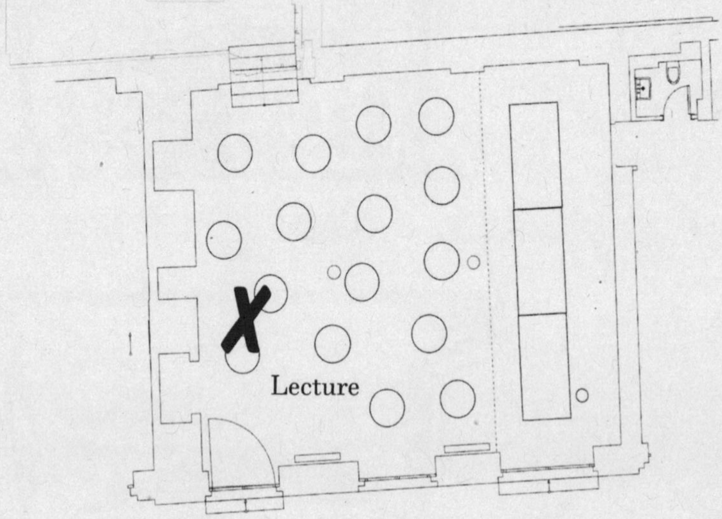

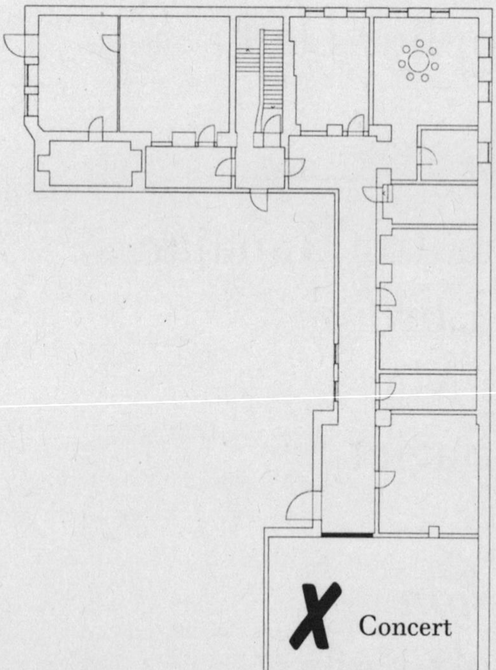

Intervention in die Ausstellung
HUMAN SCALE *REMEASURED*
(16. Januar – 20. Mai 2021)

Corporeality – Körperlichkeit

Unter Körper verstehe ich einerseits den menschlichen Leib, andererseits ein Ding. Der entscheidende Unterschied zwischen beiden ist klar: Um ein Ding kann ich herumgehen, um meinen Leib nicht. Der Leib ist mir kein Äußeres, wie das Ding. Indes, wo mein Leib mein Sein mit und als Welt ist, so geht er nicht in dem physisch erlebten Körper auf. Der Leib ist Überschuss. Er scheint sich beständig meiner Reflexion zu entziehen. Vielleicht ist er mir am gegenwärtigsten, wenn ich etwas tue.

Im Hinblick auf das Ergründen der Dinge bedeutet Körper, etwa in der Geometrie, jedes begrenzte dreidimensionale Gebilde. Mit dieser Deutung klingt jene Idee des Behälters an, die sich als allgemeiner Ausdruck für die Körper der Dinge eingebürgert hat. Ich sage ›Ich gehe in der Stadt spazieren‹ und denke mir gewöhnlich die Stadt als einen Behälter, ›in‹ dem man sich bewegt. Topologisch resultiert daraus eine Setzung, die einen Unterschied zwischen einem Körperinneren und einem Körperäußern behauptet. Ich spaziere in der Stadt und verlasse sie, wenn ich die ausgeschilderte Stadtgrenze überschreite. Eine solche zunächst aufs Ding bezogene Auffassung wirkt auf die der lebenden Körper zurück. Verstanden in diesem Sinn, denke ich zum Beispiel den menschlichen Körper als eine gegenüber einer Umwelt abgeschlossene Einheit – auch wenn dies der weiter oben angerissenen Deutung der Leiblichkeit widerspricht.

Die Idee des Körpers als Behälter spiegelt sich auch im Architektur- und Städtebaudiskurs wieder. Zwei Dimensionen des Körpers haben hier ihren Platz gefunden: Es ist von Baukörpern die Rede, wenn man von Gebäuden spricht. Gleichzeitig können gebaute Körper menschliche Körper wie auch Dinge in sich aufnehmen, die zueinander und zum Gebäude in Beziehung stehen. Die moderne Stadtplanung versteht demgemäß die Stadt als einen Körper, der Stadtteile enthält, die in Funktionen zusammenwirken.

Entlang dieser Linien ist seit der Renaissance das Verhältnis, das der menschliche Körper zur Architektur unterhält, von besonderem Interesse. Hinsichtlich der Fähigkeit, Raum zu denken und darzustellen, liefert die Wiederentdeckung und Kanonisierung der *Zehn Bücher über Architektur* von Vitruv den zentralen Motor einer dramatischen und verunsichernden geistesgeschichtlichen Zäsur. Kein Architekturtraktat der Renaissance kommt ohne jenen Verweis auf die von der Antike vollzogenen Transfers zwischen dem menschlichen Körper und der Architektur aus, die Vitruvs Bücher der Nachwelt als Wissensform bezeugen. Zwei Modi des Raumdenkens bilden hier das Herzstück: einerseits der Anthropomorphismus, der den menschlichen Körper als Figur interpretiert und andererseits die Anthropometrik, die die numerische Übersetzung der menschlichen Körper in Nummern (etwa in Elle, Fuß, Hand), Proportionen und geometrische Körper vollzieht.

Wie bekanntermaßen Vitruvs Schriften ohne visuelle Darstellungen auskommen, so schafft die Renaissance in deren Wiederaufnahme prominente Illustrationen dessen, was der römische Architekturtheoretiker einst als *homo ad quadratum* und *homo ad circulum* wie folgt definiert hatte: »Ferner ist natürlicherweise der Mittelpunkt des Körpers der Nabel. Liegt nämlich ein Mensch mit gespreizten Armen und Beinen auf dem Rücken, und setzt man die Zirkelspitze an der Stelle des Nabels ein und schlägt einen Kreis, dann werden von dem Kreis die Fingerspitzen beider Hände und die Zehenspitzen berührt. Ebenso, wie sich am Körper ein Kreis ergibt, wird sich auch die Figur eines Quadrats an ihm finden. Wenn man nämlich von den Fußsohlen bis zum Scheitel Maß nimmt und wendet dieses Maß auf die ausgestreckten Hände an, so wird sich die gleiche Breite und Höhe ergeben, wie bei Flächen, die nach dem Winkelmaß quadratisch angelegt sind.«[1] Derlei modular gedachte Raumordnung schreibt sich mit der Neuzeit in eine anthropomorph konstruierte Weltproduktion ein, die die europäische Raumrevolution und ihre praktischen und epistemologischen Spannungen – wie etwa die zwischen humanistischem Postulat und mechanistischer Technik – von nun an begleitet.

Wie man weiß, bindet im frühen 20. Jahrhundert Le Corbusiers Proportionslehre vom Modulor[2] (1948) die Figur des Menschen in das modulare Doppelquadrat eines morphenden goldenen Schnittes ein. Ziel dessen ist jedoch nicht die Wiederkehr anthropomorpher Architektur. Vielmehr wechselt letztere über ins Register einer anthropometrischen Organisation, die der normierten Typisierung in vorgefertigten Bauteilen entspricht. Es ist jetzt die industrielle Standardisierung, die es erlaubt, eine minimale Anzahl verwendeter Einheiten zu maximalen Variantenanzahl zu kombinieren, das was bei Le Corbusier »Modularkoordination« heißt. Die moderne Stadt ist ein »Neues Schauspiel.«[3] Den neuen Maßen, die nicht mehr auf der mechanischen Komposition Durands beruhen, sondern sich an der »mechanischen Harmonisierung«[4] orientieren, liefert das von Edgar Varese in die zeitgenössische Musik eingebrachte Glissando eine neue Tonleiter. Sie soll jetzt in der Lage sein, die Zerrissenheit der »Arbeit der Menschen« [5] zu beheben.

Demgegenüber erscheint mit Ernst Neuferts bereits 1936 in erster Auflage erschienener *Bauentwurfslehre*[6] – der wohl weltweit einflussreichsten Baulehre – der *homo ad quadratum* ohne unterlegtes *grid* zurück, jetzt als wohnender Produzent, standardisiert und normalisiert im Rahmenwerk industrieller Warenproduktion. Was sich hier offenbart, ist nicht nur die bereits im 19. Jahrhundert sich manifestierende Warenwerdung des Wohnraums, sondern auch die biopolitische Inwerksetzung des Normalen am Wohnen als gesellschaftlicher Regulierungsapparat. Hygiene und sanitäre Ordnung, Lichteinfall und Luftzirkulation dominieren jetzt die Diskurse um die Typisierung des Lebensraums, in der Überwachung und Anordnung der einzelnen Körper und die biopolitische Kontrolle der Bevölkerung konvergieren. Orientiert am normativen Gerüst der Kernfamilie, sorgt die funktionalistische Vermessung der Körper an Stellflächen, Abstand und Bewegungsflächen für das Parallellaufen der Naturalisierung des Wohnraums und der Naturalisierung des Sozialen, deren kleinste raumpolitische statistische Einheit der »Haushalt« ist. Man kann sagen, dass diese körperliche Normierung einer der entscheidenden Punkte ist, gegen die die feministische Bewegung der 1960er und -70er Jahre mit dem Slogan »Das Private ist politisch« den weiblichen Körper als differenzierendes Performativ in Stellung bringt, während sie gleichzeitig die Kernfamilie als normatives Lebensmodell grundsätzlich in Frage stellt.

Was aber ist heute – wo, egal ob im bezahlbaren oder im Luxuswohnen, noch immer die Kernfamilie als Grundlebensmodell des Wohnungsbaus herhält und die funktionalistische Bauordnung die Ordnung der Stadt bestimmt – aus der Körperlichkeit geworden? Ließe sie sich in neuer Weise wiedergewinnen? Und welche Formen der Politik und welche gesellschaftlichen Praxen würden den neuen Weisen der Körperlichkeit entspringen? Würde nicht, wenn beispielsweise statt Funktion der Gebrauch ins Zentrum des Interesses rückte, die Vielfältigkeit und Heterogenität von Körperlichkeit in den Blick kommen? Oder wie wäre Stadt neu zu denken, wenn keine Körperlichkeit repräsentativ wäre? Bestünde darin nicht gerade nicht das Ende, sondern die Öffnung des Politischen?

Literatur

1 *Vitruvii De architectura libri decem – Zehn Bücher über Architektur.* Hg. v. Curt Fensterbusch, Darmstadt 1964, 3. Buch, 1. Kapitel. Von den Symmetrien der Tempel 3. Absatz.

2 Le Corbusier: *Der Modulor. Darstellung eines in Architektur und Technik allgemein anwendbaren harmonischen Maßes im menschlichen Maßstab.* Stuttgart: Cotta 1953 (Teil 1) und 1958.

3 ebda., S. 44.

4 ebda., S. 54.

5 ebda., S. 17.

6 Ernst Neufert: *Bauentwurfslehre. Grundlagen, Normen, Vorschriften über Anlage, Bau, Gestaltung, Raumbedarf, Raumbeziehungen, Maße für Gebäude, Räume, Einrichtungen, Geräte mit dem Menschen als Maß und Ziel; Handbuch für den Baufachmann, Bauherrn, Lehrenden und Lernenden; mit Tabellen,* Wiesbaden: Springer 2016 (1936).

B
A

BHF
Birs

trb
c.l.b.
arco
al.b.
freier
sul pont
ord
pizz
Star Nr. 143, 10 Systeme®

FORMBLOCK 32 a) 22. 2. 2021

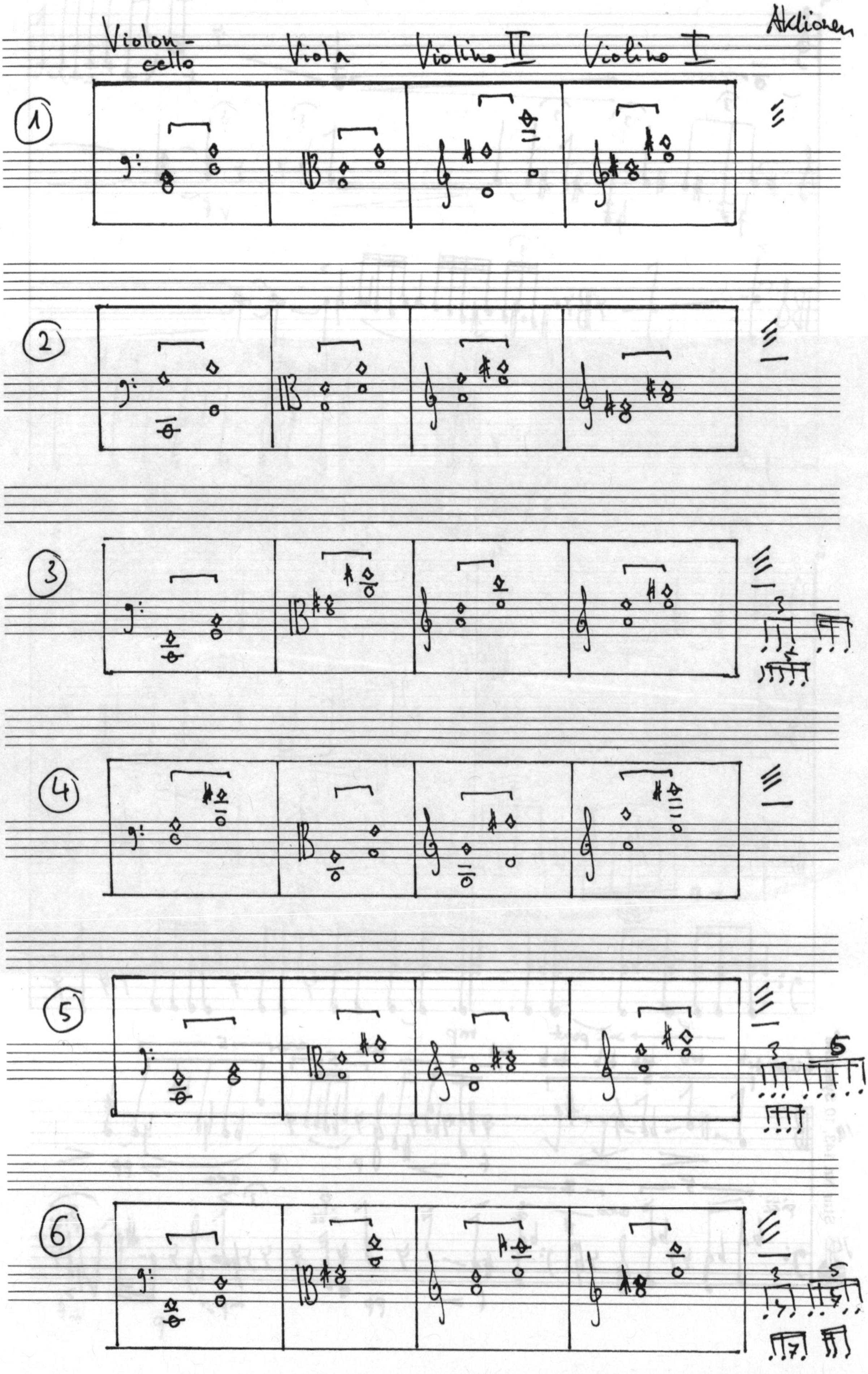

S. 3
Soziometrisches Diagramm
»Performatives Vorgehen«,
denkstatt sàrl, »Zentrale Pratteln«

S. 4
Zukunftskonferenz/Zukunftswerkstatt,
denkstatt sàrl, »Zentrale Pratteln«

S. 5
Christopher Dell: Streichquartett No. 2, S. 27
(2000)

S. 6
Christopher Dell: Formblock 32 a (2021)

Christopher Dell lebt und arbeitet als Theoretiker, Musiker und Komponist in Berlin. Studium der Philosophie, Musik, Komposition und Organisationsentwicklung an den Universitäten Darmstadt, Hilversum, Rotterdam, Boston und Kaiserslautern. Er lehrte Architekturtheorie u.a. an der Universität der Künste, Berlin und der Architectural Association, London und war Gastprofessor für Stadttheorie an der HCU Hamburg und der TU München. Sein Forschungsinteresse gilt Praxen und Organisationsverläufen der zeitgenössischen Stadt. Dell ist Gründer und Leiter des ifit, Institut für Improvisationstechnologie, Berlin. Dell gilt laut Reclam Jazzlexikon als der führende Vibraphonist Europas. Dell ist und war beteiligt an zahlreichen CD-Veröffentlichungen und Tourneen weltweit. Seine Arbeit wurde mit zahlreichen Preisen ausgezeichnet, wie z.B. dem Downbeat Allstar Award, Gary Burton Award, Preis der Deutschen Schallplattenkritik, Grammy Nominierung und Musikpreis der Stadt Darmstadt.

Chatschatur Kanajan, geboren 1971 in Moskau, ist seit 1998 Mitglied des ensembles mosaik. Er studierte Violine in Moskau, Dresden und Berlin, unter anderem bei Marina Jaschwili und Ilan Gronich. Es folgte ein Dirigier- und Kompositionsstudium bei Friedrich Goldmann an der Universität der Künste Berlin. Kanajan war Stipendiat der Akademie Schloss Solitude in Stuttgart und der Cité Internationale des Arts in Paris und erhielt den 1. Preis für Interpretation beim Hanns Eisler Preis für Komposition und Interpretation. Er war von 1997 bis 2007 Mitglied des Kairos Quartetts, seither ist er regelmäßiger Gast bei der musikFabrik, beim Neuen Ensemble und beim Ensemble Insomnio (NL). Mit dem ensemble mosaik gastierte er bei vielen der wichtigsten internationalen Festivals für zeitgenössische Musik und wirkte bei zahlreichen Rundfunkaufnahmen und CD-Produktionen mit.

Karen Lorenz ist Gründungsmitglied des ensembles mosaik, mit dem sie seit 25 Jahren bei vielen der wichtigsten internationalen Festivals für zeitgenössische Musik auftritt. An der Universität der Künste Berlin studierte sie im Hauptfach Viola bei Rainer Kimstedt und Hartmut Rohde, Barockgeige bei Christine Busch und absolvierte zusätzlich das 1. Staatsexamen für das Lehramt Musik. Darauf folgte ein Kammermusikstudium beim Alban Berg Quartett an der Hochschule für Musik in Köln. Von 1999 bis 2002 war Lorenz Gründungsmitglied des Berliner Athena Quartetts mit dem sie 2001 den 3. Preis und den Publikumspreis beim Concours de Genève gewann. Neben der zeitgenössischen Musik ist ein zweiter Schwerpunkt die Alte Musik, der sie sich unter anderem mit der Berliner capella vitalis und der Merseburger Hofmusik widmet.

Der Cellist **Mathis Mayr,** geboren 1972, ist seit 2008 Mitglied des ensemble mosaik. Er widmet sich hauptsächlich der Neuen und improvisierten Musik, mit speziellem Interesse für Mikrotonalität und traditionellen musikalischen Traditionen verschiedener ethnischer Herkunft. Er spielt außerdem Oud, Viella und Viola da Gamba mit Interesse an experimenteller elektronischer Rockmusik und historischer Aufführungspraxis. Gemeinsam mit Sebo Flaig (Percussion) und Bastian Duncker (Saxophon/Ney) gründete er die Band »Pain Perdu«; Kammermusikalisch spielt er regelmäßig mit Antonis Anissegos (Klavier), dem Synthesizer- Krautrocker Jochen Irmler, den Komponisten Carl-Friedrich Oesterhelt und Richard van Schoor, Jongsuk Kim (Klavier) und im Trio mit Ernst Surberg und Liping Ting (Performance, Vocal) zusammen.

Tabea Michaelis ist Staudengärtnerin, diplomierte Landschaftsarchitektin und M.Sc. Urban Designerin. Nach dem Diplom in Landschaftsarchitektur an der Technischen Hochschule Rapperswil (CH) arbeitete sie für verschiedene Schweizer Landschafts-/Architekturbüros und als wissenschaftliche Mitarbeiterin am Institut IRAP im Forschungsprojekt »zone*imaginaire – Zwischennutzungen in Industriearealen«. In ihrer Forschungsarbeit »Programm Möglichkeitsraum« setzt sie sich mit der Fragestellung gegenwärtiger Möglichkeitsräume auf der Hamburger Elbinsel Wilhelmsburg auseinander. Neben ihrer Berufspraxis bei denkstatt sàrl unterrichtet sie als Gastdozentin an verschiedenen Schweizer Hochschulen, hält Vorträge und forscht zur Fragestellung kooperativer Gestaltungsprozesse. Bei B/IAS engagiert sie sich für die Vermittlung von kooperativen Gestaltungsprozessen, Prozess-Architekturen und Freiraumstrategien.

Ben Pohl hat einen handwerklichen, einen sozialwissenschaftlichen und einen gestalterischen Ausbildungshintergrund. Neben Studium und freier Berufspraxis in Berlin und Hamburg, war Ben Pohl im Zeitraum von 2010 bis 2015 als Lehrbeauftragter und wissenschaftlicher Mitarbeiter am Lehr- und Forschungsbereich Urban Design der HafenCity Universität und der »Universität der Nachbarschaften« (UdN) in Hamburg tätig. In seiner Berufspraxis verbindet er soziologisch-analytische Zugangsweisen zu Stadt, mit Werkzeugen und Techniken aus Architektur, Design, Fotografie und Film. Seit September 2016 arbeitet er im Team der denkstatt sàrl in Basel in den Kernbereichen »Sozialräumliche Entwicklungskonzepte«, »Dialogformate« und »Urbane Kommunikation«. Seit 2018 engagiert er sich bei B/IAS – Basel Institut für angewandte Stadtforschung.

Sarah Saviet ist amerikanische Violinistin aus Berlin. Sie ist Mitglied des ensemble mosaik Berlin und Gründungsmitglied des Saviet/Houston-Duos und des Londoner Riot Ensemble. Saviet war Gastkünstlerin der Universität der Künste Berlin, Huddersfield University, Manhattan School of Music, Goldsmiths University of London und Harvard University. Vor kurzem erschien ihre Einspielung des Violinkonzerts Speak, Be Silent von Liza Lim mit dem Riot Ensemble beim Label HCR/NMC Recordings. Zu ihren nächsten Veröffentlichungen zählen Portrait-CDs der Komponisten Evan Johnson und Joseph Lake, eine Solo-CD bei Coviello Classics sowie ein Duo-Album mit Werken für Klavier, Violine und E-Bow, die in Zusammenarbeit mit Joseph Houston komponiert wurden.

Die Reihe **dialogue concerts: conceptual research on architecture and music** präsentiert zum 40-jährigen Jubiläum des Aedes Architekturforums ein medienpluralistisches Format, das die Erforschung des Städtischen neu in den Blick nimmt. Architektonisches Arbeiten tritt in den Dialog mit der Praxis der Musik.

Angelegt als Montage von Vortrag, Konzert und Diskussion untersucht *dialogue concerts* an sechs Veranstaltungen, wie der Stadtraum unser Miteinander bestimmt. Hier ist Stadt nicht als fixiertes Objekt definiert, sondern als dynamische und kollektive Konstellation, die performativ produziert wird.

Kuratiert vom Vibraphonisten, Komponisten und Stadttheoretiker Christopher Dell tritt *dialogue concerts* als künstlerische Aussage sowie als kritisches Dispositiv auf. Ab Dezember 2019 sind internationale Architekt*innen und Musiker*innen eingeladen, ein Jahr lang verfahrensstrategische Zusammenhänge über Disziplingrenzen hinweg zu thematisieren. Ausgehend von Fragen der Medialität, Körperlichkeit, Interaktion, Materialität, Struktur und Transformation entfaltet *dialogue concerts* einen diskursiven Raum, der die gesellschaftliche Relevanz beider Disziplinen auf neue Weise sichtbar zu machen sucht.

Konzept/Moderation: Christopher Dell
Organisatorische Projektleitung: Saori Kanemaki
Gestaltung: Helmut Völter
Controlling: Melanie Rossmann
Öffentlichkeitsarbeit: Ari Kanemaki

Das Team *dialogue concerts* dankt dem Aedes Architekturforum herzlich für die freundliche Kooperation, besonderer Dank geht an Kristin Feireiss, Hans-Jürgen Commerell, Christine Meierhofer, Mathias Schnell und Dunya Bouchi.

Cover: Cessna Pilot Center: *Professional Manual of Flight,* 1975, S. 12–25

dialogue concerts

1	*Mediality*	12. 12. 2019
2	*Interaction*	6. 2. 2020
3	*Transformation*	14. 8. 2021
4	*Structure*	17. 9. 2020
5	*Corporality*	20. 4. 2021
6	*Materiality*	9. 9. 2021, 18:30 Lecture: Ton Maton Concert: Christopher Dell, Lotte Anker, Sofia Eftychidou

Aedes Architecture Forum
enw
ifit Institut für Improvisationstechnologie
Senatsverwaltung für Kultur und Europa | be Berlin
MUSIKFONDS
Gefördert vom Musikfonds e. V. mit Projektmitteln der Beauftragten der Bundesregierung für Kultur und Medien.

dialogue concerts

6

conceptual research on architecture and music

Materiality

9. 9. 2021
18:30

Lecture
Ton Matton

Concert
Lotte Anker,
Sofia Eftychidou,
Christopher Dell

Discussion

Aedes Architecture Forum

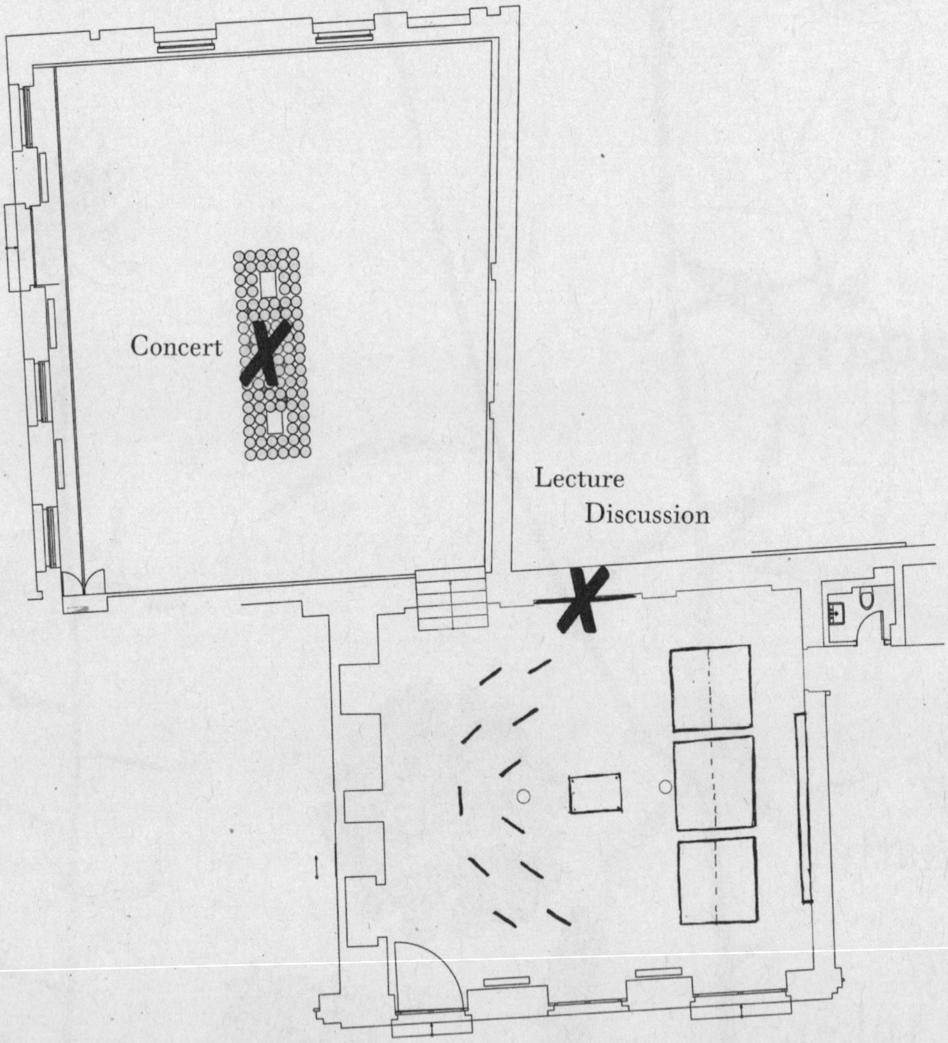

Intervention in the Aedes exhibition spaces of Kéré Architects, Berlin: *Arbre à Palabres*, and Ursula Schulz-Dornburg: *Vanished Landscapes* (17 July – 9 September 2021)

Materiality

'What matters?' – Posed ever so often, this seemingly universal question might touch several realms: the ethical, political as well as the epistemological or the ontological. In all of these realms, the question of what matters relates to inquiries on the material constitution of humans and non-humans, and about the way they exist as bodily and sensually perceivable phenomena.

In the discipline of music, every acoustic phenomenon can become musical material, but any acoustic phenomenon as such is not yet musical material. Being at hand, it has to be framed, contextualized and formally integrated into a composition. This explains, why the definition of material in music is a historically and culturally situated one. During the epochs and across cultures, different acoustic phenomena have been chosen as musical material, be it tone pitches (in form of rows, modes or scales), tone durations, dynamics, sound colours to mention a few. No musical material can be described as being "natural" or "authentic" or "found" for its catalogue and canon is always socially produced. In this sense, musical material is the compositionally framed phenomenon of sound and duration. That a phenomenon, such as a tone, can be deconstructed in parameters has been demonstrated vividly by the late modernist serialism. Today, for one who wants to compose, each parameter, be it pitch, duration, sound colour or dynamic, is in principal on equal level. Consequently, musical composition can be defined as the choice and the organization of musical material. Analogue to music, one can say, that also in the discipline of architecture no material is found as such. Even wood, stone and other so-called "natural materials" are subject to transformation in the architectural composition process. Concrete may be seen as an example of how, through a remix of materials, the question of properties such as resistance to water is tackled. Whether in music or in architecture, materials and their properties are always subject to social construction, whereas materiality can be coined as the relationship between a phenomenon and human practise.

Materialism of the Ornament.
Truth in Modern Architecture and Music

The moment Hegel declared in his *Aesthetics*, that the unity of inner meaning and external shape of architecture had become obsolete, marked a deep shock for the architectural discipline in the early 19th century. In the eyes of Hegel, architecture – undermined by the classicist will to use and to support a strict separation of means and ends – is bound to decline: "It cannot be numbered amongst the proper forms of art." (Hegel 1975, 423) In these terms, architecture as an art that was once symbolic in essence had now been degraded to pure ornament. As is known, it was Gottfried Semper who heroically countered this tendency by introducing a materialist notion of ornament to architecture, and thereby changing the meaning of architectural material itself. Semper's first move was to reintroduce the ornament as logical and truthful bodily display. The second move followed as a consequence: according to Semper, it is the will to material adornment that fundamentally distinguishes the human from the animal. "By adorning anything, be it alive or inanimate, I bestow on it the right of individual life. By making it the center of relations that pertain to it alone, I elevate it to the rank of a person." (Semper 1889, 77) On one hand, the material of ornament emerges here not only as foundation of architecture. It also points to the fact, that structuration and division of social space are produced through material dressing, embedding and incrustation. On the other hand, the elevation of material dressing to a monumental form that represents "the true essence of architecture" (ibid., 252) leads to a shift from material as matter to a materiality as a relationship that humans maintain with matter. What appeared as loss of monumentality in the perspective of Hegel – the very primacy of the dressing – is turned on its head by Semper's materialism of the ornament, which asserts foundational symbolic power to the latter.

One might claim that Semper's materialist legitimization of the ornament inspires and correlates with Adolf Loos' quest of its refusal. Against the *Potemkin City* of the *Gründerzeit* historicism of the late 19th century, which nails facades on built volumes and thereby hides their modern nature, Loos promotes an "authentic style" that displays "modernity" as architectural truth. (Loos 1982) In an article published in the *Neue Freie Presse* in September 1898, Loos aims at laying bare the modern life by revealing the distinction between built volume and façade enclosure through using materials that emphasise the difference between "the material clad" and mere "cladding". (Loos 1982) Loos' ethics of the ornament is far from eradicating ornamentality as such. Rather, by radically accentuating its materiality, Loos folds the ornament into the structure of the modern building. Such a materialism of the relational obviously resonates with Otto Wagner's outline of modernity in his book *Modern Architecture* from 1895. Wagner calls for a shift in the way architecture is considered: "we must become fully aware, that the sole departure point for our artistic work can only be modern life." (Wagner 1988, 60) Loos' famous text *Ornament and Crime* from 1908 is a modernised version of Semper, transposing the performativity of the primordial hut and its textile structures to the level of the industrial assembly line. However, the Austrian architect's statement that "untruthful" architecture, as in architecture that hides its modernity, is "a waste of human labour, money and material" reads in the light of today's debates as a very plea for a sustainable use of material. (Loos 1975, 21)

How this idea resonates into the *Neue Bauen* of the interwar period is exemplified the internationally disseminated magazine *Das Neue Frankfurt*, which accompanied the building process of the immense state-driven construction program of the same name. The magazine's pedagogical impetus was directed towards educating the broader public about "modern design", thereby covering a wide range of then contemporary disciplines such as theatre, photography, film, art and industrial design. Ernst May, the protagonist of the Frankfurt program, who had studied under Raymond Unwin in London and worked as planner in Wrocław/Breslau, states in the magazine: "Everywhere we notice the purposeful struggle for a bold new design, for honesty in the use of materials (*Materialgerechtigkeit*), and for truth." (May 1984)

Maybe from there one can illuminate the idea of truth in Theodor W. Adorno's aesthetics as truth of materiality. As is known, for Adorno the "truth content" (*Wahrheitsgehalt*) of the art work suspends concepts such as correspondence, coherence, or function, that is propositionality. Rather, artistic truth operates in a non-propositional mode. The one who wants to judge an artwork, has to understand both, the artwork's complex internal dialectics of form and material and its socio-historical context. To explore an artwork's truth content then means to neither look for a metaphysical idea nor an essence. Is truth arbitrary then? Far from it, since Adorno's argument is, that the truth of the work is materially and historically situated. One should insist on the fact, that the main point here is the work's materiality: this materiality is by nature non-propositional. Yet, and this is nowhere better exemplified than in architecture and music, this materiality – as a relational diagram that unfolds between the humans and the work – calls for discourses, that is, where propositional claims are being made and negotiated about.

To further enlighten the argument, I want to draw the attention to a text that Adorno wrote about the question of form and content in music. In "Vers une musique informelle" Adorno argues from a historically perspective when he places the historicity of the social against the immanent truth of the musical material, in order to introduce moments of a new, material-appropriate history. To refer only to material, however, would be to surrender oneself to the reification of consciousness. In order not to lose oneself in reified expression, composition must renounce the purely affirmative subjectivity of the idealistic ego. This in turn affects the reality of musical material itself: "With the increasing mastery of the material the events at the subjective pole of music inevitably unsettle the opposite pole, the musical material itself." (Adorno 1992, 271 f.) The point is, that Adorno does not treat material as something "in and of itself", but defines it as going hand in hand with production. Material is that with "which the composer operates and in which he works." (ibid. 281) Adorno's argument sounds modern in the sense that it makes utopian claims. It is in this sense, that the truth content of any architectural or musical work is the mode in which it simultaneously might challenge a status quo, while exemplifying how this status quo is materialized and produced. (see Dell 2020)

Literature

Theodor W. Adorno, "Vers une musique informelle." Trans. Rodney Livingstone. In: *Quasi una Fantasia*. (London: Verso 1992) pp. 269–322

Christopher Dell, "Improvisation (according to Adorno)" in Christopher Dell, *Das Arbeitende Konzert/ The Working Concert* (Leipzig: Spector Books, 2020)

Georg Friedrich Hegel, *Aesthetics. Lectures on Fine Art,* transl. T.M. Knox (Oxford: Oxford University Press, 1975

Adolf Loos, "Potemkin City", in: *Spoken into the void: Collected essays 1897–1900*, trad. J.O. Newman and J.H. Smith (Cambridge: MIT Press, 1982) p. 95–96

Adolf Loos, "The Principle of Cladding", in: *Spoken into the void: Collected essays 1897–1900*, trad. J.O. Newman and J.H. Smith (Cambridge: MIT Press, 1982) pp. 66-69

Adolf Loos, "Ornament and Crime", in: Ulrich Conrads, ed., *Programs and Manifestos on 20th-Century Architecture* (Cambridge: MIT Press, 1975)

Ernst May, "Das Neue Frankfurt" (*Das Neue Frankfurt 1* / 1926–27) in Heinz Hirdina, ed., *Neues Bauen, Neues Gestalten* (Berlin: Elefanten Press 1984) pp. 62–77

Gottfried Semper ,*Development of Architectural Style*, trad. J. W. Root, The Inland Architects and News Record 14, No. 7 1889

Otto Wagner, *Modern Architecture*, trans. H. Malgrave (Santa Monica: Getty Center, 1988) p. 60

Tribsees' Zukunft machen!
ZWEIFELN
machen!
SCHLAFEN
PFLANZEN
mehr machen!
SINGEN
TRINKEN
ESSEN
LESEN
TANZEN
Kunst universität linz

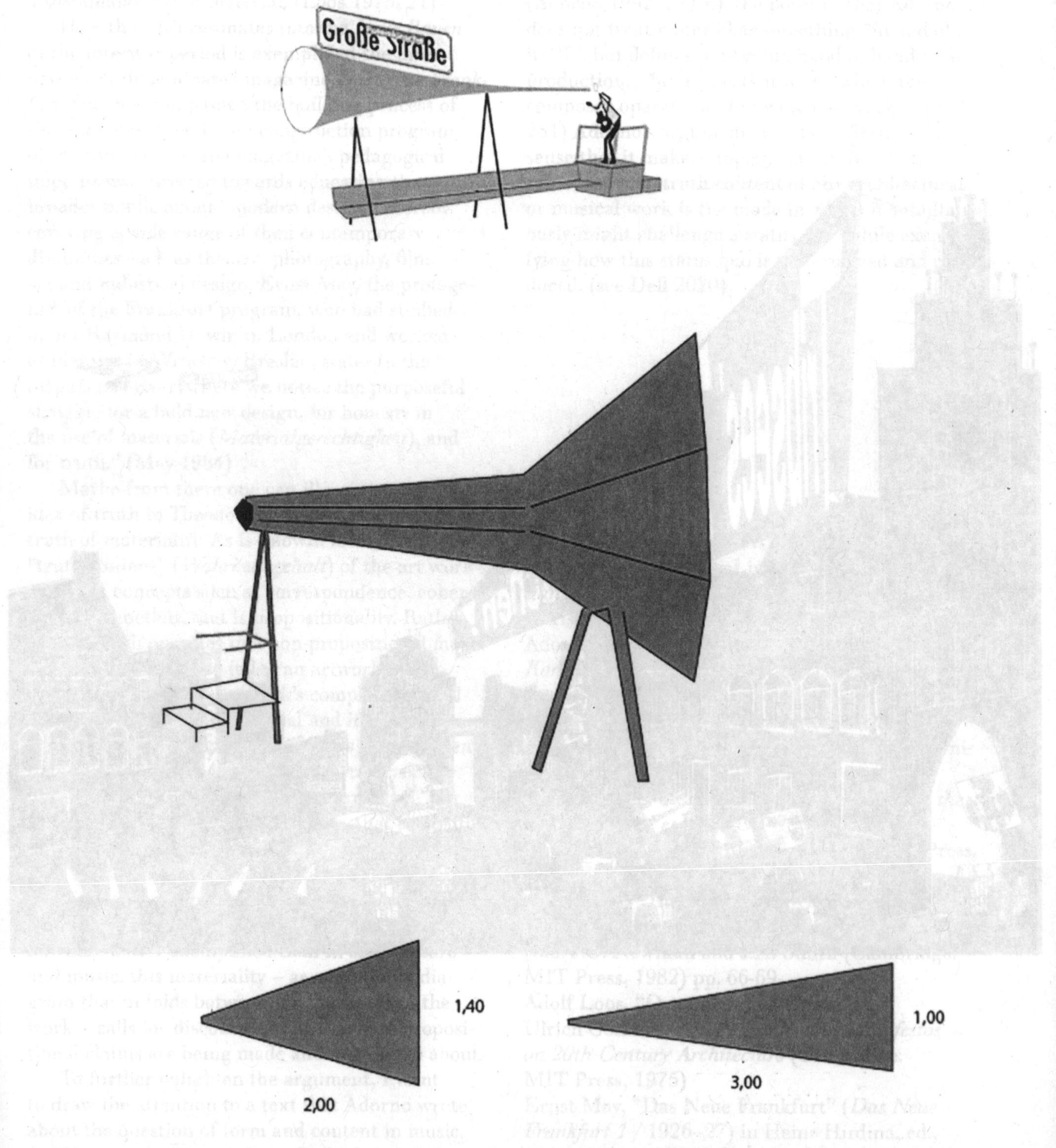
Große Straße
1,40
2,00
1,00
3,00

FORMBLOCK 31 c)
CD 8.3.2020
① 0:00"
1:10"
opt. transpose, repeat
ppp
fff
② 0:50 min.
③ 1:40 min.
④ 1:00 min.
pp
⑤ 0:45 min.
pppp

ORGANICS P.3
steg
ord.
mf
ppp
pizz
arco
mf
ppp
pizz
arco
→ steg
→ sul tasto
s.t. Bogendruck erhöhen
→ Geräusch
ord
crescendo
f
ppp
pizz
L.H.

p. 3
Ton Matton: Tribsees Postcard (2021)

p. 4
Ton Matton: Red Toot (2021)

p. 5
Christopher Dell: Formblock 31 c

p. 6
Christopher Dell: Organics for Bass solo, p. 3 (excerpt)

Lotte Anker is a Copenhagen-based saxophonist/improviser/composer working in the field between improvisation, experimental jazz and contemporary composed music. Recent years own groups/collaborations e.g.: Anker,Taborn,Cleaver (w Craig Taborn and Gerald Cleaver), What River Ensemble (w ao Phil Minton, Fred Frith, Ikue Mori, Chris Cutler, Garth Knox) Electric Habitat and Sub Habitat (Sofia Jernberg, Mazen Kerbaj, Andrea Neumann, Sten Sandell, Katt Hernandez, Nina de Heney, Ikue Mori, Burkhard Beins, Thomas Lehn, Michael Vorfeld ao), Lotte Anker & Fred Frith. Other past and present collaborations: Okkyung Lee, Ute Wasserman, Andrea Parkins, Magda Mayas, Joelle Leandre, Cristof Kurzmann, Jakob Riis, Sylvie Courvoiser, Ikue Mori, Evan Parker, Torben Snekkestad, Frelosa (Fred Frith & Sam Dühsler), Paul Lovens, Johannes Bauer, John Edwards, Nate Wooley, Mokuto Trio, Life and Other Transient Storms, Fire! Orchestra ao Performances/workshops ao in Europe, USA, Canada, Russia, Asia, Africa and the Middle East. Commissions and premieres at Huddersfield Contemporary Musicfestival, Gong Tomorrow, Donaueschingen New Music Festival ao.

Christopher Dell works in Berlin as a theorist in urban design and architecture, as musician, composer and as artist. Since 2000, Dell has been head of the Institute for Improvisationtechnology in Berlin. He held professorships in Urban Design Theory at the HafenCity Universität Hamburg and the Technical University Munich. At the moment he teaches Urban Design and Urban Renewal at the University of Fine Arts, Berlin. The Reclam Jazzlexikon hails him as one of Europe's leading vibraphonists. Dell has recorded numerous CDs and toured worldwide. His work was honored with several awards. e.g. the Downbeat Allstar Award, the Award of the Deutsche Schallplattenkritik, the JazzArt-Award—Music of the 21st Century, the Musicprize of the City of Darmstadt, German Jazz Prize and a Grammy-Nomination. He has published numerous CDs, articles, and books.

Sofia Eftychidou (1994) is a greek bass player, currently living in Berlin. She first studied classical music with Vassilis Papavassiliou in Athens and soon began to participate in orchestras and ensembles. At the age of 18, she started playing Jazz and moved to Germany, where she studied at the HfMT Köln from 2015 to 2021 under the guidance of Dieter Manderscheid and Jonas Burgwinkel. Concerts with multiple ensembles such as Bräumer/Klewer/Eftychidou have led her through numerous countries in Europe, f.e. Austria, Poland, Czech Republic and Greece. Besides her own projects, she has collaborated with artists such as Ronny Graupe, Oli Steidle and Ignaz Schick.

Since **Ton Matton** was fed up of Dutch Suburbia spatial planning, the former German Democratic Republic village-school of Wendorf is the base for his office. Inbetween Hamburg and Berlin Ton Matton makes inside the small-village structures a huge areal of ateliers, workshops, co-working-& living spaces, animals and plants. Inside the hypermodern living inbetween big-city-behaviour and wood-stove heating, Matton is looking for connections between the traditional living on the countryside and contemporary mega-city-lifestyle. "The fact that I live in Wendorf doesn't mean that I can't be reached. I live in Central Europe. I have a satellite Internet, a Lada Niva four-wheel drive, and a mobile phone, like everyone else in the Global Village." (A10 Magazine, Wonderland 2006) With the Heterotopie Wendorf Academy Ton Matton tries with ever changing guests to find the small Utopias and interruptions of daily life, where nature is an object to aesthetical mediation from crisis situations in society. Mattons work is situated somewhere between object-design, society-shape, ecological urban planning and artist-actionismus. At the moment MattonOffice is researching the possibilities of a 'slow development plan' and preparing the last phase of the Great potemkin Cirkus in the small shrinking city of Tribsees in Mecklenburg Vorpommern. As soon ex-prof. space- and design STRATEGIES Matton works since 2015 with his team on a.o. the subjects: Cow (shrinking villages), ~~NOT~~ WELCOME! (refugee research), BayWatch (see level rising)

On the occasion of Aedes Architecture Forum's 40th anniversary, the series **dialogue concerts: conceptual research on architecture and music** presents a pluralistic media format, re-envisioning urban research. Architectural practice will enter into a dialogue with musical praxis.

Designed as a montage of lectures, concerts and discussions *dialogue concerts* is a series of events that will examine the interplay of urban space and communal life. Set up as an experimental interdisciplinary format, the *dialogue concerts* series is comprised of 6 events from December 2019 through December 2021. In this context, the city is not defined as a fixed object, but as a dynamic and collective constellation that is performatively produced.

Curated by the vibraphonist, composer and urban theoretician Christopher Dell, *dialogue concerts* is presented as artistic statement and critical dispositif. International architects and musicians are invited to address aspects of procedural strategies across disciplines in a series of six *dialogue concerts*. Taking questions of mediality, corporality, interaction, materiality, structure and transformation as starting points, *dialogue concerts* creates a discursive space seeking to illustrate the societal relevance of both disciplines in a new way.

dialogue concerts is organized by Christopher Dell in cooperation with the Aedes Architecture Forum, funded by the Senate Department for Culture and Europe and the Musikfonds e. V. with project funds from the Federal Government Commissioner for Culture and the Media.

Concept / Moderation: Christopher Dell
Project Management: Saori Kanemaki
Graphic Design: Helmut Völter
Controlling: Melanie Rossmann
Public Relations: Ari Kanemaki

The Team of *dialogue concerts* would like to thank everybody at Aedes Architecture Forum for the friendly cooperation, especially Kristin Feireiss, Hans Jürgen Commerell, Christine Meierhofer, Dunya Bouchi and Mathias Schnell.

Cover: Candy-Tuft, in: Henry Irving, Edward F. Strange, *Flowers and Plants for Designers and Schools* (London: Hodder and Stoughton 1907) plate 87 [p. 76]

dialogue concerts

1	*Mediality*	12. 12. 2019
2	*Interaction*	6. 2. 2020
3	*Transformation*	14. 8. 2021
4	*Structure*	17. 9. 2020
5	*Corporality*	20. 4. 2021
6	*Materiality*	9. 9. 2021

Aedes Architecture Forum
enw
ifit Institut für Improvisationstechnologie
Senatsverwaltung für Kultur und Europa
be Berlin
MUSIKFONDS
Gefördert vom Musikfonds e. V. mit Projektmitteln der Beauftragten der Bundesregierung für Kultur und Medien.

Twenty years ago I was invited to work on a project in São Paulo as an architect and urban planner. And we came up with the idea that I visit the city like we architects do, wondering: What's the problem? How can we solve it? And one of the problems was that a lot of street children live in this city and there is no place for them to stay. Normally, the street is filled with parking or with shops. We came up with the proposal to draw playing fields on the streets. It's like when you are in a school gymnasium and you have different colors of lines on the floor, and when the teacher says, "we'll play basketball," so then everyone knows that it's now the red lines that are relevant for the game. If they say, "we'll play volleyball," then everyone knows it's the blue lines. Transposing this system onto the street, we decided that if it's the green lines, it's a parking space, if it's the white lines, it's children's play, and so on. That was our idea. We discussed it with the architects in São Paulo and sent them the drawings and the ideas in advance. I arrived in São Paulo on Friday evening, went to the opening site, and nothing was built. Saturday morning was the opening. What to do? Flying half way around the world for an opening, bringing my best suit. You're standing there and you know tomorrow morning there will be no project. I was disappointed, yes, but there was a lot of energy. And the next morning, I went to the street. I bought a piece of chalk and just started to draw on the streets what I had in my mind. Immediately, there were some street children who came and said, "What are you doing?" So I tried to explain it to them, and they started helping. And then after a while there were more children and more people coming, and they started helping. There was no plan. There was just me in my best suit doing funny things on the street. And then I realized, now I have to buy paint. I went to a shop. I bought paint

and brought it there, but I only had green. Nevertheless, the idea of different layers came into play since the white lines of the parking lots were already there. And that was this moment where there was good energy, and everyone was helping and laughing. I bought food and drinks, and we worked really hard, a whole day long. And in the night, we stopped. It was finished. The next day, all of a sudden a truck came, delivering trees. I had ordered them months ago, but since they hadn't arrived yet, I thought they would never come. However, we arranged them at the site—and now it was a project. The next day I was there, and I saw that the children wanted to play, but there was a car parking on this spot. Of course, the green territory becomes a children's playing field. The children went up to the guy who owns the car and said, "Hey now it's this new playground. You have to remove your car." And it worked. What happens is that the materiality itself appears as an argument in a spatial negotiation procedure. Painted on the asphalt and symbolically charged, the color on the street gave the children the argument to convince the guy to remove his car, because he realized that "the teacher now says it's basketball and not parking."

In fact, it became a very important project for me, because I realized that during all those months of preparation, I was thinking only about material. I was thinking only about how to draw color. How to make a nice graphic design on the streets. That it looks nice, that it looks proper. But in the end, I realized, it was this moment of being there. It was this moment of discussing with them, respecting the people, creating energy in concert. This way of material cooperation, of putting material into action together, is what becomes decisive. And then it doesn't matter that the line is not drawn very properly.

This was a key moment in my way of understanding what urban planning is. It may be about thinking, and it may be about having ideas. But in the end, the most important thing is to be close to the people with whom you are working. And that has become the essence of what I am doing.

Twenty years ago, I moved from the Netherlands to Germany. From that moment on, I was suddenly an international urban planner. And it was at the same time when globalization became normal. When I did this project, we were really proud: "A project from Rotterdam to São Paulo and now we are famous." But of course, today it is normal. We do projects all over the world and we're flying to Denmark for breakfast.

Another project I did some years ago involved moving a rather famous East German type of house, the TYP EW 64. It was the most built family house in the East German countryside. And I removed one of these houses. Since it was empty, I tore it down and moved it to the Netherlands.

When this project was over, I remember that one Sunday morning we were having breakfast at home. My wife was reading the *Süddeutsche Zeitung*, an important German newspaper, and suddenly she said: "You should read this. Here's your next project." It was a story about a small village in Ghana on the coast at the ocean. This village is slowly disappearing. The sea level rises every year. There are loads of sand coming in, and the mayor of this village, the chief, says, "We can't just take the village and move it." And then I realized that's just what I did with the house. Took the house and moved it. We put it on the truck, and we brought it from eastern Germany to Holland and rebuilt it there. With that article in my mind, I now said to the students—I was teaching in Linz, Austria, at the art university at the

„We can't go somewhere else and just say: here we are! Even when we find a place for a village, it needs houses, a school, a church, a water treatment plant."
– Chief Agbakla

With this quote in „Süddeutsche Zeitun Theophilus Agbakla, the Chief from the Village Totope in Ghana, convinced us Prof. Ton Matton and some students of space&designSTRATEGIES of art univers Linz, exactly to do this: try to move the village to a safe place!

time—this is our next project. We'll go there, and we'll move the village. Let's see.

Located on a lagoon right at the ocean, behind a small strip of sand, is the village. There is no place for this village to move. They are there and they are trapped. There's like 20 or 30 centimeters of sand brought in by the ocean every year. The image says it all. And of course, it's a very romantic village. Going there as a guy from Rotterdam, seeing this, you feel like, what are you doing? The moment the fishing boats come in and you hear the voices through the village, "Hands, hands, hands, hands," and then everyone stops what they're doing and they all go to the beach, helping to get the fish in, knowing this is the food for the coming days. It's a very far away culture. We realized, of course, that we did not have any idea how to save this village.

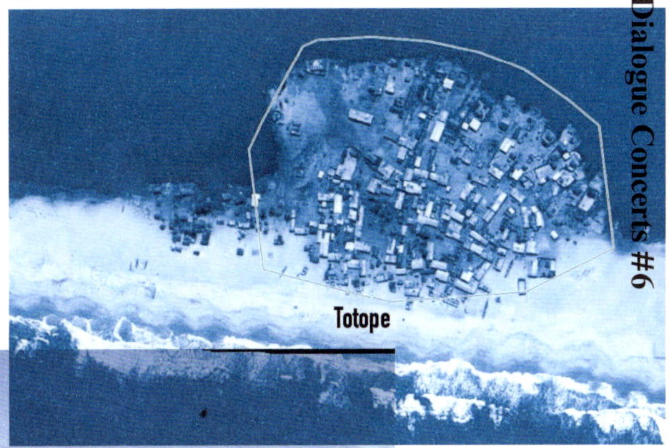

It was just a very interesting story against the background of climate change, of the rising sea level. And then the opportunity, knowing that there's a chief in this village who is looking for help. That's why he was launching the topic in the German newspaper in the first place. And we contacted him, and he said, "Yes, please pass by and we'll see what happens." And we met the chief. He explained to us what is going on, and he said that in earlier days there were palm trees near the coast. And the palm trees were blocking the wind. And they were blocking the water as well. And as a child, he said, he could climb in the trees and then see on the horizon that the ships were coming in with the fish. The ships today are huge fish factories that catch in one day what the village fishermen fish in one year. Now they feel that they have to move to the lagoon; they try to make new land there, and they do that with a lot of plastic waste, which is of course problematic.

But being there, you can also understand that a little bit. So, we talked to the community of the village. And we tried to find out what is going on, if maybe there could be a role for us, if we can help them or if we can understand or whatever.

I'm not saying this in order to emphasize the romantic side, which is certainly there, but rather to show the conflict we were confronted with as so-called "designers." On the one hand, we were naive by just going there. But on the other hand, that's the consequence of globalization. That's the inverse consequence of, for example, the refugee crisis: we can go there and think that we know in a couple of days what's going on, which of course is not true.

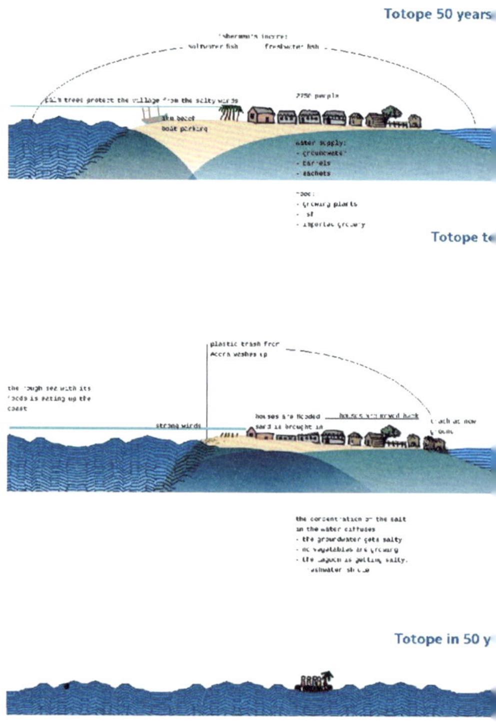

We were there. We visited. But we also had a lot of information. Since I'm Dutch, I grew up with dikes; for me it's normal that there's a dike and that I'm living with the rising water. Rotterdam is minus 6 or 7 meters below sea level. Back in Linz, I decided to invite a Dutch engineering company to discuss the problems with the students. What can we do? There's an ocean, there's the lagoon, and fifty years ago there was still a forest and the beach, which served as a harbor for the locals boats. In fifty years, there will be no village anymore.

The next year we went back to the village, and we arrived there with ideas. And one of the ideas, since we are an art university, was that we should declare the village to be art. The idea was inspired by the fact that the village was about the same size as the marketplace of Linz. The university is located on this marketplace. We proposed to the mayor: we invite you and the whole village to come up here to Linz and we will make it art. We'll put the village on a boat. We do not know how to do it. Or we will make a copy of the village on the main square of Linz. The mayor refused. But he liked the idea. Another idea was to think the future on a boat. I'm Dutch. I know how to build a dike. But you can also go back 1,000 years; back then you made the dike by hand. It's a lot of work and you need sand. Or we could put the village on pylons. The last idea was to put the village on a pedestal and lift it about 3 or 4 meters. We could make the pedestal intelligent. We could

Utotope – Utopian ideas to save a village

Move

In the naivity we started this project, this was the first idea, to move Totope to Linz. Chief Agbakla already researched this option as not realistic. Not only because of finance, but actually most of the inhabitants don't want to leave Totope

San-Trotope

A hotel for tourists who visit the rescued village could be integrated. Bringing in all social-, environmental-, economical- and sustainable issues in an intelligent socle, the village Totope becomes more then an declared art-village in a Marcel Duchamp way – it becomes an utopian village.

Arch Noah

If the village is floating, by building Totope on boats, the village will rise with the seelevel. But every time the see floods the village, a new layer of sand will cover everything. So even the gardens, chicken and and goats have to get their own ship. Or built it or a yacht like the „streets of Monaco".

Pylons

Not only an traditioral way of builcing in the water, also a classical modernistic way of architecture (Corbusier), lift the village lift Totope on pylons and the landscape can go under it.

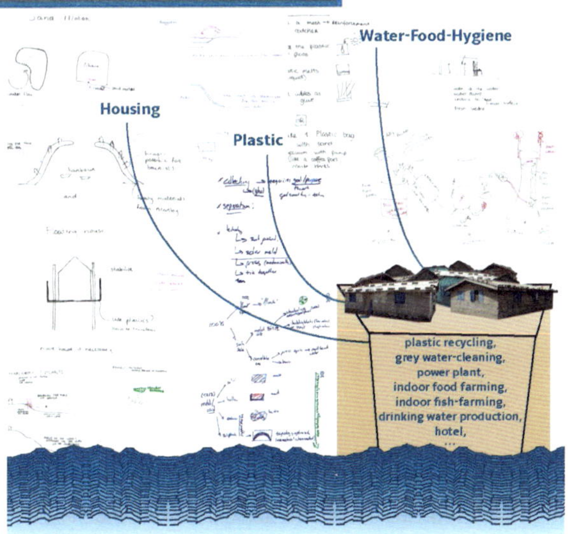

Dike

Continue the dike towards Totope in the same way it is builc some 100 meters further. Bring back the ships ard finish the work. If the dredging ships not come, then Do It Yourself!

try to use plastic recycling, drain water. For us, this would have implied investing in all the environmental issues that we are aware of nowadays, and that lead you to the creation of a model village idea. We thought of a heterotopia inside a world where climate change brings the world down. Let's make an art piece of the future village.

In order to start, one of the students did a project where he put a line as a calendar of sorts through the village, with a blue stone every 6 meters, so that you know that next year the sea will be here or this year there. Next year the sea will be here, so you can calculate in fifteen years that my house will be gone. Another student tried to make a gauge. If you go to the Netherlands—or to Austria if there's flooding—then there's always someone who marks it on a gauge so that you can remember. It's good to have these moments so that you realize what is at stake. So that you are aware it can come back next year. So that you work on the village memory of history.

Another thing that we observed in the village was that they have this poster of the European Champions League on the wall of a house. Then we found out they have a cinema in there. Inside the house is a television where they watch European football. Inspired by the cinema, one of the students organized a football competition. He organized some local

equipment, and we made a video of the games. The student synchronized the video material, imitating serious football commentators. And we showed the film to the villagers.

Though all in all, it's not about this project, but about how to reach the people. Because it was us who were feeling alienated there. As I said, it was like being an inverse refugee. You go to this place, and you realize that everything is different than what you had thought it was. And how to get into contact, how to somehow get a feeling for what is bothering them or what the situation is.

On the occasion of the presentation of our projects in the village, we put on Baywatch costumes and walked in slow motion to the beach as the opening event. And we built a chair in remembrance of the mayor's story that as a child they were climbing the trees. We interpreted the chair as a kind of monument to the land, to the trees that were gone.

Then I talked to them. I said, this is such a big problem you have. You are such a small village. It's like David and Goliath. You can't fight global climate change as a small village. You need help. You can't solve this problem on your own. Let's ask Ghana's most famous person for help, which at the time was Kofi Annan. We invited him. An artist from the village made a painting for us overnight. He painted Kofi Annan. We sent Annan the invitation, and we got the answer back that night that he was not able to come.

We went back to Linz, and we held our annual exhibition featuring some art projects. We again did our Baywatch theater, and by that time Kofi Annan had died. Since we had the painting of him, we created a scene with the picture of Kofi Annan sitting next to the mayor and the minister of Linz. This was in 2018, and we had left the village with the promise to the mayor that we'd come back, and that we wanted to build a

hotel. You don't have to build a hotel with an architect and a project developer and a lot of money. In that village, this doesn't make sense. There is sand. You start with putting sand on a pile.

Then, of course, with the coronavirus pandemic and all that stuff, the university lost its liveliness. I left our university. If there's anyone who has an idea, let's go to the village and do the hotel. It can be good.

Now I want to speak about the project that Christopher took as a reference to talk about the materiality of bricks. Tribsees is a small village in the east of Germany, close to Rostock, two hours from Berlin. It's a very typical eastern German village. It is covered by a lot of material, but there is a sort of vacuum of ideas. Which means that of the 200 houses in the inner Tribsees town, seventy are broken, amounting to one third. And broken means that they are piles of bricks. It's dead. It's empty. This is how it looks.

The general layout of the town looks very romantic, I would say. It has two brick towers from the medieval times. A central street, 400 meters long, with beautiful houses. The houses that are renovated look okay, but there are a lot of unrenovated houses. The model shows the situation. All of the blue and the green houses are empty or broken. In fact, the situation of the town has similarities to the village

in Ghana. It's broken and no one knows what to do with it. Is there anyone who maybe is interested in living here? How much do you pay for a house in Tribsees? Some cost 30,000. I would say it's very cheap. I guess if you would negotiate, though, you could even get one for a single euro.

But if you know that, then why are you still here? Curiously enough, for one of the houses they are asking 400,000 euros, but that's because the owner is divorced, and he and his ex-wife each want 200,000. I don't think they will sell it. Another house has a long garden like 50 meters. And it features an outlook over the valley of the river Trebel, which is a nature reserve. It is so beautiful, and you can have it for 5,000 euros. And I don't understand why it is empty. If all of those people in Berlin who are looking for a cheap place to live—and there's a lot of them—would go to Brandenburg, then they would pay like 100,000 euros or more, but if they would travel just half an hour further, then they would have it for free. And you wouldn't have to work forty years to pay the money to the bank to own a house in Berlin. Instead, you could work forty years to renovate this house.

We went to the village. We talked to the mayor, and the mayor had a problem with it as well. And we said, yes, it's not so purposeful that all the houses are empty and everyone is talking about the bad stories related to this village. We proposed to go there with a group of students from Linz and with artists. Our goal was to change the stories by occupying the empty houses and doing something in the houses that changes how we understand or read them. That was the strategy. To change the framing of a given situation. For example, they say, yes, you can buy the house, but the couple is divorced. Another one you can have but the owner is not known. He's far away. These are difficult stories. Our strategy was to go there and implement a restaurant or a cinema. By doing this, we create other stories and other people will get interested.

Certainly, such a strategy is connected to a certain way of doing. It has a history, by which I mean that it develops over many years of practice and has many diverse influences. For example, the project to occupy a house is what we did in the 1980s in the Netherlands. You just enter a house, and you squat it. The mayor of Tribsees is not allowed to squat a house, but we as artists are.

In Tribsees, we opened a house. We went in. We knew that this house actually is stray or *herrenlos*. In Germany, this means that the house exists but has no owner. You can have it for free if you go to the city administration and say you want to have it. The only thing is that there is someone who still has a mortgage of 100,000 euros on this house. The bank had a mortgage on the house and sold the mortgage. I thought it was just an American system that you can sell your debts—one of the main drivers of the subprime crisis in 2008—but apparently it happens in Germany as well. In our case, someone has 100,000 euros in debt on this house. If you buy it, you will have to pay this debt to the person. That is the risk that the house carries. But since we didn't own it, we only took it, went in and installed our office there. We invited all people in the village to join us in a collective brainstorming on initial concept ideas of what we could do with the empty houses. It was the beginning of the coronavirus pandemic and we had to reorganize how people can meet.

I was doing a lecture on the street. We asked the people who came to build a model of the village with us, with which we could notate and display all the houses. They built the model, and we got the history of who had been living there and what happened to the houses, et cetera. We did a remake of the model, and we painted all the houses in the model green. We installed the model as a permanent exhibition in another house, and we mounted a huge postbox outside and asked everyone to put in their wishes. What do you want in this village to change, to happen? So that we could get some kind of information. We got about 300 postcards with all the wishes and, of course, a lot of them sounded like this: we would like to have a restaurant, we would like to have a café, we would like to have a shop and a bakery and all those things. We had a meeting and then I asked them back: Where do you buy your bread? And of course, everyone buys the bread in the supermarket, which is located outside the center of the village, and no one went to a café every week to drink a coffee and have a piece of cake. There was one school class. They all together said, “We want to have a McDonald’s.” It was quite clear that wishes existed, but there was no possibility of realizing them. You would have to really go far back to reconstruct the basic functions of the village.

Because of the pandemic, the students from Linz were not allowed to go abroad. So they decided to make illuminated advertisements. I bought a lot of Christmas lights and sent them to Austria. The students processed them and sent them back. For example, we had a McDonald’s logo, but also many others. Subsequently, during Christmas, on the facades of all the empty houses, we installed light sculptures so that at least the lights were illuminating those houses. And then Christmas was gone, spring jumped up, and the students were still not allowed to go to the village. And so we said that if the students were not allowed to visit the village, then the village should go to the students. The universities were closed, but construction sites were still open and running. I declared five of my students as employees of my architectural office, and from that moment on, they were allowed to go to Germany and work on our so-called “construction site” in Tribsees. The normative transformation that took place was that the students were not students anymore, but laborers instead. We decided to take a house down, put it on a pallet, and bring it to Linz. We did. We brought a truck filled with the house—that is, the house’s parts. This is where the question of materiality comes in. In fact, where Christopher said, “Hey, you are operating by charging and mobilizing material. By dismantling the house down to its parts, and putting them on display, you are thematizing the house’s materiality; not its form, but its structure. The effect is that, by this reframing, the focus shifts to the producedness of the house.” However, for me, this is not material. We sent the truck to Linz with the task: “Don’t rebuild the house but rebuild the atmosphere of Tribsees.” That is what we need. We want to understand the village. We want to understand how it is to live in a broken village like this, and that is what we need to show the students who are not able to go there. They can work with this atmosphere import.

This image we produced is a fake. It's a print. But this other photograph of the university is real, and this situation depicted here is all real. The university is quite new. It's a building where there was still a fear of putting something on the wall. And we came in with this huge amount of "trash"—the broken-down bricks—and it worked. The students started building with it in the foyers of the university staircases,

and they started to develop the atmosphere of this village. In this way, they represented at the university the work they had done in Tribsees. Then we brought this work of representation back to the village and showed it there as well. For instance, one of the students knew that they all wanted to have a McDonald's. From the village material now located in Linz, he made a "Tribsees Burger" which was then reimported to the German village and it became a favorite. He was a Chinese student by the name of Peiyan Zhang. He was in Linz, and we wanted him to go back to Tribsees. I knew that he's a very good cook. I said, "Peiyan, you have to go there." We had planned a lot of events in Tribsees and we called it a centennial. We followed the biennial concept, which has become a ubiquitous feature of the contemporary fine arts circuit, but slowed the timing down from every two years to every 100 years. You only have to do it once. During the centennial we had a vernissage, a midissage, and a finissage. Peiyan started to think about how to produce bricks from tofu. As conceptual point of departure he took the traditional procedure of brick-making, which means to mix ground clay with water, form the clay into a desired shape, and dry and fire it. Accordingly, Peiyan modeled the tofu like a brick and cooked it and baked it and I don't know what else. And he created a new dish: the real big McTrebel, and one weekend he was feeding all of the people living in Tribsees with it. The centennial got a lot publicity; the newspaper came, the television. At the opening, even Mecklenburg-Vorpommern's secretary of state came as well. Actually, he is the head of the energy ministry, but he also engages in the social structuring of the countryside, of villages, which make up a big part of the state. He had the courage to invite us in the first place, to invite a bunch of students from an art school and myself to go to Tribsees and do all these projects. Maybe he's desperate. But either way, he still did it, and he paid for everything. And that's why we could work like this. We had about six openings, and he was always there. He came not only in his official capacity, but also as a private guy, because he really enjoys the approach to rethinking this urban planning that we are doing.

Nonetheless, you can imagine that if you live in Tribsees and you see it every day, it might make you depressed. In the beginning, all the villagers were complaining: Why is the mayor not doing anything? After a year of working with him, I know that the mayor can't do anything. In the case of one house ownership is not transparent, other houses have other problems, and the economic situation is devastating. As a mayor, you can't do anything. You only can wait,

and that's what they do. But waiting on seventy houses is quite a lot. And the secretary said, in fact, about us squatting the houses, that of course it's not allowed but it's the best thing you can do.

It's a very difficult situation. But we are now quite close to the point that we have pushed them so far that they are at least occupying two or three houses. It makes me sort of proud that, coming from the 1980s, when occupying houses was more or less a criminal act, you can now do it and the secretary of state comes and says, "Hey, good idea."

We also created the grand hotel Tribsees, but it is very DIY. Bring your furniture and your stuff, and then you have your hotel room. In fact, the only thing we do is we open the door and then it's open, and then we give you the courage to do it. Some students came and brought their beds. They made bathrooms. Of course, there's no water, there's no electricity. Electricity you can borrow from the neighbors. It's quite easy. Water is always a bit more difficult. You take a bowl of water and you have a bathroom. Concerning the showers, we constructed a wellness area and spa with a small solar-energy panel and hot-water bags. In the back is the Trebel River, so you can fill the bags in the river. In the morning, you fill them, you let them hang in the sun, and then, in the evening, you can go for a warm shower.

Audience 1 How long has this project been going on?

Ton Matton We started in October 2020 and we finished last week. Of course we're going to make a documentation. We'll come back at Christmastime to show all the video material to the people there. We try to encourage them to really pull through. The secretary of state also wants the people to continue. He doesn't want me to continue. He knows now what I can do, or we as a group. But the goal now is that the people living

there have the courage to do something. We built a cinema, we reopened the old GDR Kaufhalle, the local department store, and now we need someone to use this space and to continue. And, of course, we have a lot of ideas of what we can do, but the minister was very clear, that's not the goal. He doesn't want to make an art project out of it. He now wants the people to use what they learned from us this past year, for them to have the guts to do it, that they do it themselves.

Audience 2 What's going to happen to the village between the sea and the lagoon which you gave a lot of hope but you abandoned?

Ton Matton No, we didn't give them any hope. I was clear about it being the other way around. We learned more from them than they learned from us. Because there is no hope. If *we* don't change, yet climate change is still going on, there is no hope. The only hope is that they move, and of course, all the boys aged twenty-five and up, they really did their best to marry one of the student girls to get to Europe. Of course, that's the hope. Get out of there. And on the other side, there is this formal structure, and living in the village for all those years and the ancestors being buried there, et cetera. But you can't leave. That's what the mayor made very clear. Although he insinuated it in the newspaper article, leaving is not an option. Rather die there and drown than leave. I don't know. Well, there is hope. One could bring more sand there. But sand is not so easy to get nowadays because we use it for skyscrapers in Shenzhen.

Let's listen to some music now.

aggressively
Wendorf

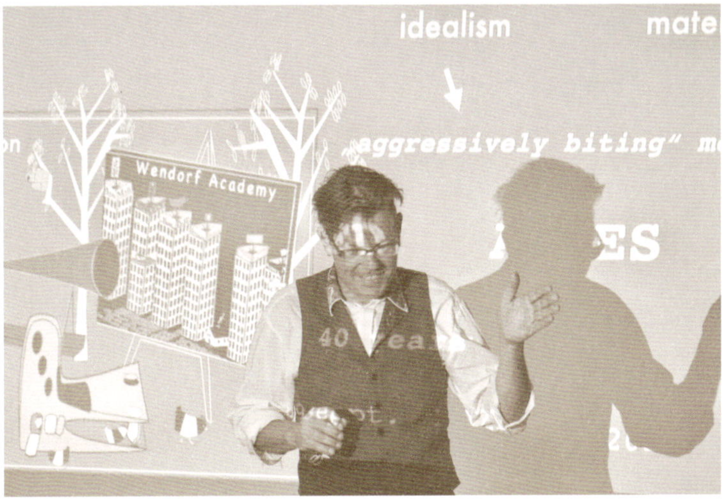
idealism
„aggressively biting“
Wendorf Academy

WORLD NEWS

Automotivo
229-9292 229-5150

Dialogue Concerts #6
Materiality
September 9, 2021
Discussion

Christopher Dell
in Conversation with
Lotte Anker,
Sofia Eftychidou,
Francis Kéré,
and Ton Matton

Christopher Dell At the outset of our discussion, it is important for me to point out that the *Dialogue Concerts* are not about the musical illustration of architecture, nor are they conceptualized with an understanding of architecture as a container for music. Instead, the *Dialogue Concerts* focus on the interaction between the two disciplines on a metalevel. In order to delimitate this rather broad conceptual outline, each event focuses on a specific theme. Today's *Dialogue Concert #6* indulges in the topic of materiality.

Since today's event is the last in a series of six, I would like to start with an observation that looks back. I can say that during the series of the *Dialogue Concerts* my playing differed each time, in resonance with the topics we explored. I assume that this fact is connected to the imaginaries that the themes evoked in me and that guided my playing. The themes seem to have the capacity to trigger a production of meaning in my music-making. However, while these imaginaries are inseparably linked to a field of knowledge, they at the same time flee the universal. The meanings they trigger can be different for everyone who perceives them. In this sense, I would argue that the themes became the material of the *Dialogue Concerts*. It was our positioning toward and our work with them, their "materiality," which guided the *Dialogue Concerts* procedures.

Ton, in your talk you emphasized that when you as an intervening urban planner are confronted with a specific situation, your approach is heavily determined by its materiality. By this is understood the way you relate to the given material, the way you are affected by it. Or, as you say, it's all emotions. Have you over the years developed a sort of technique or method of affect? How do you operate when you arrive for the first time at a site that you have earmarked for a project or research? How do you open yourself to what is there? How do you train or condition yourself toward being affected by the materiality of the situation?

Ton Matton It's wonderful that you played the music after my lecture, because I think, in fact, the concept is the same. You know, I come into the exhibition space here, and Francis Kéré said he wanted to build a tree, I see his installation here and the way you as musicians have located yourself in relation to it, and I said, this *is* the tree. And then you start to play, and it's sort of that. Of course, it's not really a tree, it's a bunch of reeds put together, but the concept of a tree is inscribed in the material on a metalevel. In a sense, it works as materiality. However, I never think of it in that way. I see the tree, or, to formulate it better, I feel the tree. And that's the same with music. You said you work with music as material. I had never thought of music as material. It's there, and you feel it, and you hear it, and you enter into an emotional state. Doing the projects like the ones I do, I think it's no coincidence that there's always a musician involved, because you feel that it's not about brick. It's about the emotion, it's about the energy, it's about how we live together in the city, and how you can play, or how you can cooperate with these emotions, which actually in music is obvious. Music is emotions, planning is not—or maybe it is?

Christopher Dell You are a planner. But obviously you have transformed your discipline throughout your work. You have expanded or changed what you learned at school. This is also guided by decisions you've made. Yes, it's about emotions, that's true, but how did you train these emotions, or how did you open yourself to these emotions? Because this an aspect that you did not learn at school, that you need the faculty of emotions to implement change.

Ton Matton You do not learn this at school. But when I confronted myself with reality, when I saw outside how the world functions, there was no other way for me than to criticize architecture and urban planning or project development or whatever. It's not even about material; it's only about money, which, one could even claim, is the densest form of material.

Christopher Dell I agree, but this way of criticizing the discipline still implies or is based on taking a position toward a situation you perceive. How did it come about that you said, "I want to criticize my own profession"? A lot of architects don't do that, or they do it in a very different way. You have developed a very peculiar way of making projects over the years. For example, exporting all the bricks from Tribsees to Linz, or bringing a house from Mecklenburg-Vorpommern to the Netherlands, which, while being a mere house, within the framework of your project means a lot more than a house. The projects demonstrate a decisive point, namely, that material can mean so much more when you displace it into a different context, when you shift it into a different framing. Normally, we are used to a concept that understands material as a passive neutral entity, but here, it's a lot more. The emotions that you talked about are mobilized by an imaginary that, for its part, is stimulated by material. They are charged with a vector, or with a drive within constellations that you create through your interventions. Was that something that you developed through your projects? Did your projects change your way of approaching situations and, if yes, how did they do so?

Ton Matton Of course my approach developed over years of doing projects, but I believe most of it is influenced by the fact that you recognize that you think in a certain way. For me, that's obvious now, that I think like that. To align the discussion back to this exhibition, you see, there's a small pile of children's bricks and they are very nicely piled up. My father was a bricklayer, so all my youth, I was piling up bricks. And then you see, just by piling up the bricks, there is this potential of what it can be. And if you have the same bricks 100 years later, falling down from a collapsing house, then there is a completely different energy in these bricks. The history of what they were is still present, but at the same time, I feel the potential of what they could be. And the question is, how do I feel it? I don't know. I mean, I feel it. It's an answer.

Christopher Dell One way is to say: the material is there, and if I cannot relate to it, then I remove it. That has been the teleology of the history of planning and of modernity in a nutshell. Tabula rasa: take it that way, or don't even recognize that it's there, but treat space as a neutral container, and plan and project over it. Your approach is the absolute opposite: you go somewhere, and first, before you start to plan or before you say I want this, you start to meditate on the situation or you get into an action or, for example, you lay a brick, you connect the material with the practice. I think that is what is ingrained as a basis in the history of your projects.

Ton Matton Yes. But I think it's the same, what you were doing here by playing, the three of you. You're all playing your own instruments, and you're reacting to each other, and you're listening to each other, and then you say, "Hey, maybe a bit more of this or this." In Tribsees, of course, the mayor of the city wanted to clean up the city, and he asked me, "Can you remove that house? You promised to bring a house to Linz." Of course, I didn't bring a house to Linz. I only brought a little bit of the house. Certainly, there was a lot of material left, and he said, "You should clean it." And then my answer was that we would build this high balcony in front of the broken house, and invite Mecklenburg-Vorpommern's secretary of state to do the opening exactly on that spot, where the mayor actually wanted to clean up. Tabula rasa, put grass over it and park some cars. We watched the mayor, we listened to him, but we also irritated him, in order to get him into this other mode. Now there's a balcony and so he doesn't have to remove the house anymore, because there's the memory (or the experience of) an opening of an exhibition, and every time he passes the balcony, he's seeing, "Ah, the secretary of state was there." The erection of the balcony and the institutional inauguration of it changed the reading of the pile of bricks behind it, and of course, one day it will be gone probably. That's what I observe in your music as well. I recognize today that it's the same when you call music material; in fact, you were doing the same thing, a bit of that, a bit more to the left, a bit more to the right, to stimulate reaction. Sometimes you look for eye contact, sometimes you get it, sometimes it's refused, but then you have to do it in another way.

Lotte Anker: The interaction between us is, it's not only improvisation, for me, at least; it's not only about making communication, but about a way of building a space, building a sound space, a sound house, you could also say. I'm actually listening better when I have closed eyes. I had to look a little bit at the music here and there, but my listening is getting more intensified and more refined. But I totally understand the method of looking at each other, because we also had to look at Christopher's cues for each section. I can only speak for myself, but you also want to build up a certain kind of tension between relations. It can be pretty lame, actually, if there's no tension, because then it gets boring. Maybe it's unconscious that, deep inside you, there is that energy; it's also using the body in a way.

Ton Matton: In a sense, it's similar to what I'm doing with the mayor of the village, putting him in this hive, knowing the secretary of state is coming, exactly positioning the camera so that he knows on the Monday after the opening the picture will be in the newspaper. Still, it is the mayor standing in front of the house that he wanted to remove, and I'm not telling him, but of course it's there.

Christopher Dell: It's the feeling of the house.

Ton Matton: Yes.

Christopher Dell: Sofia, I confronted you with the material two days ago; you came by and we rehearsed a certain pile of material, maybe a brick of material. And we thought about what part of that material could work for the performance today. How was it for you to play, and while playing to interact, but at the same time, being confronted with the material somehow? How does the material affect your playing, or how do you go about that aspect?

Sofia Eftychidou: Interesting for me were the things you told me about your music and the concepts that you had in mind, that you explained, and to work on it. Yes, you get a piece of paper with a bunch of notes, but that means nothing if you don't have the context. One aspect that you referred to very much two days ago really stayed with me: to create landscapes and to dive into that. And today, after having practiced that and after trying to understand your thoughts about the music and your ideas, it was really interesting and felt really nice playing. As we said before, it's like interacting and playing together, but you also go opposite to the other, because I felt like you put things, like you put bricks into the musical space.

Ton Matton I have the feeling that you are rather the cement in this concept. Maybe that's also the instrument, because it was always there, as a basic layer. I don't want to compare music with cement, but I was observing, thinking about materiality, and then this image came to mind.

Lotte Anker The bass is always the anchor.

Ton Matton This character belongs to the instrument?

Lotte Anker The low frequency is solid.

Sofia Eftychidou Even if the music we played today is a bit more abstract in a way, the character of the instrument stays. I think it's the nature of the instrument.

Christopher Dell For me, the theme of character relates to the issue that there is always a material, but there is also always a way of involving yourself with it, in the sense that materiality is defined as a relationship between human beings and whatever is there—wood, or fire, or water, bricks, and so on. This leads me to the next question. Lotte, you were talking lately about the difference between structure and texture. And it struck me that you linked the definition of texture with the tactile. Could you elaborate on that?

Lotte Anker Firstly, I would say that it's difficult to talk about sound. It's difficult to describe a sound like (*sings a tone*), except by saying that this is a voice, for example. What is the quality of that sound? In the context of this question, it has been very helpful for me to use vocabulary which derives from the visual arts. That's also where materiality comes in, in a way. If we are not even talking about texture, if we are just talking about the sound itself inside every little sound, then there's also a micro-texture, of course, of different frequencies, which gives that sound its special quality. How can you explain that? As is known, a lot of people would describe a sound as maybe soft, or hard, or smooth on the surface, or as having friction. These are all words that are coming from materiality, even though we're talking about air that's pushed, waves in the air.

From a music-historical perspective, one can say that a lot of musicians, including myself, often, when trying to describe music, mix up musical structure and musical texture. At the moment I'm doing a research project in Copenhagen on texture and form. I read and googled around to find out what different composers had said about that difference. Because, at least in the Danish language, structure can mean a lot of things. One may speak of "social structure" for example. But you cannot say "social texture." Texture is related to a material, and to tactility and quality especially. In this sense, texture for me means the quality of something.

There are some composers who would say that musical or sonic texture is a mass in which you cannot define the single elements. If you could, then it would be a structure. This is a thesis the famous Hungarian new music composer György Ligeti advocates. Then I asked a friend who is a painter, and she said, "I would say that structure is what holds or carries what is the texture." This definition helps me to have a certain picture in my head. Maybe it might not be so important if you confuse structure and texture in music; rather, I'm interested in the quality of sounds, and sometimes also in being able to describe them with my own words.

Christopher Dell If the material changes according to the context, then this effect is also influenced by the imaginary or emotions you have toward the material. And that's what brings me to your technique, Ton, of taking things apart. When we see the image of that torn-down house, and the mayor is in front of it, you are actually positioning him in the midst of what for most people would seem like a formless hunch. It's not a house, but a formless pile of bricks. Yet for you, it's a completely different thing; it can become a structure of a next possibility. And this opening is created by a disassembling of a situation, which I see as a core part of your work. How do you train this method with the students? Do they immediately understand it?

Ton Matton The training is you nudge them into the water, and they have to swim. And if you can't swim, then you drown. Is that a training, or not really?

Christopher Dell What are the qualities that you're looking for?

Ton Matton Of course, the quality is that people are living there in Tribsees; they know how to continue, they understand what you're doing, they are grateful for what happened, and they move on. And then, of course, there's the other quality of needing these twenty-five good pictures to convince the state secretary that it's a good project, and that you can continue the next year with new funding, doing the next project. It's all in this mixture.

To come back to teaching: I never studied at an art university. I studied architecture and urban planning, but in recent years I have been teaching at an art university. And suddenly, because I'm probably not thinking in architectural methodology, I ended up in the art context. I realized that it's art projects that I'm doing. However, for me, it's also urban planning, because it's obvious that this is what urban planning should be about. Of course, realizing what I studied and knowing what's going on in the world, you see that urban planning is not yet about this. On the other hand, what I want to teach the students is to break down that art ego and open up to what the world is telling you. Yes, you need your ego to do your things, and to be a zombie—you spent a huge amount of your life behind that computer machine. Therefore, you have to have the ego; that is what you want to do. If you do a project like we did, it's not about showing up in a broken village and demonstrating how beautiful you can paint a wall. I try to teach the students that this is not the goal—by bringing them in and inviting them to sleep in dirty, broken houses without water. Of course, they complain. Of course, they want to go to the hotel in the next village. In this case I say, "OK, but that's not the project. Go to the hotel in the next village and stay there, no problem. There are people there who want to have exactly the painting on the wall that you are able paint. But in my project, I'm sleeping in this house with broken furniture and without water." Maybe one of the reasons why I stopped teaching for the time being is that, in my mind, the ego of the student as an "artist" makes no sense. Because for me, to dwell where you do your project is all part of the experience; it's also part of going into what Lotte calls the texture, so that you really feel the dirt and the mud or shit of the house. Sometimes, it's also dangerous, of course, so you have to be careful and double-check. If a student gets hurt or breaks a leg and you have squatted the house, I'm aware that that's the end of my career as a university professor. They will fire you immediately, and probably sue you afterward. So, that's also all a part of the game.

Christopher Dell I think this is a good moment to open up the discussion.

Hans-Jürgen Commerell I have a question for Francis Kéré. Since we have situated this rendition of the *Dialogue Concerts* amidst your installation, I was wondering, Francis, what is your relationship to the material and materiality in the way you approach an architectural question or task? And how is the question of sound ingrained in your work?

Francis Kéré Today, by playing the concert in our installation, you created a bridge. I'm not a musician, but I love music, I love sound. If you create an installation that is an echo to sound, then it creates a sort of labyrinth, where sounds can resonate. And, of course, if you deal with architecture, then you always deal with sound. Especially here at Aedes, if you talk about acoustics, about the texture, about enhancing the echo. I think there's a connection, a very strong link, not only talking about the concert as a whole, but I'm talking about even the choice of material.

Hans-Jürgen Commerell Francis, you're also creating spaces like schools, and places for health care, and other things in which sound plays a role and is dependent on the material you are using.

Francis Kéré Yes, the material we applied—reed—can suit very well or can be a structure for sound; it can support it. I am happy to see you guys play under this canopy. I like it. What I always want is to not work against sounds. I feel like right now, it is good. We used a very simple balanced material. People use it for their balcony in summertime. I remember I was running late with the project, and then I had to run from the office myself with some guys to travel around all the Bauhaus hardware stores in Berlin, counting all of the reeds, and I kept collecting, driving. You have to make a joke when people are saying, "What the hell are you doing with all of these materials." No, we're going to make an installation in an art museum.

Hans-Jürgen Commerell This canopy has a meaning, also in the history of your work. You bring people together to talk below this canopy. This comes back to the issue of sound. You use the canopy to come together and communicate.

Francis Kéré Exactly. And using really natural material, you know—even in the West we have it—it's not expensive. Of course, if you want a lot, then you need a Bauhaus store next to your place.

Lotte Anker Can I ask? This is the same material that a lot of farmhouses in Denmark have for their roofs?

Francis Kéré Yes, exactly. It's like going back to the roots. Simple, traditional material. Okay, we needed some element of pulling it together, and a lot of people! That also relates to your work, Ton: creating a community. We get students, some people from my team, and at the end we do improvisation. People just love it and start to help us put these things together and cut them. That is what I understand as a participatory process, very simple.

Christopher Dell Which can evolve around a material.

Francis Kéré Yes.

Ton Matton The moment you go back to the material is decisive. If I want to build a house and I need a bricklayer, and I ask you to help my bricklayer, you will say, "Oh, I don't know." If you build a house out of straw balls, and you ask people, "Can you help?," then there's twenty people coming up immediately and saying, "Yeah, I want to help, that's fun." And they start helping you. Although it's almost the same, laying a brick or placing a strawball. But the moment it's some local material that you are not afraid of, then it's very easy to join in. And the moment it's a brick, you sort of get afraid of the brick. Saying that, I have a question as well. Halfway through the concert, when we were immersed in emotion, you suddenly stopped, and I had a feeling of wanting to applause, but I was afraid of doing it.

Christopher Dell That clapping was not allowed?

Ton Matton That was the feeling. Why not? How come?

Christopher Dell In classical music, when you play a symphony, you don't clap between its movements. That was the idea. But, I mean, if you had clapped, nothing bad would have happened.

Ton Matton No, but I was wondering, why was I afraid? Is it really a cultural taboo? Or is it something you are doing as well?

Christopher Dell I think we definitely did something. We kept the tension.

Lotte Anker And, of course, you gave some cues sometimes, but even without the cues, that's one of the enchanting things with improvisation—when a group of people can suddenly stop in the middle of a movement. I'm not talking about fading out slowly, but a moment in time that, while playing, suddenly everybody feels, or knows: okay, it's over. That's a very special intuitive entity.

Ton Matton But I'm in the audience. And you're reaching me in a sort of emotional way, and then you stop, and I think, "Oh, that was fun, oh, no oops." I felt that there is no space for this emotional intervening. And I was wondering why.

Christopher Dell It's about how we act toward the space. And that's the whole thing, because we were still in the playing, so to speak, we didn't resolve. I think it's a bodily movement. You can see it when we resolve. Then the audience knows that. It also happens sometimes after we have finished the performance, that we still keep a couple of seconds in bodily tension and then resolve.

Ton Matton But I'm wondering, did more people have the feeling I had during the concert today, that there was the possibility to break the silence by clapping? Okay, next time we'll do it.

Christopher Dell Sofia, Lotte, Ton, everyone who came, especially Francis, and everybody at Aedes, thank you very much.

Dialogue Concerts: Preliminary Series

Christopher Dell (vibraphone)

Aedes Architecture Forum, Berlin

The series *Dialogue Concerts* indicated in this book was preceded by a preliminary experimentation series under the same name. Within this series the vibraphonist, composer, and urban design theorist Christopher Dell entered into an interdisciplinary dialogue with different exhibitions held at the Aedes Architecture Forum between 2012 and 2013.

In a series of concerts and lectures, each taking place with a new exhibition at the Aedes Architecture Forum, Dell interacted over a span of one year with the concepts, forms, materials, and spatial constellations of each different exhibition and architectural language. In that way a sensual experience of cross-disciplinary dialogue unfolded. Dell composed new music for each concert, performed, and also explained how—and which musical means and materials—he had chosen to interact with in the given architectural and discursive situation.

Situated in the midst of the exhibition installations, each conversation concert took up the atmosphere and discursive space of the exhibited architectural works. Dell introduced every concert with a lecture-performance. Within this framework, the focus was on the procedural-strategic connection between architecture and music and ranged rather far from the question "How does architecture sound?" Serial wiring, motivic work, collecting, collaging, de- and re-composing, typological ordering—these are just a few examples of powerful strategic correlates.

In fascinating concert talks, Dell enabled the audience to experience the particular strategic spaces of the exhibition through the convergence of music and architecture and their procedures. In this way, the *Preliminary Dialogue Concerts* offered the possibility of discovering new relations of, as well as new perspectives on, the diverse contexts of the architectural practices shown in the respective exhibitions, which can be pursued on a thematic, formal, and subjective level.

https://cms.baunetz.de/cms/aedes/de/suche?suche=dialogue+concert

Preliminary Concert #1
DRA: Christopher Dell (vibraphone), Christian Ramond (bass), Felix Astor (drums)
October 18, 2012

Exhibition: agps clues,
September 7 – October 18, 2012

Preliminary Concert #2
Christopher Dell (vibraphone)
November 27, 2012

Exhibition: White Mountain – Contemporary Chilean Architecture,
October 26 – December 2, 2012

Akron Art Museum
Central Los Angeles Area High School #9
for the Visual and Performing Arts

Preliminary Concert #3
Christopher Dell (vibraphone)
February 28, 2013

Exhibition: COOP HIMMELB(L)AU: 7+, Wolf D. Prix & Partner: Say himmelb(l)au, December 12, 2012 – March 3, 2013

Preliminary Concert #4
Christopher Dell (vibraphone)
May 7, 2013

Exhibition: Julia Schulz-Dornburg, Modern Ruins – A Topography of Profit, Stranger than Paradise – Towards a Political Economy of Living, March 22 – May 9, 2013

Preliminary Concert #5
Christopher Dell (vibraphone)
June 19, 2013

Exhibition: Motion Matters – UNStudio, Amsterdam, May 18 – July 4, 2013

Preliminary Concert #6
Christopher Dell (vibraphone)
October 9, 2013

Exhibition: The Poetics of Boxes – Mathias Klotz, Chile, September 13 – October 17, 2013

MUSSER

Acknowledgments

It was in the autumn of 2017 that I met Daniel Libeskind at an Aedes Architecture Forum festivity on the occasion of the exhibition *Drawing Ambience: Alvin Boyarsky and the Architectural Association* at the Tchoban Foundation in Berlin. Mr. Libeskind and I soon got into an in-depth discussion on architecture and representation, and we especially elaborated on the drawing cycle *Chamberworks*. We both agreed that it would be fantastic to perform the *Chamberworks* with a music ensemble in a concert format at the Aedes Architecture Forum and to perspectivize and contextualize the work with a lecture and a discussion. When sharing the idea with Kristin Feireiss and Hans-Jürgen Commerell, they proposed: Why not make a series of it? That was the moment that sparked the actual *Dialogue Concerts* series. In this sense, I owe a special thank you to Daniel Libeskind—not only for participating in the series, but also for triggering it.

Since the series drew on a preliminary smaller version of *Dialogue Concerts* from 2012 and 2013, I am also indebted to Beate Engelhorn, who collaborated with me in curating this initial series.

A project such as the *Dialogue Concerts* would not be possible without support. I am thankful for the funding received from Berlin's Senate Department for Culture and Europe and from the Musikfonds e. V. and Gregor Hotz with project funds from the German Federal Government Commissioner for Culture and the Media.

A big thank you also goes to Saori Kanemaki for project management, Melanie Rossmann for controlling, and Ari Kanemaki for public relations.

Furthermore, I would like to thank everybody at the Aedes Architecture Forum for the fantastic cooperation, especially Kristin Feireiss, Hans-Jürgen Commerell, Christine Meierhofer, Dunya Bouchi, and Mathias Schnell. Without the generous hospitality of the Aedes Architecture Forum, this endeavor would not have been possible.

In making this book, I owe a great deal of thanks to everyone who participated in the *Dialogue Concerts*: Oda Pälmke, Karen Lorenz, Jonas Westergaard, Christophe Hutin, Kathrin Pechlof, Christian Lillinger, Daniel Libeskind, Elisabeth Coudoux, Pascal Klewer, Bernd Kniess, Sarah Saviet, Mathis Mayr, Chatschatur Kanajan, Tabea Michaelis, Ben Pohl, Lotte Anker, Sofia Eftychidou, and Ton Matton.

My gratitude is also extended to Helmut Völter for the superbly detailed design of this book, to Ruth Hommelsheim for the very precise photography, and to Anne König and Jan Wenzel of Spector Books for publishing the book in their fine and exclusive publishing house. All of these individuals have strongly influenced the visuality and materiality of this publication.

I also thank Dawn Michelle d'Atri for her meticulous copyediting and Anna Richter for her fine translation into English of the lectures and discussions that were held in German.

My thanks moreover go to the individuals who have supported or influenced this work: Ulrich Stock, Gregor Dotzauer, Katja Blomberg, Anne Elisabeth Toft, George Lewis, Kristín Guttenberg, Francis Kéré, Kaye Geipel, Christopher Williams, and Olaf Nicolai.

Installation Views, Dialogue Concerts:
Ruth Hommelsheim
Installation Views, Preliminary Concerts:
Aedes Architecture Forum

Lecture #1 Oda Pälmke:
All copyrights by Oda Pälmke
The photographs, snapshots mostly, were taken on the road and collected in albums and data files. The illustrations were drawn by Anna Hugot, Esther Wiens, Jana Gretz, Jana Wesely, Katharina Diehl, Kim Zimmermann, Pascal Lange, Philip Becker and Sarah Zemelko in September 2019.

Lecture #2 Christophe Hutin:
All copyrights by Christophe Hutin Architects

Intervention:
Water Garden by Junya Ishigami & Associates
All copyrights by Junya Ishigami & Associates

Lecture #3 Daniel Libeskind:
Chamberworks: Architectural Meditations on Themes from Heraclitus
All copyrights by Daniel Libeskind

Lecture #4 Bernd Kniess:
https://coronavirus.jhu.edu/map.html
Developing-Urban-Futures-Urban-Age-conference-newspaper.pdf
https://www.mcc-berlin.net/fileadmin/data/clock/carbon_clock.htm?i=3267263, last accessed 11.09.2020
United Nations Climate Summit 23.09.2019 © Reuters / A. Hofstetter
Alexandra Arènes, Architectural Design at the Time of Anthropocene: A Gaia-graphic Approach to the Critical Zones, The University of Manchester, PhD (supervisor: Albena Yaneva), MARG (Manchester Architecture Research Group)
Alexander von Humboldt, diagram of a cross-section of the earth's crust, 1841, from Heinrich Berghaus, Physikalischer Atlas (Gotha: J. Perthes, 1852)
http://ud.hcu-hamburg.de/projects/annual-theme/urgent-matter-s-taking-care-of-urban-futures-2019-2020
Riken Yamamoto, Local Community Area, in Arch+ 208, 2012, p. 102, Statistical
Statistical Office North, Statistical Yearbook Hamburg 2018/2019, own diagram
Aron Bohmann, Charlotte Herbst, Katrin Hovy, Weiterwohnen: Haus- und Lebenszyklen in Alt-Kirchdorf; Urban Design Project II Research and Design: Wohnen als Praxis 2012
Wajiro Kon, Objects I, Survey of Things in a New Household, 1926
Diskutieren und Arbeiten: Grundriss eines Einzelzimmers, Studentendorf Eichkamp, Georg Heinrichs, Ludwig Leo (drawing), Hans C. Müller, Berlin 1958, in Arch+ 183
Sarah Wigglesworth and Jeremy Till, Increasing disorder in a dining table, 1998
Atelier Bow-Wow, Graphic Anatomy, 2007
Nora Fanderi Chicago 2012, The People's Plan, urban design master's thesis, 2013
Marius Töpfer and Rebecca Wall, The Polis was a Party Tent: Retroactive Montages, urban design thesis project, 2018
Atelier Bow-Wow & Tamutso Ito, The Bazaar X the living rooms, 2018
Marco Mijatovic, Sarah Hablützel, Jeep Rohde, Cooperative Review Process: Building a Proposition for Future Activities, 2017
Rebecca Wall, folder structure, 2018
Marius Töpfer and Rebecca Wall, Planung als Vektor, Skript und Sichtbarmachung: Projektarchäologie eines Begegnungshauses, Everyday Urban Design 6, Berlin, 2020

Lecture #5 Christopher Dell:
Leon Battista Alberti, Façade design for the Palazzo Rucellai in Florence, started in 1455, in Paul von Naredi-Rainer, Architektur und Harmonie (Cologne: Dumont, 1982) p. 170
Cesare Cesariano, homo ad quadratum, commentary to Vitruvius, 1521
Cesare Cesariano, homo ad circulum, commentary to Vitruvius, 1521
Claude Perrault, Vitruvian commentary synopsis of the five column orders, 1684
Francesco di Giorgio Martini, Church floor plan according to the measure of man, 1480–90
Francesco di Giorgio Martini, Church façade according to the measure of man, 1480–90
Francesco di Giorgio Martini, Treatise on Architecture, Magliabechiano, manuscript, Dinocrates, ca. 1485
Antonio di Pietro Averlino aka Filarete, Design for the ideal city Sforzinda, 1457
Jean-Nicolas-Louis Durand, Précis des leçons d'architecture données à l'École royale polytechnique, "composition en general," 1809
Le Corbusier, Modulor Measurements, 1950, in Paul von Naredi-Rainer, Architektur und Harmonie (Cologne: Dumont, 1982), pp. 102, 188
Ernst Neufert, Bauentwurfslehre (1936; repr., Wiesbaden: Springer Vieweg, 2016), pp. 23, 34

Lecture #6 Ton Matton:
All copyrights by Ton Matton

Christopher Dell
Dialogue Concerts: Conceptual Research on Architecture and Music

Graphic Design: Helmut Völter, Paulina Mohr
Lithography: Dotgain
Copyediting and Proofreading:
Dawn Michelle d'Atri
Printing: Gutenberg Beuys Feindruckerei

Concept: Christopher Dell
Project Management: Saori Kanemaki
Controlling: Melanie Rossmann

The team of the *Dialogue Concerts* would like to thank everybody at the Aedes Architecture Forum for the friendly cooperation, especially Kristin Feireiss, Hans-Jürgen Commerell, Christine Meierhofer, Dunya Bouchi, and Mathias Schnell.

Published by
Spector Books
Harkortstraße 10
04107 Leipzig, Germany
www.spectorbooks.com

www.christopher-dell.com

Distribution:
Germany, Austria: GVA, Gemeinsame Verlagsauslieferung, Göttingen GmbH & Co. KG, www.gva-verlage.de
Switzerland: AVA Verlagsauslieferung AG, www.ava.ch
France, Belgium: Interart Paris, www.interart.fr
UK: Central Books Ltd, www.centralbooks.com
USA, Canada, Central and South America, Africa: Artbook / D. A. P., www.artbook.com
South Korea: The Book Society, www.thebooksociety.org
Japan: twelvebooks, www.twelve-books.com
Australia, New Zealand: Perimeter Distribution, www.perimeterdistribution.com

Printed in Germany
ISBN 978-3-95905-741-7

Aedes Architecture Forum
enw
ifit Institut für Improvisationstechnologie
Senatsverwaltung für Kultur und Europa
be Berlin
MUSIKFONDS
Gefördert vom Musikfonds e.V. mit Projektmitteln der Beauftragten der Bundesregierung für Kultur und Medien.